Brian Turner was born in Halifax and brought up in Morley, West Yorkshire, where he began his cooking career – aged twelve – in his father's transport café. This early introduction to the preparation of hearty British food was followed by a formal training in Leeds, then a move to London where he honed his culinary skills at several of the capital's top hotels and restaurants, starting with Simpson's in the Strand. He worked for the Capital Hotel for fifteen years, and in his career has opened several of his own restaurants, including Turner's, in 1986, and in 2003 Brian Turner Mayfair at the Millennium Hotel.

One of the country's most popular chefs, in 2002 Brian was awarded the CBE for his services to tourism and to training in the catering industry. He is President of the Academy of Culinary Arts – actively involved in numerous schools and environmental projects – and enjoys an ambassadorial role with two of Britain's leading cooking brands, Stoves and Belling, as well as with hospitality tabletop supplier, Steelite International, some of whose products are featured in the photographs in this book.

Brian has written two previous books for Headline: *A Yorkshire Lad: My Life with Recipes* (2000) and *Brian Turner's Favourite British Recipes* (2003).

DEDICATION

This book is dedicated to a real friend, someone who understood hospitality and had a great love of quality in food and drink. His passion for meeting people and spending hours around a table, eating and drinking and enjoying life, was second to none. He was my great mate, Michael E. Mills, 1942–2009. Gone but never forgotten, old boy.

GREAT BRITISH GRUB

BRIAN TURNER

headline

Photographs © 2009 Noel Murphy except for pages 27, 40, 45, 74, 93, 117, 121, 128, 131, 135, 143, 173, 179, 187, 230, 249 © William Shaw Author photograph by John Deehan

First published in 2009 by HEADLINE PUBLISHING GROUP

Cataloguing in Publication Data is available from the British Library

ISBN 978 0 7553 1878 0

Typeset in Gill Sans and Farnham
Edited by Susan Fleming
Designed by Ant Gatt and Nick Venables
Photography by Noel Murphy
Art direction by Wendy Birch
Home economy by Gerard O'Sullivan and Brian Turner
Styling by Nel Haynes
Colour reproduction, printing and binding
by Rotolito Lombarda S.p.A. in Italy

Headline's policy is to use papers that are natural, renewable and recyclable products and made from wood grown in sustainable forests. The logging and manufacturing processes are expected to conform to the environmental regulations of the country of origin.

HEADLINE PUBLISHING GROUP
An Hachette UK Company
338 Euston Road
London NW1 3BH

www.headline.co.uk
www.hachette.co.uk

Contents

Introduction

A few years ago I had great fun exploring, researching and pulling together a book that became *Brian Turner's Favourite British Recipes*. The cooking of Britain has long been a passion of mine: I may be classically trained (which means my professional culinary knowledge is mainly French), but I have still managed to remain true to my British roots. They say you never lose sight of things you learned early on in childhood, and in Yorkshire I was brought up eating, and then later cooking, simple British fare. So to be asked to write a follow-up to that first book was a delight, and it has been even more of a delight in the writing.

Great British Grub delves into the same rich subject, and it has been hugely enjoyable filling in the gaps that inevitably punctuated the last book, and exploring other, sometimes less familiar, seams of British food and eating. For instance, the eating patterns we know in our country today have evolved over many years, and I was astounded to discover that lunch, for instance – we tend to think of Sunday lunch as a long-established institution – is a fairly recent arrival in our eating day. Coming from the north of England, I was always confused about the differences between 'tea', 'dinner' and 'supper', and I think I have found the answer now. I was aware too of the basic traditions attached to various days of the calendar year – such as Hallowe'en and Mother's Day – but I hadn't realised how historically rich they were, combining Christian thinking with ideas that were much more ancient.

As a result of all these discoveries made during my research, I have organised the book into chapters on traditional (often unique) British meals (breakfasts, teas, high teas, suppers and lunches) and chapters on specific times of the year when cooking and eating are to the fore, and again very traditional (Christmas, New Year and Easter, for instance). Interspersed with these are smaller features on specific British festivals, when we might make and eat particular foods, and these include St Valentine's Day, Burns Night and Shrove Tuesday. What I have done, really, is try to go through a typical calendar year of British eating, unearthing the history and any snippets I thought were interesting.

While once again exploring the traditional foods of Britain – the roasts, the stews, pies, puddings, cakes and breads – I have gone a little further as well, recognising and acknowledging the influences that have been absorbed from other cuisines into ours. Our colonial past and our rich history have had a distinct effect on the way we eat and celebrate, as indeed have the many and varied new ingredients which have been introduced from around the world. Although the Great British way of eating is far from dead, all these different strands are celebrated here.

As always, in any book on home cooking, what we eat ought to be based on what is available seasonally. In the good old days we had no choice: we had to eat what we grew, killed, trapped or acquired (by means fair or foul). Now we have supermarkets, for whom seasons do not seem to exist, but it still makes sense, both price and health wise, to stick to what is naturally available. I also think that, whenever possible, we should buy local produce; it's good to know where the food comes from and how it has been nurtured. I say this having spent most of my working and cooking life in London. If we applied that theory too rigidly, I wouldn't have had much access to seafood or meat (how many fish swim up the Thames, and how many herds of cattle, sheep and pigs do we see in Central London parks?).

Our produce in Britain is second to none, but do we use it properly? I'm afraid that, on the whole, we don't, because many people just do not have the requisite skills or knowledge. They say an army marches on its stomach, but the same could be said of a nation, and we desperately need to educate the next generation on how to appreciate the food products available,

and how to transform them into healthy, nutritional, well presented and tasty meals. If we cannot bring about this change in food education, then I and many others fear for the future of this great nation. This book is hardly an antidote to these problems, but it contains recipes that my mum and grandma would have known, and which they would have hoped would not disappear. It is vital that we look to the future, but at the same time we must not forget the past.

I hope the recipes here – some of which are old, some new, some familiar, some apparently strange – will please you. None of them is too difficult to achieve, for many of them are not sophisticated in the least (good food can be made from simple ingredients and simple techniques), and quite a few use up leftovers. Finally, in the testing, I was delighted and relieved to find out how *good* all the recipes taste. I hope that you will enjoy this book – use it well, and cook and eat well.

Brian Turner

NOTE   Good-quality ingredients are the key to good eating. In moderation, I am not averse to stock cubes – they can work well instead of stock. Wine and water are good too. All the eggs throughout, except where stated otherwise, are medium. And while I'm at it, I think you have to use your common sense when cooking. I urge you to read the whole recipe through first before starting, and work out the steps mentally.

Breakfast is probably the meal for which we British are best known internationally. Most visitors would know the typical breakfast platter of bacon, egg, sausage, black pudding, fried bread, tomatoes and mushrooms. Whether they would begin their meal with porridge and end it with toast and marmalade would probably depend on constitution and appetite!

Breakfast must be the time of least culinary understanding between nations. The French fondness for a *café au lait* with a chocolate *croissant* would have made the average Briton shudder, as would the Italian penchant for bread, olive oil, garlic and tomatoes. But the average Briton is probably not familiar with his own country's breakfasting history. Around 1500, an English gentleman would break his fast in the morning with beer and salted fish, while the English, Irish, Scots or Welsh peasant would possibly have a bowl of grain and water (milk if he were lucky, the forerunner of porridge) or some bread and cheese. At the beginning of the eighteenth century, people of fashion dined on spiced bread with one of the two new drinks, coffee and chocolate. By the end of the century, tea had become the rage, and it would be accompanied by plain bread or toast and butter.

It was not until Edwardian and Victorian times that the Great British breakfast as we now know it came to be established. A larger meal was thought necessary to start the day off, and keep one going until the main meal in the evening. Mrs Beeton herself suggested that, for the 'comfortable meal called breakfast', her readers should offer 'cold joints, collared or potted meats, cold game, veal and ham pies, broiled fish, mutton chops and rump steaks, kidneys, sausages, bacon and poached eggs, muffins, toast, marmalade, butter'. Then, without irony, she adds, 'etcetera, etcetera'.

This was the time when eggs and bacon came to the fore as breakfast foods (although 'collops' or slices of bacon with an egg had long been a favourite complete meal for the working man). Traditional and new foods were included in the spread: black pudding was eaten in the north, devilled chops in the south; Arbroath smokies or Finnan haddies were poached in milk in Scotland; smoked haddock was flaked into rice for the new-fangled, Raj-inspired kedgeree in the south. The novelist Somerset Maugham once said that to eat well in Britain you had to eat breakfast three times a day. On a scale such as described above, that would be rather daunting, so the introduction of brunch in the late 1890s must have come as something of a relief (as well as dietary sense). Although it is usually thought of as an American invention, it might have originated in Oxford, where the students were notoriously late risers.

The Great British breakfast may have changed over the years, but it has become an undeniable institution. In fact, making breakfast is how I started my career, in my dad's transport café, at the age of twelve! And I once won a prize for cooking the best breakfast in London, a meal that was judged by brickies (and reported in no less than *The Times* newspaper). Breakfast remains one of my favourite meals – it's a meal I enjoy both at home and away, and a bacon sarnie in a warm restaurant kitchen is a necessity with which to start a hard-working day. In this chapter there are old favourites, mainly British obviously, but some recipes have a flavour or influence from elsewhere in our culinary heritage, and these I hope will become new favourites.

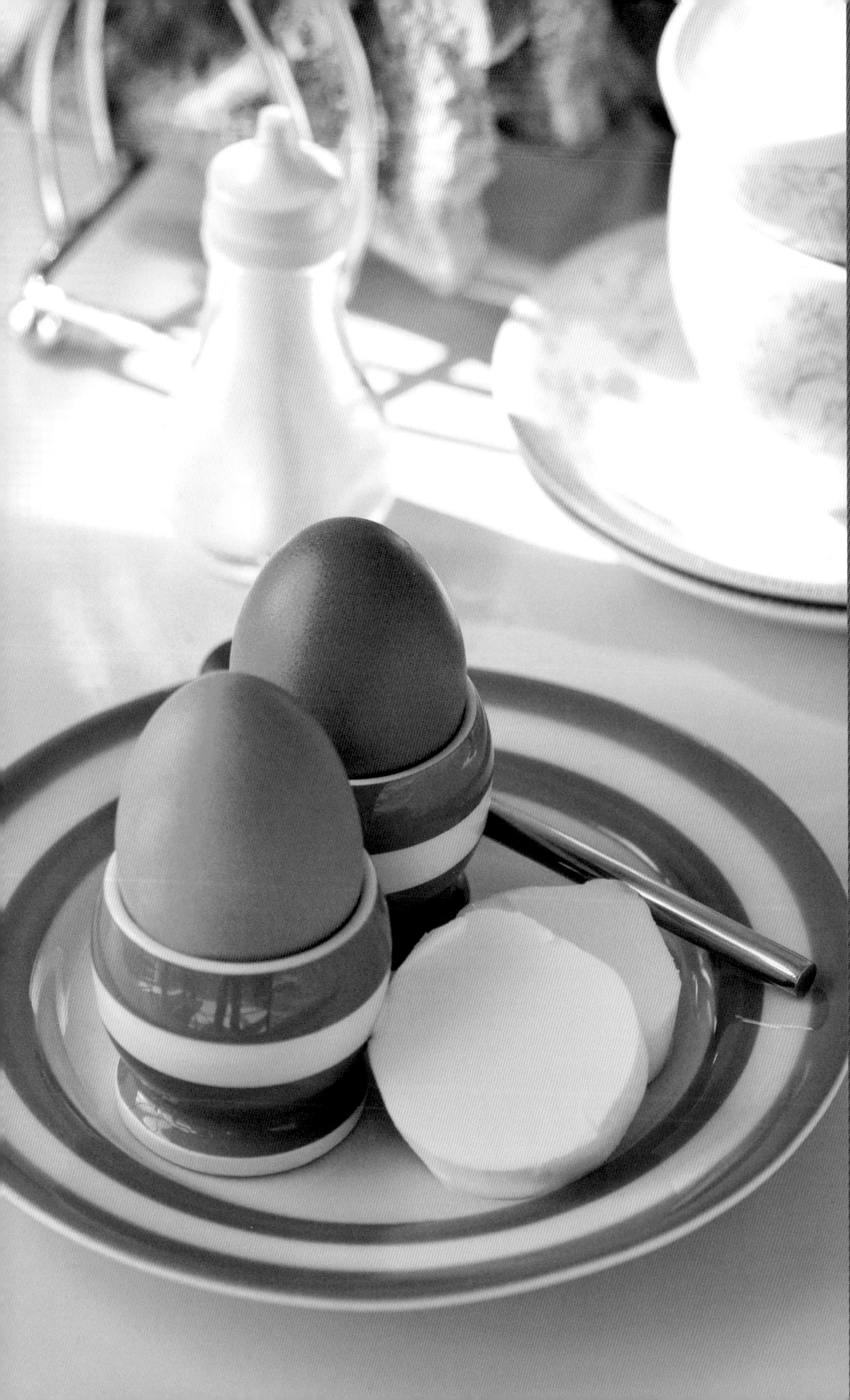

1 Breakfasts & Brunches

Kedgeree

Although generally thought of as essentially English, kedgeree came to us via India, and was 'invented' during the days of the Raj. The original *'khichri'* was a vegetarian combination of rice and lentils, eaten as a breakfast dish. English army officers stationed in India – or their local cooks – adapted it to be a rice-only dish, and are credited with adding pieces of dried or salted fish (Englishmen *do* like their protein). Smoked haddock is the fish most commonly used now, and I have occasionally made kedgeree with salmon. It makes a substantial breakfast dish, but I quite like it for supper too, or a light lunch.

SERVES 4

550 g (1¼ lb) smoked haddock fillet

600 ml (1 pint) fish stock

1 bay leaf

juice of 1 lemon

salt and freshly ground black pepper

25 g (1 oz) unsalted butter

1 onion, peeled and finely chopped

225 g (8 oz) long-grain rice

1 tsp curry powder

a pinch each of cayenne pepper and freshly grated nutmeg

a pinch of saffron strands (optional)

4 hard-boiled eggs, shelled

1 tbsp chopped fresh coriander

1 Preheat the oven to 180°C/350°F/Gas 4.

2 Make sure the haddock fillet is skinned and boned totally. Put into a large ovenproof dish. Bring the fish stock to the boil, and pour over the fish. Add the bay leaf and lemon juice, and season well. Cook covered in the preheated oven for 5 minutes until just cooked. Strain off the stock, and reserve.

3 Meanwhile, melt the butter in a saucepan, add the onion and sweat without colouring for a few minutes until soft. Add the rice and stir, then cook until the rice is completely coated with butter. Add the spices.

4 Pour in the strained fish stock topped up with enough water to make twice the volume of the rice. Cover with buttered greaseproof paper and cook in the preheated oven as above for 18 minutes.

5 Take out of the oven, leave to sit for 2 minutes, and then stir with a fork.

6 Cut the eggs into big chunks, add half to the rice and stir in. Check the seasoning of the rice, then pour into a warmed serving bowl. Flake the smoked haddock over the top, sprinkle with the rest of the eggs and the coriander, and serve.

Kedgeree Cakes with Poached Eggs

When I was growing up, using up leftovers was an important part of daily cooking, especially as my dad would bring stuff home from the café. Mashed potato mixed with meat, fish or veg, and made into cakes, was one way of using leftovers, and fishcakes are classic. You could just use leftover kedgeree here, with a little leftover mashed potato (and follow the recipe from step 4), but these cakes are good enough to make from fresh. Ideal for breakfast, they would also be good for high tea or supper.

SERVES 4

vegetable oil, for shallow-frying

4 large eggs

FISHCAKES

225 g (8 oz) mashed potato

55 g (2 oz) cooked long-grain rice

225 g (8 oz) cooked smoked haddock (see p. 10)

15 g (½ oz) unsalted butter

½ onion, peeled and finely chopped

¼ tsp curry powder (or more if you like)

2 hard-boiled eggs, shelled and chopped

2 eggs, beaten

1 tsp chopped fresh parsley

salt and freshly ground black pepper

25 g (1 oz) plain flour

85 g (3 oz) fresh white breadcrumbs

1. Have ready the cooled mashed potato and the cooked rice (simply cook according to the instruction on the packet). Flake the smoked haddock, and make sure it is free of skin and bone.

2. Melt the butter in a pan, add the chopped onion and sweat, without colouring, for a few minutes. Add the curry powder, stir and cook gently for 1 minute before adding the haddock. Stir and cook, but try not to break it up too much. Take this mixture off the heat and leave to cool.

3. Mix the haddock mixture into the mashed potato. Mix in the chopped hard-boiled eggs and rice. Drip a little of the beaten eggs into the fishcake mixture then add the parsley, some salt and pepper, and mix.

4. Divide the mixture into eight even-sized pieces, and mould into balls. Flatten to a fishcake shape using your hands.

5. Put the seasoned flour, the remaining beaten egg and the breadcrumbs on three separate plates. Coat the fishcakes first in flour, then egg and breadcrumbs. Pat with a palette knife to make sure any loose breadcrumbs stick properly.

6. Heat the oil until it is hot (see below). Shallow-fry the fishcakes until golden, about 2 minutes on each side. Drain well on absorbent paper.

7. Meanwhile poach four eggs in simmering water with added salt and white wine vinegar. This will take about 10 minutes altogether, if you are doing four (see below).

8. Serve the cakes on warm plates, with a poached egg on top.

☞ To make sure a fat is hot enough to properly shallow-fry or deep-fry, heat until near the smoking point of the fat, when a thermometer registers at least 180°C/350°F. The smoking point of animal fats can be a little higher, while some vegetable oils (peanut and corn) can go higher still, up to 220°C/425°F.

☞ To judge temperature without a thermometer, heat the oil and test it by popping in a cube of fresh bread. If it turns golden brown in 1 minute, the oil is at about 180°C/350°F; if it browns in less time than that, the temperature is obviously higher. Try not to go too much higher, as fat ignites very easily; it is a dangerous cooking medium.

☞ To poach eggs without a poacher pan (the one with little containers), bring a small pan of water up to the boil. Add some vinegar and salt. Use the freshest eggs possible (as there is nothing else to contribute flavour to poached eggs). Break the egg into a cup first, then when the water boils, stir it, then slide in the egg. Only do one or two eggs at a time. Cook for a few minutes, swirling the water, until the white completely encloses the yolk. Remove with a slotted spoon and serve immediately. If cooking in advance, or working on a breakfast conveyor belt, store in a bowl of ice-cold water. Warm up in hot water when ready to serve.

☞ When serving, you can snip the eggs with scissors to allow the yolks to run out – great effect!

Creamed Tomatoes on Toast

Too often we ignore simple good food, feeling we have to make everything too sophisticated. This is a classic example of a simple, traditional family dish (better than baked beans, I think), which I have actually cooked in one of my demonstrations in South Africa. It probably originated as an after-dinner savoury, another British meal course which is as unique as the Great British breakfast and afternoon tea. See pp. 127–31 for a few more savoury ideas.

SERVES 4

25 g (1 oz) unsalted butter

1 shallot, peeled and finely chopped

½ tsp dry English mustard powder

350 g (12 oz) tomatoes, cubed

a splash of white wine vinegar

½ tsp caster sugar

2 tbsp natural yoghurt

2 tbsp double cream

salt and freshly ground black pepper

1 tbsp finely chopped fresh parsley

TO SERVE

4 slices wholemeal bread

55 g (2 oz) unsalted butter

4 sprigs fresh chervil

extra virgin olive oil (optional)

1 Melt the butter in a medium pan, and add the shallot. Sweat gently for a few minutes, but do not allow to colour.

2 Stir in the mustard powder along with the tomato cubes, vinegar and sugar. Simmer until the juices start to disappear.

3 Add the yoghurt and cream and boil to a spreading consistency. Season with salt and pepper, and stir in the parsley.

4 Meanwhile, toast the bread and spread with butter. Cut the crusts off if you like. Spoon the tomato mixture on top.

5 Serve with a sprig of chervil, possibly sprinkled with some good extra virgin olive oil.

☛ Creamed mushrooms on toast is another breakfast favourite – and would probably have served its turn as an after-dinner savoury as well. You simply fry 450 g (1 lb) button mushrooms in 25 g (1 oz) unsalted butter until golden brown. Add a chopped shallot and 150 ml (5 fl oz) dry sherry, and boil to reduce the sherry by two-thirds. Add the same amount of double cream, and simmer until the cream starts to thicken. Season with salt and pepper, sprinkle with chopped chives and serve on toast as above.

☛ In the restaurant we might take refinement a step further, and cut circles out of each slice of toast as the base for the tomatoes, as for *Scotch Woodcock* (see p. 128).

Scrambled Eggs with Toasted Brioche

Scrambled eggs have been with us since about the fifteenth century. An early dish called 'herbolace' was a mixture of beaten eggs and herbs, which was stirred over heat to cook it (the English predecessor of the soon-to-be-introduced French omelette). There is an art to making scrambled eggs, an easy art, but think of those ghastly piles of yellow goo in motorway cafés that pretend to be scrambled eggs. This is a rich recipe, because it uses both whole eggs and egg yolks (Italian eggs, with their bright yellow yolks, are good here). Scrambled eggs are traditionally served on toast, but I have used the French brioche, which you can buy anywhere these days.

SERVES 4

6 eggs

4 egg yolks

salt and freshly ground black pepper

55 g (2 oz) unsalted butter

150 ml (5 fl oz) double cream

TO SERVE

4 slices brioche loaf

55 g (2 oz) unsalted butter

1   Whisk the eggs and egg yolks together in a bowl, then season them.

2   Melt the butter in a solid-based pan. Add the eggs to the pan, and cook, stirring frequently, but be very careful not to overcook. They want to be soft. When just starting to scramble, stir in three-quarters of the cream.

3   Meanwhile toast the brioche then cut into circles (if you like). Butter the toast generously.

4   When the eggs are ready add the remainder of the cream and stir in. Pile on to the buttered toast and serve immediately.

☛ There are any number of variations on this simple basic dish. You could add anchovies, smoked salmon, sun-blush tomatoes, garlic and parsley, chives or chilli. Chop and mix into the eggs, or sprinkle over or under the eggs. Just use your imagination!

☛ I use brioche, because I like the hint of sweetness with the eggs. Sally Lunn could be used instead (see p.38), or any Italian bread, a tomato or olive bread, for instance.

Scrambled Egg with Spicy Sausage

Where I come from, we have tomato sausages. I remember going to collect the week's order from my dad's butcher, Ernie Ward (I saw him recently, not long before he sadly died): they were coloured by tomato sauce, so weren't spicy, but still tasted good. I would watch Ernie painstakingly fill the sausage skins with meat, tie them and wrap them. I would then take them back to my dad's café, where he would painstakingly remove the meat from the skins, and halve the sausages. They cooked quicker, apparently! This combination of *chorizo* and scrambled egg is more Spanish in feel, strictly speaking, than British – but I love the idea of *red* scrambled eggs, and the flavour is great.

SERVES 4

6 eggs

2 egg yolks

salt and freshly ground black pepper

55 g (2 oz) unsalted butter

225 g (8 oz) *chorizo* sausages

75 ml (2½ fl oz) double cream

1 tbsp chopped fresh parsley

1 Beat the eggs and yolks together in a bowl and season them with salt and pepper.

2 Melt the butter in a small frying pan. Cut the sausages into dice and colour gently in the butter for a couple of minutes. When cooked, take out of the pan, using a slotted spoon.

3 Pull the pan to one side, keeping the fat, and add the seasoned eggs. Return to the heat and stir frequently to scramble. Add and stir in the cream. Do not overcook: the eggs should be soft.

4 When ready, add the sausage and stir in. Check the seasoning, add the parsley and serve.

☞ You could use pork sausages instead of the *chorizo*. Cook first in a tsp of vegetable oil and allow to cool. Cut into dice and continue as if using *chorizo*. Add a pinch each of good chilli powder and paprika (for colour) just before taking out to drain, and be careful not to scorch the spices.

Crab and Spinach Omelette

Omelettes came from France, probably in about the sixteenth century. There was some debate as to whether an omelette – known for some time here as 'amulet' – should be cooked on one side or two, like a pancake. I've heard of another debate. Albert and Michel Roux used to test would-be chefs by asking them to make an omelette. Easy enough, you would think, but not when one of them liked it golden brown on top, the other with no colour on top. Peter Chandler, their first British apprentice, never knew which one he was making an omelette for, and said he always got it wrong...

Here I have incorporated two special British ingredients – crab and spinach – into the eggs to make a dish which is great for breakfast, but would also be good for high tea or supper.

SERVES 4

---

225 g (8 oz) young spinach leaves, washed and dried

55 g (2 oz) unsalted butter

½ garlic clove, peeled and crushed

freshly grated nutmeg

10 eggs

salt and freshly ground black pepper

4 tbsp double cream

1 tsp made Dijon mustard

55 g (2 oz) dark crabmeat

175 g (6 oz) white crabmeat

---

1   Roll up the spinach leaves and shred finely. Melt a third of the butter in a medium pan, and quickly cook the spinach with the garlic and a little grated nutmeg. Take out, drain and leave to cool.

2   Beat the eggs and season them with salt and pepper.

3   Meanwhile boil the double cream. When starting to thicken, take off the heat and stir in the mustard and dark crabmeat. Heat gently, then add the white crabmeat, heat again, and put to one side.

4   Put a quarter of the remaining butter into a 20 cm (8 in) omelette pan, and add a quarter of the spinach and a quarter of the egg. Stir gently over the heat, then leave to set. When almost set, put a quarter of the crab mixture in the middle, fold over and then turn out. Repeat to make three more small omelettes.

☞   You could also make one big omelette which you would have to cut in four. Use a 30 cm (12 in) non-stick frying pan.

Ham and Eggs

In the Middle Ages, a collop or slice of bacon would have been a rare treat for the working man, and when it was accompanied by a new-laid egg, even better still. That combination of ham or bacon and eggs is still with us now, and it is a dish for which the British are known the world over. Here I have moved slightly away from the famous 'fried' element, and baked the ingredients instead. (In fact, fried eggs were considered unwholesome at one time, and the eggs were separately boiled.)

If you use the best ham and the best eggs, you will have a dish second to none. I first came across the idea when I was working in Switzerland at the Beau Rivage Hotel, and the following recipe was how the dish was served in the restaurant. (In the kitchen we cooked this for ourselves in a huge frying pan: sliced sausage then sliced ham with twelve eggs broken on top. We ate from the pan.) Later I used to cook it for Richard Shepherd when we got together late at night after our respective services, and we were starving. Now we still enjoy ham and eggs (and chips), and eat it regularly in his posh restaurant, but we make sure that we don't eat after eight o'clock at night.

SERVES 4

85 g (3 oz) unsalted butter	8 eggs
8 slices boiled ham	salt and freshly ground black pepper

1 Preheat the oven to 200°C/400°F/Gas 6.

2 Melt the butter in a large heatproof and ovenproof dish and put in the ham. Turn the slices over so both sides are buttery.

3 Crack the eggs on top, season and then bake in the preheated oven for about 6 minutes until set. Serve immediately, with lots of bread.

☛ You could put the ham and eggs into smaller ovenproof pans or individual ovenproof dishes and, if you liked, sprinkle some breadcrumbs on top for an extra texture and flavour.

Crispy Bacon with Mushroom Pancakes

These pancakes are very useful, especially for breakfast or tea (see the sweet version on p. 249): they are more like drop scones than Shrove Tuesday lemon pancakes, but they are easy and you can make them in bulk in advance (always useful when you have people around). The ingredients here may be conventional but the combination is less usual.

SERVES 4

25 g (1 oz) unsalted butter	15 rashers streaky bacon	1 tsp baking powder
115 g (4 oz) button mushrooms	1 tbsp chopped fresh parsley	½ tsp salt
salt and freshly ground black pepper	**SAVOURY SCOTCH PANCAKES**	1 medium egg, beaten
	225 g (8 oz) plain flour	150 ml (5 fl oz) milk

1 Preheat the oven to 200°C/400°F/Gas 6.

2 Melt the butter in a medium pan. Cut the mushrooms into small dice and cook in the butter until drying out, about 4 minutes, then season.

3 Cook the rashers of bacon in the preheated oven until well done and crisp. Take out and chop three of the rashers into fine bits, leaving the others whole. Add the bacon bits to the mushrooms, along with the parsley.

4 Now for the pancakes. In a bowl mix together the flour, baking powder and salt, then make a well in the centre and add the beaten egg. Stir, adding enough of the milk to make a stiff batter. Stir in the mushroom, bacon and parsley mixture.

5 Heat a griddle or frying pan and place on it a 5 cm (2 in) greased metal ring. Using a tablespoon, drop a spoonful of batter into the ring on the griddle, and leave to set and colour for a few minutes. Remove the ring, turn over and allow to cook on the second side. Each pancake takes about 5 minutes to cook. Store inside a tea towel until all are cooked. You should have about twelve pancakes.

6 Stack three pancakes per plate, with pieces of halved rasher between each pancake (three whole rashers per three pancakes).

☛ To serve, pour over a little melted butter with chopped parsley and garlic, if desired.

Thick Toast with Bramble Conserve

Sweet preserves such as jam are common and traditional all over Europe. Before sugar became more readily available, in the eighteenth century, honey would have been used to preserve wild and cultivated fruits such as quinces, cherries, plums, damsons and raspberries. At one time these jams would have been made with gluts of fruits, and they would last, hopefully, until the fruit season came round again. This isn't a conserve in the pure sense of the word. It is something to keep in the fridge for a few days and to eat fairly quickly. If you want to keep it for longer, sterilise the jars and seal them correctly.

SERVES 4

	BRAMBLE CONSERVE	
1 loaf wholemeal bread	900 g (2 lb) blackberries	2 tbsp water
175 g (6 oz) unsalted butter	225 g (8 oz) apples, peeled, cored and diced	900 g (2 lb) granulated sugar
		juice of ½ lemon

1 Put several small plates or saucers into the freezer quite a while in advance of starting the conserve (see p. 27).

2 Put 450 g (1 lb) of the blackberries into a large preserving pan with the diced apples and water. Simmer gently until tender, about 35–40 minutes, then pass through a fine sieve into a bowl. You can let the mixture drip through, which will take ages (but will give you a clear preserve), or you can push the mixture through (which makes the preserve cloudy, but much fruitier and punchier).

3 Clean the pan and return the mixture to it. Add the rest of the berries, put back on the heat, and cook until the fruit starts to soften, about 10 minutes.

4 Add the sugar and return to a big heat. Boil quickly, stirring rapidly until the sugar melts. The timing will depend on the fruit, but 5–10 minutes usually. Take a small plate from the freezer and add a spoonful of conserve – it is ready when your finger pushed through it leaves wrinkles in its wake. If it doesn't, keep boiling and test with another cold saucer in a few minutes.

5 When ready, pour the conserve into clean jars and allow to cool.

6 When you want to eat the conserve, cut the wholemeal bread into 2.5 cm (1 in) thick slices, and toast and butter them well. Pile jam on top, and cut in half.

All-day Breakfast Bap

The English breakfast is famous the world over, with its egg, bacon, sausage, fried tomato, fried mushroom and fried bread – cholesterol on a plate! Done well, though, it is delicious, but I have played around with the basic idea here to come up with something completely different. The egg, bacon, sausage, tomato and mushroom are served together in a bun, rather like a burger with lots of different seasonings to taste. I've even added some cheese. It tastes wonderful, at any time of day!

SERVES 8

8 bread buns

FILLING

450 g (1 lb) Cumberland or Lincolnshire sausages

6 slices best-quality back bacon

vegetable oil

8 button mushrooms

25 g (1 oz) butter

salt and freshly ground black pepper

3 hard-boiled eggs, shelled and roughly chopped

5 sun-blush tomatoes, cut into fine strips

a handful of fresh parsley leaves, finely chopped

1 tbsp tomato ketchup, bought or home-made

1 tbsp brown sauce

55 g (2 oz) Cheddar, grated (optional)

1 Remove the outer skin from the sausages, and put the meat in a bowl, gently mix together, and place to one side.

2 Discard the rinds, and cut the bacon rashers into lardons. Fry in a hot pan in 1 tbsp of the oil until golden brown. Drain and cool.

3 Remove the stalks from the mushrooms and cut them and the caps into quarters. Gently fry in the butter and another tbsp of oil. Season and cook until just done. Cool.

4 Incorporate all the ingredients into the sausagemeat, season and mix well together. Shape the mixture into eight equal-sized patties and store in the fridge for half an hour or so before cooking.

5 To cook, heat a couple of tbsp of oil in a frying pan, to a moderate-high temperature. Add the patties, in batches if necessary, and seal both sides. Cook through well, for about 4–6 minutes each side.

6 Meanwhile, warm the buns through in a low oven, and butter them if you like (I don't). Serve a hot breakfast patty in each bun.

St Valentine's Day Breakfast

For a country not particularly known for romance, we in Britain seem to go mad in February, on the 14th to be precise, the day we know as St Valentine's Day. Apparently on and around that date, we send almost as many cards through the post as we do at Christmas. And, as if that were not enough, in this new era of mobile telephonic communication, we send more text messages that day than on any other day of the year!

The tradition of St Valentine dates back to ancient Rome, and there are several theories. The most potent is the one concerning a Christian priest, Valentine, who lived in the third century AD. The emperor, Claudius, had decided to forbid marriage, because he believed that conscripted soldiers were braver and bolder if they remained single. Valentine, believing in the power of love, secretly continued marrying couples, and for this he was later beheaded and martyred. Since then, the date on which he died, 14 February AD 269, has become inextricably associated with love and marriage. As the date is also very close to the times of ancient festivals which honour Juno, queen of the gods (also goddess of women and marriage), and Lupercus (the god of fertility), the conjunction of ideas is not too surprising.

Food and love have long been linked: we all cook food for people we love, and eating together plays such an important part in the early stages of relationships –'Would you like to have dinner with me?...' And of course many people think that a romantic dinner, especially at the start of a new relationship, is the essence of St Valentine. However, for many lovers, a breakfast together is *the* way to celebrate. That is the route I have taken, thinking of delicious treats for breakfast on the day itself: a selection of tiny *blinis* with tasty toppings, or a French toast stuffed with fruit, or simply some bread and jam or marmalade. And don't forget the champagne and orange juice, a buck's fizz.

Irish Soda Bread

Ireland is famous for its simple baking. In the absence of sophisticated raising agents like yeast, and domestic ovens, other means of raising and cooking had to be utilised. At one time buttermilk and other leavens (including sourdough and fermented potato juice) would have raised breads. It was only after the introduction of baking chemicals such as bicarbonate of soda and cream of tartar in the early nineteenth century that the full range of Irish soda breads began to be baked. They are simple to make, and delicious to eat, and are also great as an accompaniment to stews.

Bread such as this would once have been baked on a girdle or griddle or in a frying pan. The bastible, an iron pot with its base in the fire, and hot coals on the lid, was an effective baking oven, still used until very recently in Ireland.

**MAKES 1
ROUND LOAF**

450g (1 lb) flour, half plain white, half wholemeal	½ tsp each of bicarbonate of soda and cream of tartar (or 1 tsp baking powder)
½ tsp salt	300 ml (10 fl oz) buttermilk

1 Lightly grease a baking tray or cast-iron frying pan, and preheat the oven to 200°C/400°F/Gas 6.

2 Sift the flour, salt, bicarb and cream of tartar into a bowl. Add the buttermilk and mix to a dough. Knead and stretch until smooth.

3 Shape into a round on a floured board, and roll flat or use your knuckles, to 4 cm (1½ in) thick.

4 Put on to the tray or into the frying pan, and cut lightly into quarters (or farls). Bake in the preheated oven for 25 minutes, then turn the oven down to 180°C/350°F/Gas 4, and cook for a further 20 minutes.

5 Take out and wrap in a cloth to keep soft. Eat quickly, as it does not keep well. In Ireland, it is made daily and eaten that day.

☛ Buttermilk gives wonderful flavour and texture to this bread. It was once quite difficult to find, but is now stocked by many delis and quite a few supermarkets.

☛ 115g (4 oz) raisins added to this is good too.

Marmalade

Marmalade is thought of as very Scottish but the idea is based on those solid and long-keeping confections popular on the Continent such as the Spanish *'dulce de membrillo'* and the French *'coing'* (in fact quite similar to our own fruit cheeses). The story goes that when Janet Keiller's husband bought some Seville oranges off a ship in their native Dundee at the turn of the eighteenth century, she made a preserve from them. This was based loosely on a recipe for *'marmelo'*, a Portuguese quince paste she had encountered previously. She altered the recipe though, making the preserve less solid, in order to fill more jars – she was a thrifty Scot after all. (The Keiller marmalade factory, which was founded thereafter in 1797, was also where the famous Dundee cake is said to have originated.)

MAKES ABOUT
1.3 KG (3 LB)

900 g (2 lb) Seville oranges	900 g (2 lb) unrefined caster sugar
1.4 litres (2½ pints) water	juice of 2 lemons

1　Wash the oranges well and put in a preserving pan with the water. Slowly boil in the water for around 1½–2 hours then take out and cool. Keep the water.

2　Carefully cut off the peel, leaving the pith behind. Mince or shred the peel – I prefer to mince it.

3　Peel the pith from the oranges with a sharp knife and discard. Take out the pips and wrap them in a muslin bag.

4　Cut the peeled oranges into halves and then slice thinly.

5　Put the orange slices into the orange water, then add the minced peel and the muslin bag of pips. Bring to the boil and simmer for 5 minutes.

6　Take off the heat, then add the sugar and lemon juice. Stir until the sugar has dissolved.

7　Put back on the heat and bring up to the boil quickly. Test for setting after 15 minutes (see opposite).

8　If the marmalade is ready, keep the pan off the heat and allow it to cool for 20 minutes. If not ready, put back on to the heat and bring back to the simmer. Check every 2 minutes.

9　When the marmalade has rested, stir, discard the pips and bottle in sterilised jars.

- Most marmalades are made from Seville oranges – and apparently most of Iberia's Seville orange crop ends up in the UK's marmalades – but this one, with less sugar, can be made from ordinary sweet oranges at any time of year.

- I test to see whether a marmalade, jam or jelly is ready by having several small saucers in the fridge or freezer. When I think my preserve has reached setting point, I take it off the heat, and put a tsp of the mixture on a cold saucer. After it has cooled for a few seconds – count to ten – I push the surface with a finger. If the surface wrinkles, the preserve is ready. If the texture is 'loose', the preserve needs to be boiled for a few minutes more and tested again with another cold saucer.

Blinis with Breakfast Tasters

Blinis are Russian, I know, but basically they are tiny crumpets – a pancake batter raised with yeast (and often made with buckwheat flour). Instead of a piece of toast with delicious breakfast things on it, here we can serve a few *blinis* per person, topped with whatever you like – or indeed a mixture. See some of the taster ideas opposite. If at first you don't succeed with the *blinis,* try, try again. Martin Blunos, a *blini* expert, says, 'The first one never works, but once the pan gets going, it all flows.' And of course these ideas are not just for breakfast, but could be made as canapés as well. And you may think this whole idea is a bit over the top, but if you can't do it on Valentine's Day, when can you? You could make just one of the 'tasters', instead of a selection, and when you have more guests than just one, you could make the *blinis* bigger.

SERVES 2

BLINIS
225 g (8 oz) wholemeal flour
225 g (8 oz) strong plain flour
a pinch of salt

25 g (1 oz) dried yeast
a pinch of caster sugar
1 tsp caraway seeds
6 eggs, separated

300 ml (10 fl oz) soured cream
600 ml (1 pint) milk
175 g (6 oz) clarified butter
(see opposite)

---

1   To make the *blinis*, sift the flours and salt into a large bowl, and make a well in the centre. Add the yeast, sugar and caraway seeds, and then the liquids – the egg yolks, cream and milk – and make into a smooth batter. (To save time, you could measure everything out the night before.)

2   Clean down the sides of the bowl, cover the top with a cloth, and put the batter in a warm place to prove. This can take quite a long time – up to about 40 minutes – and you will know when it is ready as the batter will produce lots of small bubbles.

3   When the batter is ready, whisk the egg whites to a dropping consistency. Fold into the batter carefully.

4   Grease the base of a griddle or frying pan with clarified butter. Drop table-spoonfuls of batter into the butter, a few at a time. Cook until the bottom of each *blini* has become golden, and the top is bubbly, about 2 minutes. Turn the *blinis* over and continue frying for a few more minutes. (You could also make the *blinis* in 5 cm/2 in rings for a neater finish.)

5   Keep the *blinis* warm, wrapped in a clean tea towel, while you make the 'tasters' to go with them.

Breakfast Tasters

Fried Quail's Eggs
Fry, perhaps three per person, in a small frying pan using unsalted butter.

Sausage and Ketchup Rings
Cook a couple of sausages, and cut into slices 1 cm (½in) thick. Smear a *blini* with tomato ketchup and put a sausage slice on top.

Bacon and Scrambled Egg
Make some scrambled egg at the last minute as described on p. 15. Cut some pre-cooked bacon into strips and add to the egg (you could use boiled ham instead of bacon) along with some salt and pepper. Take off the heat, mould on to *blinis* and decorate with a sprig of chervil.

Black Pudding and Horseradish Cream
Slice a small black pudding and fry in oil or grill until cooked on both sides. Smear the *blinis* with horseradish sauce or cream, top with black pudding and brush lightly with olive oil.

☞ You clarify butter to purify it, to get rid of butter solids that might burn if heated to frying temperatures, or simply to have a clear butter, which will look good topping a dish. Put a 225g (8oz) pack of unsalted butter in a small pan, and gently melt. You will see pale solids towards the bottom of the pan, golden clear butter at the top. What you want to do is pour the golden liquid into another pan, very carefully, leaving the pale solids behind, which you discard. It is a wasteful process: you will end up with only about 175g (6oz) clarified butter.

Cranberry and Raspberry Stuffed French Toast

French toast is just another name for eggy bread, and that is so much part of my childhood that I just had to include it – although I admit I have refined it a little! It was the Norman French who introduced to Britain the idea of *pain perdu*, or 'lost bread', and over the centuries we went well over the top, adding sack (wine or sherry), spices and cream, steeping the bread for an hour, before frying it in lavish butter, then spreading it with butter to serve. Adding fruit, as I am doing here, makes it a simpler, more sensible dish, and the basic fruit jam could be useful in many other ways.

SERVES 4

---

115 g (4 oz) unsalted butter, softened	2 tbsp double cream	75 ml (2 fl oz) water
8 thin slices white bread	25 g (1 oz) caster sugar	140 g (5 oz) caster sugar
3 eggs	**STUFFING**	115 g (4 oz) raspberries
	175 g (6 oz) cranberries	

---

1 For the 'stuffing', put the cranberries, water and sugar together in a pot and bring to the boil. Simmer until cooked, about 10–15 minutes, then take off the heat and add the raspberries. Leave to cool.

2 Using about half of the butter, butter lightly one side of each piece of bread. Spread the cranberry mixture on top of half of the buttered slices, then sandwich together with the remaining slices, buttered-side down (i.e. butter on the inside of the sandwich).

3 Beat the eggs and cream together, then add the sugar.

4 Heat the remaining butter gently in a frying pan or more than one pan. Dip the sandwiches carefully into the egg mixture, and place equally carefully into the frying pan or pans. Fry for about 2 minutes, then turn over and fry for a further 2 minutes. You want the eggs to start to crisp and colour.

5 When cooked remove from the pan, drain on kitchen paper, and serve.

☞ If cranberries are not available, just use raspberries alone. And you don't have to make French toast (although it's delicious), you can just serve the fruit with ordinary toast.

☞ When dipping the sandwiches in the egg, if left for 30 seconds to soak they become softer and more delicious, but beware – they will then have to be treated carefully as they could easily break up.

I can't imagine anything more leisurely than a proper morning coffee or afternoon tea: both drinks are usually taken by me on the gallop in the kitchen from a chipped mug or, even less attractively, on a train, from a plastic or paper cup.

Coffee as a drink was first introduced to Britain in the late seventeenth century, and became such a hit that very soon there were hundreds of coffee houses in London and other cities. In these, men (and only men) would meet to discuss the weather, read the news-sheets and exchange gossip. Coffee houses were, I suppose, the forerunners of today's gentlemen's clubs, and indeed the one-time male-only bastion of Lloyd's originated as a coffee house. The ceremony of morning coffee now, though, is seen as more of a female preserve, and the concept comes from Europe, from the great coffee-drinking cities of Vienna, Budapest and Berlin. There, before the Great War, ladies used to meet in the mornings (or indeed afternoons) to discuss parties, fashion and children, either in their own homes or in one of the famous coffee shops (think of the Café Sacher in Vienna, for instance). Sweet cakes and pastries were always part of the occasion, and any of the recipes in this chapter would be ideal to offer, and you should look too at the other cakes and biscuits throughout the book. Just remember that, because coffee is more robust in flavour than tea, you should choose cakes, pastries and biscuits that are slightly stronger in flavour as well.

Afternoon tea, as is well known, is a uniquely British institution. Tea, like coffee, was introduced to Britain in the late seventeenth century, and was popularised by Catherine of Braganza, Charles II's queen, who brought the tea-drinking habit from Portugal. A man called Thomas Twining (a familiar tea name) opened a tea shop in London in 1717, in which ladies could meet and gossip in much the same way as their husbands were doing in the coffee houses. Food didn't play much of a part, it is said, until Anna, the seventh Duchess of Bedford, in the early nineteenth century, got too hungry to wait for her dinner, and ordered some bread and butter to accompany her afternoon cup of tea. The idea spread quickly, and by the end of the century the meal was well established, with toasted breads, sandwiches, muffins, teabreads, crumpets and cakes accompanying the cups of tea.

Despite the plethora of coffee shops in this country – most of them American now – the concept of morning coffee is usually home-based, as is that of afternoon tea. But why, I wonder, are there so few 'tea' shops around, apart from places like the Ritz Hotel? There, afternoon tea in the Palm Court is booked up weeks in advance, mostly by visitors from around Britain as well as from abroad. Tea has always outclassed coffee as a popular drink in Britain, and indeed drinking tea is well known to be our national habit. So come on, my fellow Brits, and anyone else who agrees, let's get back to having a proper and civilised afternoon tea.

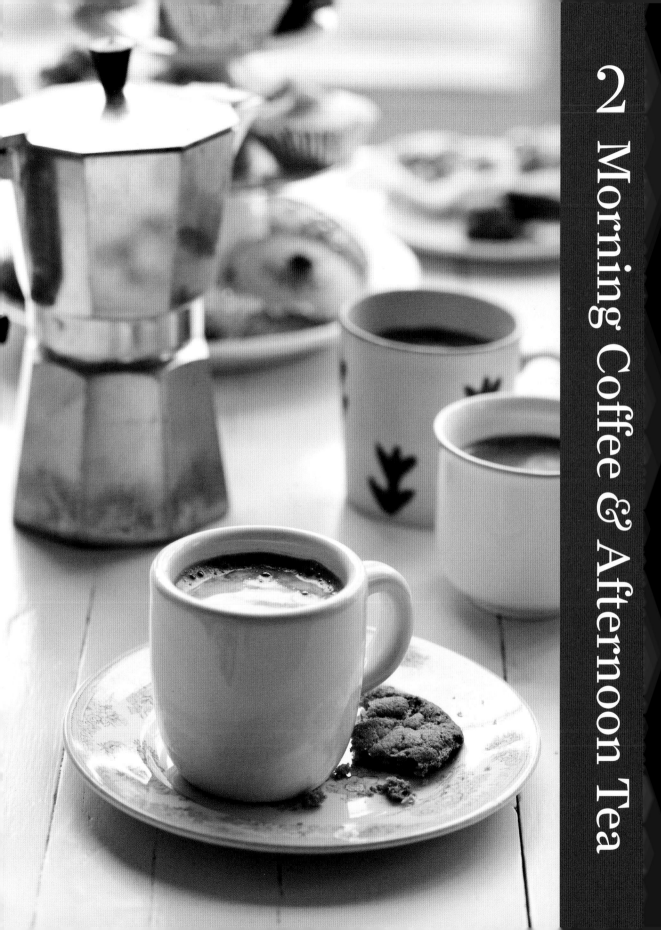

Peach and Banana Scotch Pancakes

Scotch pancakes are what are known as drop scones in England. Traditional English pancakes are thin and wide, made with a runny batter, and can be wrapped round fillings (see p. 248). Drop scones are made with a much thicker batter, and spoonfuls dropped on to a hot griddle pan will make what looks more like a crumpet or Welsh pikelet (although both these latter two are leavened with yeast). The pancakes can be eaten by themselves of course (and they can be savoury, see p. 20), instead of topped with fruit as here – and food snobs hold back, canned peaches are delicious...

SERVES 6

1 recipe *Scotch Pancakes* (see p. 249), omitting the syrup	12 canned peach halves	1 tbsp lemon juice
3 bananas	150 ml (5 fl oz) raspberry purée, sieved	2 tbsp chopped pistachio nuts
a little vegetable oil		

1   Make the sweet Scotch pancake batter as described on p. 249.

2   Peel and purée one of the bananas. Stir this into the pancake batter, and cook as soon as possible.

3   Heat a griddle or griddle pan and brush with a little oil. Drop a tablespoonful of the pancake mixture on to the griddle and leave to set and colour, about 5 minutes. Turn over and cook the second side for a further 3 minutes. When cooked, store the pancakes inside a clean tea towel to keep warm whilst cooking the rest. You should make about twelve pancakes.

4   Slice the bananas and put some decoratively around the edges of each pancake.

5   Put a peach half in the middle, and top with a little raspberry purée, mixed with the lemon juice. Sprinkle with pistachios and serve.

☛ To serve the peach halves warm, you could heat them through gently in a little of their syrup.

☛ Clotted cream would be a great accompaniment.

Madeira Cake

From the 1600s, sweet wines were very popular in Britain, many of them made from the 'malvasia' grape, which was grown all over southern Europe. The Portuguese grew malvasia grapes on the island of Madeira, and the resultant wine was imported into Britain, where the name 'malvasia' was corrupted to 'malmsey' (and in a butt of which the Duke of Clarence was said to have drowned in the Tower). Madeira malmsey was most enjoyed in tandem with a rich sponge cake, which was the eighteenth century's equivalent of lunch; a century later, the custom – of the upper classes only! – became more of a snack. The cake is named after the wine, rather than the reverse, and the recurring theme is the lemon – or probably originally citron – flavour and peel topping.

MAKES 1 CAKE

225 g (8 oz) unsalted butter	4 eggs, beaten	**TOPPING**
225 g (8 oz) unrefined caster sugar	250 g (9 oz) plain flour	4 pieces fresh lemon peel
1 tsp finely grated lemon zest	1 tsp baking powder	4 tsp unrefined caster sugar
1 tsp lemon juice	a pinch of salt	1 tbsp water
seeds from ½ vanilla pod		

1   Preheat the oven to 170°C/340°C/Gas 3–4. Grease an oblong 900 g (2 lb) loaf tin and line with greaseproof or parchment paper.

2   Cream the butter and the sugar with the lemon zest, lemon juice and vanilla seeds. Beat the eggs slowly into the mix. If it starts to separate, don't panic, just sprinkle with a little flour.

3   Sieve the flour and baking powder together, then stir carefully into the butter mixture. Mix in the salt.

4   Fill the prepared tin with the mixture, and smooth the top. Bake in the preheated oven for 45 minutes.

5   Meanwhile heat the pieces of lemon peel, 2 tsp of the sugar and the water together gently on the stove top.

6   Remove the cake from the oven and sprinkle the peel and sugar on top. Return to the oven and bake for a further 45 minutes, for 1½ hours in total. Allow to cool slightly in the tin then take out and cool on a wire rack. Sprinkle the remaining sugar on top.

Popovers

Batter puddings and cakes are a long-established part of the British culinary heritage, and the most famous of these is *Yorkshire Pudding* (see p. 73). Popovers are a sweet version of Yorkshire pud, and although we associate them mainly now with America, they began here.

As for Yorkshire pudding, the way of getting my recipe exactly right is to use cups, thus volume, rather than weight. Be sure, though, to use the same cup to measure all the ingredients! A teacup works very well.

MAKES 12

groundnut oil, for cooking	**POPOVER BATTER**	a pinch of salt
85 g (3 oz) strawberry jam	2 cups plain flour	2 tsp caster sugar
Greek yoghurt	2 cups milk	
icing sugar	2 cups eggs, beaten	

1   For the batter, sieve the flour into a bowl, and make a well in the centre. Pour in the milk, then add the eggs, salt and sugar. Beat to a smooth batter, then strain into another bowl and allow to stand for 30 minutes.

2   Preheat the oven to 220°C/425°F/Gas 7. When ready to cook, heat one of those Yorkshire or popover trays (with twelve holes) in the preheated oven with a little oil in each.

3   When hot, remove the tray from the oven and pour in the batter as fast as possible. Bake in the oven for about 30 minutes. Do not open the door.

4   Turn the oven down to 180°C/350°F/Gas 4, and cook the popovers for a further 5 minutes.

5   Put 1 tsp of jam into each popover, and finish cooking for about 10 minutes.

6   Take out of the oven, and serve two per person, spooned over with yoghurt and sprinkled with icing sugar.

Sally Lunn

Solange Luyon was a French Huguenot, who came to Georgian Bath and opened a bakery. Her house still exists, and is a world-famous tea shop in the city centre. She baked a brioche-like bun/cake (a dough enriched with egg), which was sold in the shop and in the streets: buyers were told to cut them open and spread them with butter (they became fashionable amongst the wealthy, and were eaten for the fairly new-fangled breakfast). The name Sally Lunn is thought to be an anglicisation of her French name, but it could also be based on the street call of the sellers: a derivation of the French *soleil et lune* (sun and moon) – because the top of Sally Lunns looks a bit like the sun.

MAKES 6

50 ml (2 fl oz) milk	450 g (1 lb) plain flour	**TO FINISH**
50 ml (2 fl oz) double cream	a pinch of salt	1 large egg yolk, for egg wash
55 g (2 oz) unsalted butter	25 g (1 oz) caster sugar	finely grated zest of 1 lemon
15 g (½ oz) fresh yeast, stirred (creamed) to a liquid	2 eggs, beaten	a pinch of mixed spice

1 Warm the milk, cream and butter together to blood temperature, just warm enough for you to stand your finger in. Add the yeast and stir. Sprinkle a little flour on top and leave for 10 minutes or so to froth up.

2 Mix the flour, salt and sugar in a bowl and make a well in the centre. Add the beaten eggs to the yeast mixture, then pour all this into the flour. Mix well and knead to amalgamate well. Put in the bowl, cover with a clean cloth and leave in a warm place until it has doubled in size, usually 20–50 minutes.

3 Knock back the dough – by putting it on the work surface and punching the air out of it – then divide it into six even pieces. Shape into round balls, put on to a baking sheet, brush with egg wash and allow to prove again, this time for about 30 minutes (depending on how warm your kitchen is).

4 Preheat the oven to 220°C/425°F/Gas 7.

5 Mix the lemon zest and spice into the remainder of the egg wash. Brush this over the tops of the buns again, then bake in the preheated oven for 15 minutes. Turn the oven down to 180°C/350°F/Gas 4, and bake for a further 10 minutes.

6 Serve warm, split and spread with whipped cream and jam.

Swiss Roll

Sponges are part of our British baking heritage, but baking them thin and rolling them around a filling seems to have been a European influence (although we do have our *Jam Roly-poly*, p. 88). Think of the French Christmas chocolate log cake or *bûche de Noël*, and there are similar ideas in many other countries. Why 'Swiss', though? One theory is that early British tourists, flown to Switzerland for the skiing, encountered a local rolled, jammy sponge cake. They brought the idea back home and dubbed it 'Swiss'.

MAKES I CAKE

3 large eggs	175 g (6 oz) unrefined caster sugar	115 g (4 oz) warm raspberry jam, sieved
I large egg yolk	115 g (4 oz) plain flour	

1 Have all the ingredients out of the fridge in good time to reach room temperature. Preheat the oven to 180°C/350°F/Gas 4. Grease a Swiss roll tray about 30 x 20 cm (12 x 8 in) then line with greased greaseproof paper.

2 Whisk the eggs, egg yolk and 115 g (4 oz) of the sugar together in a mixer to double in volume, then continue whisking until the ribbon stage (see below).

3 Sieve the flour twice on to paper (which makes it super smooth). Pour the flour gently into the egg mixture and mix in carefully with a metal spoon.

4 Pour the mixture gently into the prepared tray then, using a palette knife, spread the mixture evenly. Put into the preheated oven and bake for about 8 minutes. To test that it is cooked properly, run your finger over the sponge: the mark made will disappear quickly.

5 Meanwhile, spread a damp tea towel on your work surface. Place a clean sheet of greaseproof paper on top and sprinkle it with the remaining sugar. Remove the sponge from the oven, and turn it out and over on to the greaseproof paper. Remove the paper from the top of the sponge.

6 Trim the edges of the sponge straight, then pour the warm jam on top. Spread with a palette knife, leaving a 1 cm (½ in) border. Carefully, using the paper and tea towel, roll up nice and tight. Leave to cool, when it will be ready to serve.

☛ The 'ribbon stage' is when you lift up the whisk and it drops trails or ribbons. If the mixture drops and disappears too quickly, the batter needs mixing for longer.

Chelsea Buns

MAKES 16

These are made from a dough not dissimilar to that of the *Sally Lunn* (see p.38), but here it is wrapped around currants and sultanas – and is indeed the same dough with which you can make *Hot Cross Buns* (see p.246), Bath buns, fruit buns etc, all variations on the same theme. Chelsea buns were the speciality of a London bakery, The Chelsea Bun House, from the middle of the eighteenth century.

BASIC BUN DOUGH

450 g (1 lb) plain flour

a pinch of salt

approx. 300 ml (10 fl oz) milk

115 g (4 oz) unsalted butter

55 g (2 oz) unrefined caster sugar

20 g (¾ oz) fresh yeast

1 large egg, beaten

FILLING AND TOPPING

55 g (2 oz) unsalted butter, melted

55 g (2 oz) unrefined caster sugar

½ tsp ground cinnamon

55 g (2 oz) currants

115 g (4 oz) sultanas

25 g (1 oz) mixed chopped candied peel

2 tbsp icing sugar

1 To make the basic bun dough, sift the flour and salt into a bowl. Make a well in the centre.

2 Very gently warm the milk in a pan, with the butter and sugar, to blood temperature. Take off the heat, make sure it's the right temperature – as for a baby's bottle – then crumble in the yeast. Stir to make sure it dissolves.

3 Add to the well in the flour, along with the beaten egg, and mix to make a dough. Knead well, cover with a cloth, and put in a warm place to prove until doubled in size, usually anything from 20–50 minutes.

4 Knock back the dough and knead until it is firm, with no air in it. Roll out into a large square about 1 cm (½ in) thick.

5 Brush the square with melted butter, leaving a 1 cm (½ in) margin all round. Sprinkle with the sugar and cinnamon, then the mixed dried fruits and peel, and carefully press these down.

6 Roll up like a Swiss roll (see p. 39) and cut into 16 x 2.5 cm (1 in) slices. Place these carefully into a greased, deep-sided baking tray about 5 cm (2 in) apart. Cover with a clean cloth and allow to prove until doubled in size, about 30 minutes.

7 Meanwhile, preheat the oven to 220°C/425°F/Gas 7.

8 Bake the buns in the preheated oven for 15–20 minutes.

9 When taken out, brush immediately with a mixture of icing sugar and enough water to make a single cream consistency. This gives the buns their characteristic white sheen.

☛ The buns will touch each other when proving and baking, and look like a sheet of buns joined together. When separated, this gives a lighter eating experience.

Cream Cake

One of my mother's favourite regular treats was a cream cake, which she bought from the local baker's, not at a supermarket. Cakes like these have been part of my culinary history. One of my earliest experiences in the baking field was working with Frank and Theo at the Glendale Bakery on Morley Top Road. We would make big six-portion cream cakes and, on Friday and Saturday, we would sell them on stalls at markets in Morley, Dewsbury, Batley and Bradford.

MAKES 1 x
2-LAYER CAKE
FOR 6 PEOPLE

	FILLING AND TOPPING	115 g (4 oz) strawberries, hulled and chopped
4 eggs	600 ml (1 pint) double cream	115 g (4 oz) strawberry jam
115 g (4 oz) unrefined caster sugar	55 g (2 oz) unrefined caster sugar	icing sugar, to dust
115 g (4 oz) plain flour	seeds from 1 vanilla pod	
55 g (2 oz) unsalted butter, melted		

1   Preheat the oven to 200°C/400°F/Gas 6. Grease and flour a 25 cm (10 in) round cake tin.

2   Whisk the eggs and sugar together over a pan of hot water. Continue whisking until doubled in volume and at the ribbon stage (see p. 39).

3   Remove from the heat, and whisk until the mixture is cold.

4   Sieve the flour a couple of times on to paper, then add slowly to the egg and sugar mixture. Fold in gently, followed by the melted butter.

5   Pour the mixture into the prepared cake tin and bake in the preheated oven for about 30 minutes.

6   Take out and leave to cool for 5 minutes in the tin then cool completely, out of the tin, on a wire rack. When cold, cut in half horizontally.

7   Whisk the cream with the sugar and vanilla seeds until thick. Mix the strawberries and jam together and put on the bottom layer of the cake. Pipe the cream on top of the jam, and put the top on the cake. Shake over some icing sugar, cut and serve.

☛ For the stalls, or just for show, we would cut the top part of the cake into eight, then put these back on top of the cake, on top of the cream, but at an angle. I loved doing that, and thought it was genius! I still do.

☛ When making a sponge over hot water, the bowl should sit in the pan but not touch the water. This is done to set the eggs slowly while allowing the volume to increase sufficiently to hold the air and make the cake lighter!

Fruit Cake

Cakes are in essence made from bread doughs enriched with other ingredients, such as butter or lard, spices, sugar and eggs. Some were raised by yeast, and even more were packed full of dried fruit – sultanas, raisins and chopped peel – which had become part of British celebratory eating since the times of the Crusades. From the mid-sixteenth century, the 'bride' (wedding) cake was a rich fruit cake; but it wasn't until much later that a similar cake became part of the Christmas feast. This one would make a good Christmas cake (see how to decorate it on p. 221).

MAKES 1 CAKE

---

450 g (1 lb) California golden raisins

115 g (4 oz) glacé cherries

115 g (4 oz) semi-dried apricots

55 g (2 oz) each of crystallised mixed peel and crystallised ginger

50 ml (2 fl oz) each of brandy and rum

50 ml (2 fl oz) infused black tea

115 g (4 oz) unsalted butter

115 g (4 oz) unrefined brown sugar

3 large eggs, beaten

1 tsp black treacle

140 g (5 oz) plain flour

a pinch of baking powder

25 g (1 oz) each of ground almonds and ground hazelnuts

¼ tsp ground cinnamon

---

1 Put the raisins in a large bowl. Cut the remaining fruit as necessary, and put into the bowl with the raisins. Slightly warm the brandy, rum and tea together, then pour over the fruit. Leave to macerate for 24 hours.

2 On the day of baking, drain the fruit, and put to one side, keeping the remaining liquor.

3 Preheat the oven to 160°C/325°F/Gas 3. Grease a 25 cm (10 in) round cake tin and line with plenty of two- or three-ply greaseproof or parchment paper.

4 Cream the butter and sugar together in a large bowl, then slowly add the beaten eggs, then beat in the treacle.

5 Sieve the flour and baking powder together into another bowl, then add the almonds, hazelnuts and cinnamon. Stir this into the butter mixture, then add the drained fruit. Carefully and thoroughly mix together.

6 Spoon into the prepared tin, and flatten the top using wet hands. Bake in the preheated oven for 30 minutes, then reduce the temperature to 140°C/275°F/Gas 1, and bake for a further 1½ hours.

7 Take out and leave in the tin. Pour the reserved liquor over, and allow to soak in before removing the cake from the tin.

Victoria Sponge

A true sponge is actually fatless – made from eggs, sugar and flour only – and is so light that it could never be used to hold any type of filling other than jam or some cream. The Victoria sponge, a 'creamed' cake, was created later, obviously named after the old Queen, and included butter 'creamed' with the sugar, and baking powder. (It's the butter that makes it rather crumbly.) I used to make these at school with Elsie Bibby, my teacher. We called them 'jam' sponges, but would sometimes use a butter cream too (icing sugar and unsalted butter). A Victoria sandwich sponge cake is good for tea, along with other cakes and biscuits, but must be very fresh.

MAKES 1 x 2-LAYER CAKE

115 g (4 oz) unsalted butter, plus extra for greasing	115 g (4 oz) unrefined caster sugar	**FILLING AND TOPPING**
115 g (4 oz) plain flour, plus extra for dusting	2 eggs, beaten	about 4 tbsp jam
	½ tsp baking powder	icing sugar

1 Butter and flour two 18 cm (7 in) sponge tins, and preheat the oven to 200°C/400°F/Gas 6.

2 Cream the measured butter and sugar together until soft and white. Gradually add the beaten eggs.

3 Sift the flour and baking powder together and lightly fold into the butter mixture.

4 Divide the mixture between the two tins and bake in the preheated oven for 10–15 minutes. Turn out on to a wire cake rack and leave to cool.

5 Spread one sponge with jam and lay the other on top. Dust with icing sugar and serve.

Parkin

Gingerbread has been made in Britain for centuries, and parkin is basically the northern form of gingerbread, but made with the local cereal, oats. Like early gingerbreads, some parkins were made as biscuits, cooked until as hard as most gingerbread men, and on the griddle. Others were made into chemically raised soft sponges that could be baked in the oven, sliced and spread with butter. Different parkins are identified by county names, and this one, inevitably from Yorkshire, and one of the most famous, is traditionally eaten on 5 November. Guy Fawkes was a York man, born and bred...

SERVES 6–8

225 g (8 oz) fine oatmeal	115 g (4 oz) unsalted butter	115 g (4 oz) black treacle
225 g (8 oz) plain flour	115 g (4 oz) unrefined demerara sugar	115 g (4 oz) golden syrup
1 tbsp ground ginger		2 tbsp milk (optional)
½ tsp baking powder	1 egg, beaten	

1 Line a 20 cm (8 in) square baking tray with greaseproof paper and preheat the oven to 160°C/325°F/Gas 3.

2 Mix the oatmeal and flour with the ginger and baking powder, then rub in the butter to a crumb consistency. Add the sugar and beaten egg.

3 Warm the treacle and syrup gently to melt, and add to the mixture. Mix to a paste, using the milk if necessary to achieve a slightly sloppy consistency.

4 Pour the mixture into the prepared baking tray and bake for 1 hour plus. Press the top with the back of a spoon: if it springs back into shape immediately, it is cooked. Take out of the oven and leave to cool a little.

5 After 5 minutes, cut into squares, and then leave to cool completely before taking out of the tin.

6 Store in an airtight container for about a week before eating. This is quite important, as the characteristics of the cake change. Eat as a cake.

☛ Syrup and treacle are notoriously difficult to get out of their tins to be measured properly. The answer is to warm the tins in boiling water (sit them in a pan) or in a low oven. The content of the tins becomes more liquid, which means it is easier to spoon or pour out – but do be careful, the tins will be hot.

Birthday Tea

In our western culture, birthdays are important. The actual day of your birth is celebrated every year, with certain years deemed to be of particular significance: the 18th or 21st, for instance, and the 40th, 50th, 60th or 100th. In other cultures, however, it is often a coming of age, or a transition into adulthood, that is more celebrated than an actual date, and obviously that is not an annual event.

Whether conventional birthday, or coming of age, these occasions always seem to be celebrated with a party. In very early, pre-Christian days, people thought themselves vulnerable to attack from evil spirits on the day on which they were born, and so they would surround themselves with friends and family. Singing, dancing and making merry would drive away the spirits (which sounds a lot like a birthday party to me!). People would bring the celebrant happy thoughts to help them through their day, and this later developed into bringing actual presents.

Why we have birthday cakes, I'm not quite sure, although any excuse for a party and a cake! Some say that the birthday cake is a relic of an old Greek tradition, when worshippers would take candle-topped cakes as an offering to the goddess of the moon, Artemis. Ancient peoples also believed that the smoke from their fires would take their wishes up to heaven: this might be related to the silent wish we make when we blow out the candles on our birthday cake. If you succeed in doing so in one breath, your wish will be granted.

Birthday cards became popular in Britain and the United States in the late nineteenth century, originally sent as an apology for being unable to attend the party. We now send cards anyway, whether there's a party or not, and millions of them are delivered every year. Another birthday tradition is the singing of 'Happy birthday to you'. This was a song written in 1893, by two sisters, with the original words 'Good morning to all'. (The present words were substituted in 1935.) The song, amazingly, is still in copyright, until 2010 (it must have made a fortune), and is ranked the most frequently sung song in the *Guinness Book of Records*.

We don't seem to celebrate birthdays as much as we used to, but probably because we are all getting older. That's why the recipes here are more for grown-ups than for children. We do hold parties still for kids, who love them, but I must admit I am getting to the stage where I think of *un*birthday parties...

Chocolate and Hazelnut Cake

The cake is the centre of any birthday tea and people love chocolate! The addition of ground nuts, which have been toasted first, adds a wonderful flavour, and they take the place of flour, making this recipe good for coeliacs. Always remember, the better the chocolate, the better the finished cake. I use Green & Black's dark, with 70 per cent cocoa butter.

MAKES I CAKE

225 g (8 oz) dark chocolate
6 eggs
280 g (10 oz) caster sugar
115 g (4 oz) ground hazelnuts

55 g (2 oz) ground almonds
I tbsp strong liquid coffee
TOPPING
115 g (4 oz) sieved apricot jam

3 tbsp double cream
115 g (4 oz) dark chocolate, broken into pieces
55 g (2 oz) unsalted butter

1   Preheat the oven to 180°C/350°F/Gas 4. Grease and line a 20 cm (8 in) cake tin with greaseproof paper.

2   Break the chocolate into small pieces, and melt carefully in a bowl standing over a pan of hot water. Do not let the water touch the bowl.

3   Separate four of the eggs. Put the yolks and the two whole eggs into a bowl, along with the sugar, and whisk until thick and creamy. In a separate bowl, whisk the egg whites to stiff peaks.

4   Toast the ground nuts quickly – do not over-colour – and leave to cool.

5   Add the toasted ground nuts, liquid coffee and melted chocolate to the egg mixture, then gently fold in the whisked egg white.

6   Pour this into the prepared cake tin and bake in the preheated oven for 30 minutes. Cover with a piece of foil, and bake for a further 30 minutes. (To check if cooked, plunge a skewer into the centre; it will come out with no uncooked cake on it.)

7   Remove the tin from the oven, and leave to sit for 10 minutes. Take the cake out of the tin, and leave to cool on a wire cake rack.

8   For the topping, melt the apricot jam in a small pan, brush over the outside of the cake, and allow to cool. Boil the cream in a small pan, then take off the heat. Add the chocolate pieces, and stir in until melted. Beat in the soft butter. Allow to cool slightly before pouring on to the cake. Use a palette knife to roughly smooth over. Leave to set a little before serving.

☛ Caramelised nuts make a nice accompaniment: just sauté with some sugar.

Scones

Rather like soda bread (see p. 25), a scone mixture would have been raised with buttermilk and cooked on the griddle until the advent of chemical leavens and domestic ovens in the nineteenth century. Varieties of scones are found all over Britain, but the name (pronounced to rhyme with 'gone' in Scotland, 'clone' elsewhere) and the basic concept are claimed as their own by the Scots.

In his café, my dad and his helper, Annie Denton, used to make large scones like this, divided into four farls. They were made to eat then and there, not to be kept.

MAKES 1
LARGE SCONE

---

115 g (4 oz) cold unsalted butter, diced, plus extra for greasing

450 g (1 lb) self-raising flour

a pinch of salt

115 g (4 oz) unrefined caster sugar

300 ml (10 fl oz) milk or buttermilk at room temperature, plus extra for brushing

---

1 Lightly butter a baking tray and preheat the oven to 200°C/400°F/Gas 6.

2 Sift the flour and salt into a bowl, and quickly rub in the cold butter. Make a well in the centre.

3 Dissolve the sugar in the milk or buttermilk and pour into the well. Gradually stir the flour into the liquid and mix to a dough. Do this as cleanly and quickly as you can. (Speed is of the essence when making scones.) Do not overmix.

4 Shape into a large round, brush with milk, and cut a cross in the top.

5 Put on the baking tray and bake in the preheated oven for 10–15 minutes.

☛ You can vary scones almost infinitely. The Welsh add 115 g (4 oz) extra butter and 225 g (8 oz) currants, and I remember Dad used to make date scones. You could also make savoury scones, adding 225 g (8 oz) grated Cheddar to the above mixture instead of the sugar.

☛ In Yorkshire we used to roll out the mixture and cut out small shapes with a fluted cutter to make individual scones. These would take slightly less time to cook.

Shortbread

Shortbread biscuits appear all over Britain (in Shrewsbury cakes and the Goosenargh cakes from Lancashire, for instance, both containing caraway seeds), but they are most associated with Scotland. They are 'short' because they contain no liquid, and may be made as 'fingers' or 'petticoat tails'. I've done the latter here, although I haven't cut out a circle from the middle in the traditional way (to prevent broken points to the wedges).

Through John Grant, whose family make Glenfarclas, my favourite whisky, I met James Walker of Aberlour, whose family make the best commercial shortbread. I have encountered him on the odd occasion since, at food exhibitions and the like, and always seem to get a box of shortbread shortly afterwards! Not that I'm complaining...

MAKES 2
ROUNDS,
ABOUT
16 PIECES

---

225 g (8 oz) unsalted butter, plus extra for greasing

115 g (4 oz) unrefined caster sugar, plus extra for dredging

225 g (8 oz) plain flour

115 g (4 oz) rice flour

a pinch of salt

---

1   Lightly butter a baking sheet and preheat the oven to 160°C/325°F/Gas 3.

2   Cream the measured butter and sugar together until light.

3   Sift the flour, rice flour and salt together, and fold carefully into the butter mixture.

4   Split the mixture in two and shape each half into balls. Flatten each with the hands and put on to the baking sheet. Crimp the edges, then cut across the top, not quite through, into eighths. Prick the centres with a fork.

5   Bake in the preheated oven for 20 minutes, then turn the oven down to 140°C/275°F/Gas 1 and bake for a further 20–30 minutes.

6   Leave to cool. The shortbread will be soft baked at this stage, but as it cools it will crisp up. Dredge with sugar before serving.

☛ The secrets of shortbread are: use the best ingredients available (there are so few) and handle the dough as briefly as possible.

Coconut Macaroons

Macaroons have been a popular sweetmeat in Britain since as early as Elizabethan times. They were probably introduced from France and Italy, where similar egg-white-raised biscuits were made with ground nuts – think of the Italian *amaretti,* made with almonds – but I really have no idea. In the old days, macaroons were traditionally served with sherry and sweet wines, but my mother's were supposed to be served with tea. However, they never made it that far, as they were always finished before they had even cooled!

MAKES
ABOUT 18

vegetable oil, for greasing	a few drops of almond essence	115 g (4 oz) desiccated coconut
2 egg whites	175 g (6 oz) caster sugar	9 glacé cherries, halved
	55 g (2 oz) ground almonds	

1 Preheat the oven to 180°C/350°F/Gas 4. Cover a baking sheet with rice paper, and grease an egg-cup with a little oil.

2 Whisk the egg whites until frothy. Add the almond essence, sugar, almonds and coconut, and stir in well.

3 Push some of the mixture into the greased egg-cup, a cupful at a time, then turn out on to the rice paper. Repeat until all the mixture is used. Top each macaroon with a half glacé cherry.

4 Bake in the preheated oven for about 15 minutes until coloured golden brown. Remove, leave to cool, then cut around the rice papers and serve. (They can keep in an airtight container for a few days.)

L unch – or 'luncheon' to give it its original and formal name – is, as we all know, a meal taken at midday (or thereabouts). We think of it as a meal cast in stone so far as Britain is concerned, but in reality it hasn't actually been around all that long.

The eating day in Britain used to be quite different from what it is now. Working people, particularly those working on the land, would rise with the sun and go to bed with the sun: they would break their night's fast when they got up at dawn (thus 'breakfast'), and have a more substantial meal in the middle of the day, which was called 'dinner'. (Many people in the north of England and in Scotland still call a midday meal 'dinner', and in this they are historically correct. And it's interesting that school lunches are more commonly referred to as 'school dinners', and the women who cook and serve it are very much 'dinner ladies'.) Before going to bed, working people might have something light for 'supper'.

The more leisured classes, however, partly because they could afford proper candles and, later, oil lamps, were able to extend their days, and therefore the hours at which they took their main meal of 'dinner'. In more sophisticated households, the dinner hour became later and later until, in the eighteenth century, people found they needed a midday snack to bridge the gap between breakfast and dinner. The *Oxford English Dictionary* gives one definition of 'lunch' as a 'piece' or 'thick piece' (a sandwich is still called 'piece' in parts of Scotland), and 'luncheon' as 'a slight repast taken between two meal-times, *esp*. in the morning'. The word may have been adapted from 'nuncheon' (a dialect word now), which derives from an Anglo-Saxon term meaning 'noon drink', and indeed early

lunches were often ale or beer accompanied by bread, and occasionally cheese (a ploughman's?).

It was only in the nineteenth century that lunch became the meal we know today. As agriculture employed fewer people, and more people worked in towns and offices, the working and eating day became increasingly determined by office hours rather than the day's natural cycle. Men working from home would eat large breakfasts and large dinners, little in between (although chop houses and men's clubs soon appeared to cater for midday appetites). It was women, who stayed at home, who became the earliest lunchers, having guests or visiting friends, hence the mildly sarcastic phrase 'ladies who lunch' – a term still used today.

Lunches now can be 'light', a 'working lunch' or more substantial affairs, when friends and family sit down to several courses, which can take most of the afternoon. This, to me, is perfect for a Sunday: people communicate with each other, help you peel the veg, eat and appreciate and, hopefully, take over the washing-up. I think it's sad that we rush through such a meal, because of the match on the TV, or miss out on it completely because the children are out. I recently auctioned myself as cook and teacher for a Sunday lunch course (on behalf of the Anthony Nolan Trust), and was amazed at the response. So many top barristers, businessmen and professional people wanted to learn how to cook roast beef. We started at 10 in the morning, and finally sat down to our well-earned 'lunch' at 6.30. That was a great day, and I hope some of the recipes in this chapter – traditional roasts, pies, stews, puddings etc – will make your next Sunday a great lunch day.

Fish Pie

SERVES 6–8

In medieval times, mixtures of fish would have been topped with pastry, both to seal in the flavour and to serve as added fuel. Although pastry can of course still be used, we now commonly use the words 'fish pie' to mean fish topped with mashed potato.

115 g (4 oz) monkfish, off the bone
175 g (6 oz) salmon, skinned
12 scampi tails, shelled
6 tomatoes
salt and freshly ground black pepper
1 tsp balsamic vinegar
2 spring onions, finely chopped

SAUCE
55 g (2 oz) unsalted butter
55 g (2 oz) plain flour
150 ml (5 fl oz) chicken stock
300 ml (10 fl oz) milk
150 ml (5 fl oz) double cream
2 tbsp chopped fresh chives
1 tbsp grain mustard

TOPPING
450 g (1 lb) baked jacket potatoes
115 g (4 oz) unsalted butter
55 g (2 oz) Cheddar, grated
25 g (1 oz) unsalted butter, melted

1 Preheat the oven to 180°C/350°F/Gas 4. Have ready a 1.2 litre (2 pint) pie dish.

2 Cut the monkfish and salmon into 2.5 cm (1 in) dice. Cut the shelled scampi in half. Cut the tomatoes into six segments each. Mix all these together in a bowl, and season with salt, pepper and balsamic vinegar.

3 For the sauce, melt the butter, add the flour and mix together. Boil the chicken stock, milk and double cream together, then slowly add to the 'roux' of butter and flour. Beat in to get rid of any lumps.

4 Add the chives, mustard and fish to the sauce, and season with salt and pepper. Bring back to the boil and then immediately remove from the heat. Put into the pie dish and allow to cool.

5 Meanwhile, for the topping, scrape the flesh from the skins of the warm baked potatoes into a bowl. Add the butter and cheese and beat into a good smooth mash. Season with salt and pepper, and put on top of the fish. Smooth over with a palette knife, dipping the knife frequently in the melted butter, then use the side of the knife to make little indentations or ridges around the pie. Brush any remaining butter over the top.

6 Bake in the preheated oven for 30 minutes until the top is crisp and brown. Take out, sprinkle with the spring onions, and serve.

- Not everyone likes cheese with fish, so you could add horseradish or mustard to the basic recipe above, or a normal boiled potato mash, and a *Bubble and Squeak* mash (see p. 142) would be quite interesting too.

- I occasionally top a fish pie with layers of lightly fried thin slices of potato, as if I were making sauté potatoes.

- I use baked potatoes because the flesh has much more flavour, and it is drier because the potato hasn't been immersed in water during cooking.

- Chicken stock helps with the flavour of the pie – i.e. not too fishy – but if serving to non-meat eaters, vegetable or fish stock both work – or even dry white wine.

Poacher's Pie

When it became an offence for the ordinary man to kill wild game, I think Britain turned into a nation of poachers! Rabbits were probably the easiest prey, and would have been a welcome addition to the family pot. When it is around, usually in the autumn, the prices are still very good.

SERVES 4

450 g (1 lb) boned rabbit meat

115 g (4 oz) back bacon rashers

2 tbsp chopped fresh parsley

1 tsp chopped garlic

115 g (4 oz) diced red onion

225 g (8 oz) potatoes, peeled

115 g (4 oz) button mushrooms

salt and freshly ground black pepper

about 450 ml (15 fl oz) chicken stock

SAVOURY SHORTCRUST PASTRY

225 g (8 oz) plain flour

55 g (2 oz) each of butter and lard

4 tbsp cold water

1 medium egg yolk mixed with a little water, for egg wash

1   Preheat the oven to 180°C/350°F/Gas 4.

2   To make the pastry, put the flour, butter, lard and a little salt into a bowl. Rub the fats into the flour using your fingertips, then use enough cold water to make a dough that is easy to handle. Mix well, cover with clingfilm and leave to rest for about half an hour minimum.

3   Cut the rabbit flesh into 1 cm (½ in) dice. Cut the bacon into fine dice and mix with the rabbit, parsley, garlic and onion.

4   Slice the potatoes and the mushrooms. Mix these together, and season.

5   Put a third of the rabbit mix into a 1.2–1.7 litre (2–3 pint) pie dish. Layer half the potatoes and mushrooms on top. Put in another layer of rabbit, using half of what you have left, then potatoes and finally rabbit. Fill the dish two-thirds full of stock only (you may not use all the stock).

6   Roll out the pastry to the shape of the top of the pie dish, but a little larger. Cut a strip from around the edges of the pastry shape. Dampen the rim of the pie dish and put the strip of pastry round the edge. Lay the pastry shape on top and seal to the pastry rim with your fingers. Brush the top of the pie with egg wash, and make a hole in the middle for the steam to escape. Pull the back of a fork several times through the egg wash to make a pattern, then brush with egg wash again.

7   Bake the pie in the preheated oven for 30 minutes. Reduce the heat to 160°C/325°F/Gas 3, and cook for a further 45 minutes. Serve hot.

Beef Cecils

This is a traditional leftover recipe, which is like a cross between a hash and a fritter – and indeed like the rissoles my mother used to make, although she deep-fried them. In old cookbooks Cecils are described as a way of using up cold roast beef that had not been done enough; it should be served with a gravy like beef olives. Its name may be associated with William Cecil (later Lord Burghley), who was a politician in the time of Elizabeth I, and who passed laws regarding food (fish days and the like). It is interesting that the Scrabble dictionary says the word 'cecils' is allowed (it's meatballs), but that it is only ever found in the plural.

SERVES 4

450 g (1 lb) cooked roast beef

1 red onion, peeled and finely chopped

55 g (2 oz) unsalted butter

1 garlic clove, peeled and crushed

1 tbsp capers, drained and chopped

1 tbsp chopped fresh parsley

55 g (2 oz) fresh white breadcrumbs

2 canned anchovy fillets, chopped

½ egg, beaten

freshly grated nutmeg

a splash each of Worcestershire and Tabasco sauces

salt and freshly ground black pepper

1 tbsp vegetable oil

COATING

25 g (1 oz) plain flour

1 egg, beaten

115 g (4 oz) fresh white breadcrumbs

1 tsp chopped fresh parsley

1   Preheat the oven to 180°C/350°F/Gas 4.

2   Mince the beef. Do it in a mincer or by hand, but do not put in a food processor.

3   In a large frying pan, soften the onion in half the butter, then add the garlic, then the beef, and heat for a minute or so. Remove to a bowl and add the capers, parsley, breadcrumbs, anchovy and egg to mix. Season with nutmeg, Worcestershire, Tabasco and some salt and pepper. Mix well together.

4   Roll the mixture into eight round balls, then flatten lightly. Put the flour and egg on separate small plates. Mix the breadcrumbs and parsley and put on a third plate. Coat each meatball with flour first, shaking off the excess, then coat with beaten egg then breadcrumbs and parsley.

5   Fry in the oil and remaining butter until coloured on one side, then turn over and stick in the preheated oven for 10 minutes. Remove from the oven, drain, and serve hot with a piquant tomato sauce (see p. 156). I like them with chips or potatoes shallow-fried with onions, and I am not averse to some HP sauce…

Onion Charlottes

This is a savoury version of apple charlotte, a typically British combination of bread with fruit or vegetable, in this case slow-cooked onions. Bread was always used to eke out other ingredients, so this is quite an economical dish (and tastes great). The name 'charlotte' has been the subject of some debate over the years. It is most likely that it was applied to dishes in honour of the wife of George III, Charlotte Sophia of Mecklenburg-Strelitz, in the late eighteenth century.

SERVES 4

140 g (5 oz) unsalted butter

450 g (1 lb) red onions, peeled and thinly sliced

150 ml (5 fl oz) vegetable stock

12 slices white bread, crusts cut off

a pinch of freshly grated nutmeg

a pinch of ground cinnamon

1 tsp each of chopped fresh sage and parsley

salt and freshly ground black pepper

TOPPING

55 g (2 oz) mature Cheddar, grated

25 g (1 oz) fresh white breadcrumbs

½ tsp dry English mustard powder

1 tbsp chopped fresh chives

1 Preheat the oven to 190°C/375°F/Gas 5. Have ready four dariole moulds, which are like rounded ramekins, with slightly higher sides (or use small ramekins), on a baking sheet.

2 Melt 25 g (1 oz) of the butter in a large pan, add the onion and allow to colour, about 4–5 minutes. Meanwhile, melt the remaining butter in another small pan, and keep to one side.

3 Add the vegetable stock to the onion pan, bring to a simmer and cook for up to 20 minutes to allow the stock to evaporate and for the onions to take on some more colour. Remove the onions from the pan, and allow to cool and drain.

4 Cut out four circles from four of the bread slices that will fit into the bottoms of the moulds. Dip one side of each circle into the melted butter then put dipped-side down into the mould. Cut four slices of the bread into 4–5 cm (1½–2 in) strips of a length to fit the height of the moulds. Dip one side of each strip into melted butter, then fit, overlapping well, into the moulds, buttered sides touching the sides of the moulds. Take care to leave no gaps.

5 Mix the cooked, cooled and drained onion with the nutmeg, cinnamon, sage and parsley, then season with salt and pepper and put to drain in a sieve. Fill the moulds with this mixture almost to the top. Cut rounds of bread from the remaining slices of a size to seal the onions in the moulds. You don't need to butter these.

6 Bake in the preheated oven for about 30–40 minutes. When cooked, take out of the oven and leave to stand for 5 minutes.

7 Carefully remove the little charlottes from their moulds by inverting them on to a small baking tray, and then put them on to a serving dish. Mix the topping ingredients together, sprinkle over the charlottes, and return to the oven for 2 minutes to melt the cheese. Serve immediately.

☛ Don't worry if the cooked onions change colour when cold, they will change back again when cooked.

Wood Pigeon Potato Cake

Wild pigeons would have been considered fair game for the ordinary man (and for poachers), because they stole grain, but they were also valued by those higher up the social scale. Many British manor houses and monasteries, dating from centuries ago, have dovecotes for raising doves or wood pigeons built into roofs or walls (an idea imported by the Romans). Potato cakes are traditional – and in fact a pigeon dumpling was once a well-loved dish in Scotland – but the basic (and quite unashamedly sophisticated) ideas here have been adapted from elsewhere: the French *confit* technique has been used for the pigeon legs, and this tasty meat flavours the potato cake, with fresh pigeon breasts served on top.

SERVES 4

---

6 plump pigeons, cleaned and plucked

2 garlic cloves, peeled and halved

enough duck fat to cover the legs

150 ml (5 fl oz) red wine

150 ml (5 fl oz) chicken stock

350 g (12 oz) potatoes, peeled

1 onion, peeled

salt and freshly ground black pepper

1 tbsp fresh thyme leaves

55 g (2 oz) unsalted butter

1 tbsp chopped fresh chervil

☛ This is, I admit, a much more complicated recipe than most of the others here, but in a way it's not so complicated as it sounds. There are really only three elements – the potato cake, the sauce and pigeon – and you just need to watch your timing. You can make the same dish using quail, partridge or even pheasant. Just be aware of size, and don't serve three breasts of pheasant per person!

☛ A less fussy way is to cook an extra pair of pigeon breasts first and use these instead of the pigeon legs if you are not worried about cost. In this case, use the legs with the trimmings in the sauce.

1   Take the crowns – the double breasts – off the pigeon carcasses, and trim.
    Cut off the legs.

2   Put the 12 pigeon legs into a small pan with the garlic, and cover with melted
    duck fat. Gently heat, approximately 80°C/176°F, and cook at a mere simmer
    for 1 hour. Take out, drain and cool. Keep the fat (to use here, and to roast
    your Sunday lunch potatoes).

3   Take all the meat off the cooled and skinned legs, and put to one side. Place
    the bones with the trimmings in a pot and colour in a little of the reserved
    duck fat. Add the red wine and stock, and reduce slowly by half.

4   Meanwhile grate the peeled potatoes into a bowl. Chop the pigeon leg meat
    and add to the potato. Grate the onion into a small bowl, and get rid of the
    juice: put the onion in a clean tea towel, and squeeze all the juices out (save
    these and use in sauces or curries instead of stock). Put the onion with the
    potato mixture. Mix together well, and season with salt and pepper.

5   When ready to cook, preheat the oven to 200°C/400°F/Gas 6.

6   Put a little duck fat into a large frying pan and put four piles of potato in
    to make four potato cakes. Push down to flatten a little and colour. When
    coloured on one side, turn over and leave to slowly cook while you prepare
    the pigeon crowns and sauce.

7   Seal the crowns by frying in some duck fat in a little heatproof and ovenproof
    pan, then roast in the preheated oven for about 8 minutes. Keep them
    underdone. When cooked, take out and leave to rest.

8   Throw away the excess fat from the pan, then add the reduced wine and
    stock and the thyme. Allow to simmer for 10 minutes, then reduce by boiling
    swiftly. Strain into a clean pan, shake in the butter, then season and add the
    chopped chervil.

9   Take the breasts off the pigeon crowns, and season them. Lay three breasts
    per person on a potato cake. Spoon the sauce over and serve.

Sea Bass with Fennel Butter

Fish was once the mainstay of the diet – at times, monotonously so, during the medieval period when three days a week at least had to be meat free. This has completely changed now, with fish an increasing luxury on our plates, principally due to its scarcity because of pollution and over-fishing. Sea bass have been highly prized since Greek and Roman times, and they have a range which extends from the Black Sea up to Norway. Because they occasionally swim a little upriver, therefore can survive in lagoons, they have proved capable of being farmed, and many fish now are farmed rather than wild. Whichever, they are wonderful cooked with the anise flavour of fennel, a herb introduced by the Romans, and often associated with seafood. Here I have used bulb fennel, an Italian introduction, for an extra bit of oomph.

SERVES 4

4 x 550 g (1¼ lb) sea bass	salt and freshly ground black pepper
2 fennel bulbs	2 tbsp lemon juice
4 garlic cloves, unpeeled	1 shallot, peeled and chopped
2 tbsp olive oil	225 g (8 oz) cold unsalted butter

☞ The two most common ways of cooking sea bass are baking it encased in salt, and grilling on the barbecue, with fennel herb inside. The moral of the story is that a good sea bass doesn't need much doing to it...

1 Preheat the oven to 200°C/400°F/Gas 6. Make a steamer by putting a trivet in a roasting tray, on which the fish will sit.

2 Prepare the bass, firstly by de-scaling. Using a sharp knife, push towards the head, taking off all the scales (any remainder can be washed off). Now with scissors take off all the fins. Cut off the head from behind where the fin was at an angle to keep as much flesh as possible. Slit the belly and clean out the guts. Use the handle of a small ladle to scrape out the bloodline from the belly and then trim the belly skin evenly at an angle. Now wash and dry the fish, and score the thickest part of the body twice on each side.

3 Trim off the outside leaves of the fennel and put these into the belly cavity of each fish along with a garlic clove.

4 Put boiling water into the roasting tray, to below the level of the trivet, and bring up to the boil. Pull to one side and leave at a simmer.

5 Mix the oil with some salt and pepper, and gently massage this around all sides of the fish. Put on the trivet in the roasting tray. Cover with foil and bake in the preheated oven for about 10–12 minutes. Do not overcook.

6 Meanwhile shred the remaining fennel finely. Put into a pot with the lemon juice and a little water. Gently cook the fennel for about 10 minutes, then drain off, but retain the liquor. Keep the fennel warm. Add the chopped shallot to the liquor, and reduce to about 3 tbsp, then beat in the cold butter. Season and add the fennel, to make a 'butter'.

7 Carefully take the fillets off the bass, which isn't all that easy. Or you could just remove the skin, and serve the fish whole (as they do in Spain). Serve on a bed of fennel butter.

Roast Chicken with Horseradish and Spring Onion

A roast chicken is one of the most traditional of Sunday lunch dishes. I remember as a child that it was served as a treat, although all too often it tasted of the fishmeal it had been fed. As with all other meats, 'roast' chicken would once have been cooked on a spit in front of a fire, instead of in an oven. A young cockerel would normally have been used, as hens were far too valuable as egg-layers. Nowadays we can get chickens aplenty, but when cooking them as simply as this – well, it's *fairly* simple – do try and buy the very best you can, preferably corn-fed and free-range.

SERVES 4

---

1 x 1.6 kg (3½ lb) roasting chicken, wishbone removed

85 g (3 oz) unsalted butter

8 spring onions, chopped

2 tbsp creamed horseradish

1 tbsp groundnut oil

salt and freshly ground black pepper

150 ml (5 fl oz) dry white wine

150 ml (5 fl oz) chicken stock

1 tbsp chopped fresh parsley

---

1 Preheat the oven to 200°C/400°F/Gas 6.

2 Melt 25 g (1 oz) of the butter in a small pan. Put half of the chopped spring onions into the butter, and cook, but do not colour. Remove from the heat and stir in the horseradish.

3 Release the skin on the chicken from the wishbone end, using a finger. Try not to make a hole in the skin. Do this on both sides, to create pockets over both breasts. Push the horseradish mixture into these pockets, then pull the skin back to chicken shape.

4 Heat the oil in a roasting tray on top of the stove. Colour the chicken on one leg, season and put into the preheated oven, laying it on that coloured leg, for 15 minutes. Turn it on to the other leg and cook for a further 15 minutes. Turn the chicken on to its back and cook for about a further 20–30 minutes. When cooked, take out of the tray and keep warm.

5 Pour off excess fat. Put the remaining chopped spring onion into the fat remaining in the roasting tray and colour lightly. Add the wine and boil to reduce by two-thirds. Add the chicken stock and boil to reduce by half. Shake in the remaining butter, cold and diced, and season. Mix in the parsley.

6 Serve the hot chicken with its gravy, some poured over.

Chicken and Quail Egg Pie

Highly spiced and dried fruit-rich pastry pies of fowl, to be eaten both hot and cold, have been traditional and popular since at least the fifteenth century, and birds such as chickens, pheasants, partridges, turkey, doves, bustards, peacocks and swans were cooked in this way – as were of course rooks (were they the 'four and twenty black birds, baked in a pie'?). Quails were also put into pies, but here I have married chicken and quail's eggs, rather than the quails themselves, and deleted the dried fruit and spices... I would have this with mashed potato and even crispy roast potatoes. If serving with mash, serve in a soup bowl with plenty of gravy.

SERVES 4–6

1 recipe *Savoury Shortcrust Pastry* (see p. 58)

1 egg, for egg wash

CHICKEN FILLING

675 g (1½ lb) skinned and boneless chicken thigh meat

1 carrot, peeled and halved

1 onion, peeled and halved

2 cloves

600 ml (1 pint) chicken stock

150 ml (5 fl oz) dry white wine

175 g (6 oz) button mushrooms, trimmed

juice of ½ lemon

55 g (2 oz) unsalted butter

55 g (2 oz) plain flour

300 ml (10 fl oz) double cream

2 tbsp chopped fresh parsley

12 soft-boiled quail's eggs, carefully peeled

1 Cut the meat into large 2.5 cm (1 in) chunks. Put it into a large pan with the carrot and onion, the cloves and stock. Bring up to the boil and skim off any scum. Add the wine, and then let it simmer for about 45 minutes.

2 After 30 minutes, remove about 150 ml (5 fl oz) of the stock. Put this into a medium pan with the mushrooms and lemon juice, and poach for about 5 minutes. Remove the mushrooms and keep to one side, reserving the poaching liquid.

3 When the chicken is cooked, remove the meat from the stock, using a slotted spoon, and put to one side. Strain and keep the stock, discarding the vegetables and cloves.

4 To make the sauce, melt the butter in a small pan, add the flour, and gently cook for a minute or two, stirring. Slowly add the stock from the chicken and beat in, then add the stock from the mushrooms and beat in. Pour in the double cream, season and then strain the whole thing into a clean, medium pan.

5 Put the chicken back into the sauce, and add the mushrooms and the parsley. Bring to the boil then put to one side to cool.

6 Preheat the oven to 200°C/400°F/Gas 6.

7 When cold put half of the chicken and sauce into a 1.2 litre (2 pint) pie dish. Add the peeled quail's eggs, and cover with the rest of the chicken mix.

8 Roll out the pastry to a little bit larger than the shape of the pie dish. Cut a strip of pastry from the edges that will fit round the rim of the pie dish, then moisten this with a little water. Lay the pastry on top, and crimp the edges to seal. Brush with egg wash and make a hole in the middle of the pastry to allow steam to escape.

9 Put the pie dish in the preheated oven for 10 minutes, then turn the temperature down to 180°C/350°F/Gas 4, and bake for a further 15–20 minutes.

10 Remove from the oven, allow to cool a little, then cut into serving portions. Serve hot.

Red Wine Braised Duck Legs, Roasted Pears and Onions

Wild duck would always have been eaten, but many landowners, monasteries and smaller, poorer households would have kept a few domestic ducks. Birds were always popular eating, especially in winter, when most of the rest of the meat and fish would have been salted, not fresh. Braised duck, sometimes with turnips, sometimes with peas (see p. 134), has been around since the eighteenth century. Here I have used only the legs (of farmed birds, they have more flesh), braised them in wine and stock, and accompanied them with some of the wonderful pears that would have been around in autumn. This recipe could also be prepared with chicken legs.

SERVES 8

2 tbsp duck fat

8 large duck legs

salt and freshly ground black pepper

1 carrot, peeled and sliced

2 onions, peeled and sliced

4 garlic cloves, peeled and chopped

6 tomatoes, roughly chopped

1 sprig fresh thyme

300 ml (10 fl oz) red wine (Cabernet Sauvignon)

150 ml (5 fl oz) white wine

600 ml (1 pint) chicken stock

55 g (2 oz) unsalted butter

ROASTED PEARS AND ONIONS

4 Comice pears

4 medium red onions

1 tbsp duck fat

2 spring onions, shredded

1   Preheat the oven to 180°C/350°F/Gas 4.

2   Heat the duck fat in a suitably sized casserole. Colour the duck legs, skin-side down, for 3–4 minutes, then take out and reserve. Season with salt and pepper. Leave the duck fat in the pan.

3   Add the carrot and onion to the fat remaining in the casserole, and fry gently to colour, for about 5 minutes. Add the garlic, chopped tomatoes and thyme. Colour these too for about another 5 minutes. Add the wines and boil to reduce by half.

4   Add the stock, bring to the boil, then add the duck legs. Put the lid on the casserole, and cook in the preheated oven for about 45 minutes or until the legs are cooked through. Take out the legs and keep warm.

5   Boil the liquor to reduce it by about half, then strain into a clean pan. Reduce again until the taste is strong enough: you will need about 150 ml (5 fl oz). Beat in the butter and season.

6   Meanwhile, for the pears and onions, cut the pears into quarters and remove the core and stalk. Peel the red onions and cut in half horizontally.

7   Heat the duck fat in a small roasting tray, and colour the pear quarters on all sides, and the cut surfaces of the onions. Season and roast in the oven until cooked, about 30 minutes, but check the pears after 20 minutes, and take them out if soft. (Some pears, of course, may be rock hard and could take even longer.)

8   Pile the duck legs on to a platter and reheat. Pour the sauce over. Arrange the pears and onions on the platter, sprinkle with shredded spring onions and put on the table for people to help themselves. Or, of course, serve on individual plates.

Roast Beef and Yorkshire Pudding

Whatever the reason for the undeniable quality of our beef, Britain wouldn't be so great without its roast beef and Yorkshire pudding. I remember we cooked 25-pound sirloins on the bone at Simpson's in the Strand, and then we took them into the dining room to be carved in front of the guests. Batter puddings are traditional all over the British Isles, and Yorkshire pudding is the most famous, originally cooked in the tray of dripping under the meat as it turned on the spit. Why it became so associated with Yorkshire, I don't know. Perhaps it was because of the renowned thrifty nature of my fellow countrymen: the pudding was served first, before the meat, in order to fill people up so that they would then eat less meat! To me its main purpose is to soak up the meat juices and gravy.

SERVES 8–10

1 x 4.5 kg (10 lb) rib of beef (5 ribs)

salt and freshly ground black pepper

YORKSHIRE PUDDING

2 cups plain flour

a pinch of salt

2 cups eggs

2 cups milk and water mixed

1 tbsp malt vinegar

1 For the Yorkshire pudding batter, sift the flour and salt into a large bowl. Add the eggs and beat well with half the liquid until all the lumps have disappeared. Add the rest of the liquid and the vinegar, and allow to stand.

2 Meanwhile, preheat the oven to 220°C/425°F/Gas 7.

3 Prepare the meat by cutting down the backbone towards the rib bones with the knife angled towards the backbone. Take a chopper and then break the backbones near the bottom of the cut (this is called chining). Lift up the fat from the back and take out the rubbery sinew. Tie the beef with string.

4 Put the joint into a roasting tray and season well. Roast in the preheated oven for 30 minutes and then reduce the heat to 190°C/375°F/Gas 5 and cook for a further 1½ hours. This will give you blood-red beef in the middle. The way to check this is by using a meat thermometer to test to 55°C/130°F or, as I prefer, by plunging a metal skewer through the middle of the beef, holding it there for 10 seconds and then running it either across the wrist or under the bottom lip. If the skewer is cold the meat is not ready: if warm, it's medium; and if hot then the meat is well done.

5   When cooked, put the meat in a warm place to rest for 20–30 minutes before carving and serving. Meanwhile, increase the oven temperature again to 200°C/400°F/Gas 6.

6   Heat some of the excess dripping from the roast in a suitably sized ovenproof pan or roasting tray. Whisk up the Yorkshire pudding batter, then pour into the tray and immediately place in the oven. Close the door quickly and bake for 25 minutes. Turn the pan round and cook on for another 10 minutes.

7   Meanwhile, carve and portion the beef on to hot plates, and make a gravy using the juices left in the roasting tray (see *Roast Grouse*, p. 78). As soon as the Yorkshire pudding is ready, serve it with the meat, along with mustard and horseradish sauce, or indeed some horseradish mustard.

☞ The bigger the joint, the better the roast, and it is better cooked on the bone. The meat should have a good covering of fat, be dark red in colour (which shows it has been hung properly), and have a good marbling of fat throughout.

☞ Sprinkling some English mustard powder over the top of the meat halfway through its cooking gives a nice heat.

☞ This Yorkshire pudding recipe works not by weight, but by volume. Use any size of cup but measure each ingredient with the same cup. I'm not sure why the vinegar is there, but that's what my gran did. It seems to work, so why change it?

☞ Yorkshire pudding is very versatile. It can be eaten by itself, with onions and gravy, or can be used in a sweet context as well – not surprising as the batter is virtually the same as that for popovers (see p. 36) and pancakes (see p. 248). In Yorkshire we eat it with sugar and jam, and that's after the pudding and the meat!

Lamb Kidneys Turbigo

This is an unashamedly European recipe, but it has been part of our culinary heritage for such a long time, a combination of kidneys, sausages and mushrooms. We used to serve them at The Savoy in the 1960s. I'm not quite sure why the name, but I suspect it must have something to do with the town of Turbigo in Lombardy, Italy: there was a battle there in 1859, during the Franco–Austrian War, which the French won. The dish would be good for a light lunch, but I quite fancy it for breakfast as well...

SERVES 4

8 lamb's kidneys

I tbsp olive oil

175 g (6 oz) unsalted butter

150 ml (5 fl oz) dry white wine

2 shallots, peeled and finely chopped

150 ml (5 fl oz) chicken stock

2 slices bread

8 chipolata sausages

115 g (4 oz) small button mushrooms

salt and freshly ground black pepper

2 tbsp chopped fresh parsley

1 Cut the kidneys in half. Take off the skin, and remove and discard the sinews.

2 Heat the oil in a small frying pan, and add 25 g (1 oz) of the butter. Sear the kidneys, then cook to keep them pink, probably about 2–3 minutes, turning over halfway through. Drain and keep warm.

3 Throw away the excess fat from the kidney pan, and add the dry white wine off the heat. Shake the pan to 'rinse' off the residue. Keep this.

4 In a clean pan melt another 25 g (1 oz) of the butter, add the shallot and sweat, do not colour, about 2 minutes. Strain the wine into the new pan, add the stock and simmer to reduce by about one-third.

5 Cut the bread into four heart-shaped pieces and pan-fry in another 25 g (1 oz) of the butter until golden on both sides. Take out and drain.

6 Cook the chipolatas in 25 g (1 oz) butter, about 5 minutes. Cut the mushrooms in halves and fry in another 25 g (1 oz) butter, about 3 minutes.

7 When ready, add the remaining 25 g (1 oz) butter to the sauce and season it.

8 Put the kidneys into a serving dish. Dip the tips of the heart-shaped croûtons into the parsley. Put the rest of the parsley into the sauce. Add the mushrooms and chipolatas to the serving dish. Pour the sauce over the kidneys, then lay the croûtons on top and serve.

Leek and Cheese Pudding with Pan-fried Beetroot

SERVES 4

Very few people make things like this pudding now, but once they would have been a major part of the diet – the protein of the cheese and eggs bulked out with bread. My father used to make a pudding like this with onions, which was delicious. I have substituted leeks, and served the pudding on slices of beetroot for a more sophisticated finish.

450 g (1 lb) leeks

salt and freshly ground black pepper

55 g (2 oz) unsalted butter

225 g (8 oz) mature Cheddar, grated

175 g (6 oz) fresh white breadcrumbs

4 eggs

a pinch of freshly grated nutmeg

a pinch of cayenne pepper

300 ml (10 fl oz) each of double cream and milk

PAN-FRIED BEETROOT

4 cooked beetroot, skinned (see p. 199)

25 g (1 oz) unsalted butter

a splash of white wine vinegar

1   Wash and clean the leeks and cook whole in boiling salted water for 5 minutes. Drain well, cool and then cut in half lengthways. Lay flat-side down on the board, and cut into 5 mm (¼ in) shreds or strips, not too fine.

2   Preheat the oven to 160°C/325°F/Gas 3. Butter a 1.2 litre (2 pint) pie dish, then sprinkle with some of the grated cheese.

3   Put a layer of leeks in the bottom of the dish, sprinkle with some of the breadcrumbs, then repeat this layering twice more.

4   Beat the eggs well together in a large bowl, then add the nutmeg, cayenne pepper, and salt and pepper to taste, along with the rest of the cheese. Warm the milk and cream together, pour over the cheese mixture then gently pour all this over the leeks and breadcrumbs in the pie dish.

5   Bake in the preheated oven for 30–40 minutes, then take out and leave to sit for 5 minutes while you pan-fry the beetroot.

6   Slice the beetroot into 5 mm (¼ in) slices, and pan-fry in a medium frying pan in the butter for about 3 minutes. Turn over, and cook for another 3 minutes. Add a splash of vinegar, and some salt and pepper, and let it evaporate over the heat quickly.

7   Arrange slices of the beetroot in a circle on individual plates, and spoon a portion of pudding on top using a large metal spoon. Serve hot.

Roast Grouse

The red grouse is said to be the king of game birds, and although the flesh is delicious, its popularity has probably got more to do with its rarity – you almost need the wealth of a king in order to shoot it, buy it or eat it. The Glorious Twelfth, 12 August, is when the season starts, and London restaurateurs still compete to have the first birds flown down from Scotland – the birds' only habitat – to be on their tables that very night. The season is short, only until 10 December (although the grouse would probably think it too long). Grouse are not raised for the shoot, as are other game birds like pheasant, but the heather moors where they live are very carefully managed to provide the right conditions, cover, nesting places and food. It is probably their diet that makes their flesh more aromatic – they eat heather shoots, flowers and seeds, as well as any wild blackberries that come their way.

SERVES 4

---

4 young grouse, with giblets

salt and freshly ground black pepper

4 thin slices pork back fat

85 g (3 oz) unsalted butter

1 tbsp vegetable oil

4 slices good bread

1 onion, peeled and sliced

300 ml (10 fl oz) game stock

4 small bunches watercress

☞ You can tell young grouse by their undeveloped spurs, and downy breast feathers. Hang them in the feather by the neck for two to three days, no longer.

☞ Try to get sheets of pork fat. They will cover and moisten the breasts better – vital with the lean flesh of game birds – and they will not flavour it like bacon.

☞ Serve with game chips, a green vegetable, fried breadcrumbs, bread sauce and redcurrant jelly. Grouse are also delicious when cold.

1   Preheat the oven to 200°C/400°F/Gas 6.

2   Season well inside the birds, and keep the livers to one side. Tie the pieces of back fat over the breasts of the birds.

3   Heat 25 g (1 oz) of the butter and the oil together in a roasting tray, and colour the birds all over on a gentle heat.

4   Put the birds in the preheated oven for 15 minutes, then turn the temperature down to 180°C/350°F/Gas 4 and cook for a further 10 minutes. Take the string and back fat off and colour the birds for a final 10 minutes. Keep medium-rare to medium. There's an art to cooking grouse. It should be pink but not bloody. Take out of the oven and leave to rest.

5   Meanwhile toast the bread, then cut 5 cm (2 in) circles from each slice.

6   Stew the livers in half the remaining butter, then put into a bowl with the rest of the butter, season well and mash together.

7   Put the onion into the fat in the grouse roasting tray and fry quickly to colour. Add the stock and bring to the boil, season and strain.

8   Put the mushed-up livers on the circles of toast and perch a bird on top of each. Put a bunch of watercress into each cavity, and serve immediately. Serve the gravy separately.

Rhubarb and Ginger Fool

In Elizabethan times, when cream was much liked, a fool was a flavoured cream mixed with eggs and heated gently until it thickened. (At this time, desserts with rather silly names, like 'trifle' and 'fool', formed part of a 'banquet' course.) Later, in the eighteenth century, fools became more like those of today, the pulp of cooked fruits beaten together with cream and sugar. Here I've allied my favourite rhubarb – from the Yorkshire 'rhubarb triangle' – and ginger. I like to serve this in martini glasses.

SERVES 4

450 g (1 lb) rhubarb	55 g (2 oz) caster sugar	300 ml (10 fl oz) double cream
55 g (2 oz) unsalted butter	1 x 5 cm (2 in) piece fresh root ginger, peeled and cut in half	icing sugar, to taste

1   Trim the rhubarb and cut it into 2.5 cm (1 in) strips. Put into a pan, and add about 2 tbsp water. Add the butter, sugar and ginger, and slowly simmer away until cooked, about 10 minutes. Remove and discard the ginger, and allow the rhubarb to cool.

2   Take out a third of the rhubarb and drain through a sieve or colander, keeping the resulting juice. Put the juice on to the heat to reduce by about two-thirds, then cool.

3   Meanwhile, divide the drained rhubarb between the four glasses. You could save some pieces whole to decorate.

4   Take the remaining rhubarb and purée using a fork: do not make a fine purée, leave some texture.

5   Whip the cream to soft peaks – do not over-whip – then sweeten with icing sugar to taste. Fold in the rhubarb purée. Using a piping bag with a 1 cm (½ in) nozzle, pipe the fool mixture in a circular fashion into each glass. Chill for 2 hours only.

6   Pour the reduced juice over the top of each glass, and serve.

☞   Rhubarb is available from January to July, the first three months forced, the latter three months outdoors.

Flummery

The original flummery – the word anglicised from the Welsh *llymru* – was made with grain. Any unhusked grain or cereal, when soaked and boiled, will give a milky liquid, which sets in a jelly-like way. (Atholl Brose, the oat-based pudding served at Hogmanay in Scotland, is a type of grain flummery.) Later, particularly in Tudor times, animal milks were used, then cream, in combination with ground almonds instead of grain, and they were set with the ingredients mentioned opposite, the forerunners of gelatine. When I first read about flummery, I thought it sounded ghastly, but I loved the name. So I have updated the original recipe, and give it here, just so that I can say, 'Let's have some flummery!'

SERVES 4

---

300 ml (10 fl oz) single cream

¼ tsp ground cinnamon

finely grated zest of 1 orange

85 g (3 oz) ground almonds

55 g (2 oz) caster sugar

150 ml (5 fl oz) sweet white wine

2 level tsp powdered gelatine

2 tbsp brandy

150 ml (5 fl oz) double cream

55 g (2 oz) shelled pistachio nuts

---

1   Put the single cream, cinnamon and orange zest into a large pan and bring up to the boil. Remove from the heat and add 55 g (2 oz) of the almonds and the sugar.

2   Warm the wine gently, then take off the heat. It must not be too hot. Pour in the gelatine and stir to dissolve. Pour this into the single cream mixture, along with the brandy, then leave to cool.

3   Whip the double cream to soft peaks. Add a quarter of this to the single cream mixture, and beat it in. Fold in the rest of the whipped cream.

4   Spoon the flummery into martini glasses, and leave to set in the fridge for about an hour.

5   Chop the cleaned pistachios in a food processor and mix with the remaining ground almonds. When the flummery has set, sprinkle the nuts on top.

☞   Try toasting the whole nuts in a dry pan for a few minutes, then cooling them, before chopping and sprinkling on top. The flavour is hugely intensified.

Yorkshire Orange Jelly

Jelly was popular in Tudor and Stuart times, forming part of the banquet course, with things like fruit tarts, trifles and fools. (This course was usually served in a separate room from the bulk of the meal, sometimes even in a specially built summerhouse.) The setting agent was isinglass, calf's foot or hartshorn, and the emphasis seems to have been on colour and look rather than flavour. I know which I would prefer, and this one has both flavour and colour!

We used to have orange jelly with canned mandarins at my gran's house when I was a kid. They were served in separate bowls, and we ate them together with Carnation milk.

SERVES 6–8

rind of 1 lemon	2 egg whites	3 tbsp sweet sherry
rind of 2 oranges	600 ml (1 pint) water	2 tbsp orange Curaçao
2 cloves	300 ml (10 fl oz) orange juice	2 oranges, segmented
225 g (8 oz) caster sugar	juice of 1 lemon	TO SERVE
1 x 2.5 cm (1 in) piece cinnamon stick	55 g (2 oz) powdered gelatine	whipped whipping or double cream

1   Put the citrus rinds, cloves, sugar, cinnamon, egg whites, water and fruit juices into a pan and bring slowly to the boil. Turn off the heat and leave to sit for 15 minutes. Strain slowly through a jelly bag or fine muslin cloth suspended above a bowl. Do not press as the resultant juice will become cloudy. Be patient.

2   Take a little of the liquor and dissolve the gelatine in it. Whisk this into the bulk of the juices in the pan and simmer carefully for 10 minutes. Stir in the sherry and orange Curaçao and leave to cool.

3   Take a jelly mould – a pudding basin works well – and splash with cold water. As the jelly cools, put a ladleful in the bottom of the mould. Dry the orange segments then drop into the mould. (I personally think there no need to make a pretty pattern, but some people would like to, especially in a jelly mould.) Put this in the fridge to set quickly.

4   Pour the rest of the liquor into the mould and put in the fridge to set totally overnight.

5   To serve, dip the mould into warm water then put a dish on top and turn over. Decorate with whipped cream and serve.

Blackberry Blancmange

White foods were very popular in cooking in the fourteenth century, and the name of this dessert comes from the French 'blanc-manger', meaning (inevitably) 'white food'. White foods often included savoury ingredients, such as chicken, but there was always an inherent sweetness – from sugar, honey, dried fruits or almond milk. Over the years the recipe developed until, by the seventeenth century, it was entirely sweet, although of course it still contained its animal setting agent, calf's foot, or today's gelatine. In the 1950s, people used to make what they called blancmange by whipping egg whites into a packet of jelly. So to me, 'blanc' didn't mean 'white', it represented more of a texture. And I've taken it a bit further: this recipe for blancmange is *any*thing but white!

SERVES 6

4 eggs	225 g (8 oz) caster sugar	TO DECORATE
juice of ½ lemon	225 g (8 oz) blackberry purée	extra whipped double cream and some whole blackberries
15 g (½ oz) powdered gelatine	300 ml (10 fl oz) double cream	some chopped pistachios, if liked

1 Have ready six 7.5 cm (3 in) ramekins on a baking sheet. Tie a collar of greaseproof paper around each, so that the paper stands proud of the top of the ramekin.

2 Separate the eggs into separate bowls. In a small pan, warm the lemon juice very gently, then dissolve the gelatine in it.

3 Whisk the egg yolks and sugar together until thickening up over a very gentle heat. Fold in the gelatine mix and blackberry purée and leave to cool completely.

4 Whisk the cream to soft peaks, and then the egg whites to stiff peaks. Fold the cream into the egg yolks carefully first, and then the egg whites.

5 Pour the mixture into the ramekins, so that it comes up over the top (but is held by the paper collar), and leave to set overnight in the fridge.

6 Take off the collars and decorate with whipped cream and blackberries.

☞ Many serve this as a cold soufflé, which is what it looks like. For adults, decorate the exposed sides with chopped pistachio nuts. You could also make in one big dish. And of course you can make this with other soft fruits.

College Pudding

Almost every Oxford and Cambridge college has a pudding named after it, and these generally contain the traditional British pudding ingredients of breadcrumbs, suet, dried fruit, often with eggs and/or milk. This one, which is most like the famous New College Oxford pudding, is not a steamed pudding, as you might expect: little dumplings of the suet mix are fried. It is definitely not for the diet-conscious...

SERVES 4

175 g (6 oz) shredded suet	55 g (2 oz) runny honey	2 tbsp good brandy
175 g (6 oz) fresh white breadcrumbs	115 g (4 oz) sultanas	1 tbsp hazelnut oil
20 g (¾ oz) baking powder	55 g (2 oz) currants	55 g (2 oz) unsalted butter
a pinch of salt	25 g (1 oz) chopped mixed peel	icing sugar and ground cinnamon, to serve
	4 eggs	

1   Mix the suet, breadcrumbs, baking powder and salt together in a large bowl. Add the honey, sultanas, currants and peel, and mix well.

2   Mix the eggs and brandy well together, and stir into the breadcrumb mix. The 'dough' should have a dropping consistency.

3   Heat the oil in a medium frying pan, then add the butter. Grease four 5 cm (2 in) metal rings, then put into the pan. Pour a good amount of the mix in each ring, and allow the bases to colour, about 4–5 minutes over a good medium heat. When set, take off the rings and turn the puddings over with a fish slice. Cook the second side for about 5 minutes.

4   Remove the puddings from the fat, and drain on absorbent paper. Keep warm while you make the remainder.

5   Dust with icing sugar and cinnamon and serve, possibly (if you dare) with cream.

☞ It's probably not a good idea to do them all at the same time in the same pan: make them in batches.

☞ You could try different oils: walnut would be good, or even sesame or pumpkin seed, but be careful with the latter two as they are very strong.

Trifle

SERVES 6

The word 'trifle' actually means something of little importance, but in this instance I would totally disagree, as I love trifle, in all its forms. I used to get a very traditional one at my gran's house, for Sunday lunch, when my Uncle Donald would watch us suspiciously, in case we took too much! In Elizabethan times the name 'trifle' was applied to a thick cream flavoured with sugar, ginger and rosewater, which became part of the banquet course (see p. 83). Later trifles consisted of custards poured over wine-soaked sweet biscuits (usually macaroons), and topped with syllabub. In this one, which is simplicity to do, I have reverted to the cream topping.

I Swiss roll (see p. 39 if you want to make your own)

2 bananas

225 g (8 oz) raspberries

I sherry glass sweet sherry

115 g (4 oz) raspberry jam

300 ml (10 fl oz) double cream

25 g (1 oz) caster sugar

55 g (2 oz) chopped pistachios

VANILLA CUSTARD

300 ml (10 fl oz) milk

300 ml (10 fl oz) double cream

I vanilla pod, split

I tbsp cornflour or custard powder

4 egg yolks

2 eggs

115 g (4 oz) caster sugar

1 Cut the Swiss roll into slices or chunks and lay in the bottom of a large glass bowl or individual glass bowls (it used to be the best crystal bowl). Peel and slice the bananas, and sprinkle the slices over the Swiss roll. Scatter the raspberries on top, and leave to one side.

2 For the custard, put the milk and double cream on to boil in a medium pan with the scraped vanilla pod and seeds. When boiled, thicken with the cornflour. Put the egg yolks, eggs and sugar into a bowl and beat well together. Pour the hot cream mixture on to the eggs and mix well.

3 Put this mixture into a clean pan and heat gently, stirring carefully, to allow the custard to thicken slightly. Do not let it curdle. Pull off the heat, put into a cold container and leave to cool.

4 When the custard is cool, pour the sweet sherry over the fruit and sponge in the bowl or bowls. Now pour the cooled custard over. Refrigerate and allow to set (overnight is good).

5 Warm the jam then allow it to cool a little, but whilst still runny, pour it over the custard. Allow to set.

6 Whip the cream with the sugar and put into a piping bag. Decorate the top of the trifle with this, then carefully sprinkle the pistachios over the cream. Serve.

Jam Roly-poly

Steamed and boiled puddings lie at the heart of the British pudding tradition. They began as savoury-sweet (a very medieval concept) puddings, made in the autumn when the animals were slaughtered: suet or bone marrow, flour, dried fruits, spices and sugar were stuffed into an animal gut and boiled, either alone, or with meat, to serve as the carbohydrate part of a meal. When the pudding cloth or bag was invented, suet puddings could be made at any time of the year, although they were not necessarily served as a separate sweet or dessert course until much later. Steamed puds such as jam roly-poly – and others like *Spotted Dick* (see p.186), Snowdon pudding, even some versions of *College Pudding* (see p.85) – are current surviving examples of these early puddings which, happily, seem to be making a comeback.

SERVES 4

225 g (8 oz) plain flour, plus extra for dusting	a pinch of salt	approx. 150 ml (5 fl oz) cold water
15 g (½ oz) baking powder	115 g (4 oz) finely chopped beef suet	175 g (6 oz) strawberry jam

1 Sieve the flour, baking powder and salt together into a large bowl. Rub in the suet and enough water to make a fairly stiff dough. Mix well.

2 On a lightly floured work surface, roll the dough out to a rectangle of about 30 x 15 cm (12 x 6 in).

3 Soften the jam by heating it in a small pan, and spread over the pastry, leaving a 5 mm (¼ in) border. Brush this border with cold water.

4 To roll, fold over the short ends and then roll the pastry from the side farthest away from you, enclosing the jam. Press the overlapping end to seal.

5 Wrap the roly-poly in a damp tea towel or muslin cloth. Put in a steamer with the water boiling fast, cover and steam for an hour. Turn down and simmer until fully cooked, about another 30 minutes.

6 Remove from the steamer, unwrap, and place on a platter. Cut into individual pieces, and serve with more warm strawberry jam.

☞ You could also bake the roly-poly. When rolled, brush the top and sides with milk and sprinkle sugar on top. Bake in a preheated oven at 200ºC/400ºF/Gas 6 for 25 minutes, then reduce to 180ºC/350ºF/Gas 4 for another 25 minutes or so.

Rhubarb and Ginger Crumble

Although we have long loved fruit pies using pastry, fruit with a crumble topping – basically sweet pastry ingredients without the water – is very much more recent. Some suggest it did not come into use until after World War Two, perhaps when sugar had stopped being rationed. And of course a crumble is much easier and quicker to make than a pastry! The idea may have developed from the Austrian *'streusel'*, a cake topping which, because it contains less flour, bakes to a crisper texture than our distinctly crumbly crumble. This one here is much more elaborate, containing oats and nibbed almonds. The whole idea of crumbles, much to my pleasure, is coming back into vogue, and we are experiencing all sorts of different fillings and toppings, both savoury and sweet.

SERVES 4

675 g (1 ½ lb) rhubarb

2 pieces preserved stem ginger, finely diced

2 tbsp syrup from the ginger

25 g (1 oz) unrefined caster sugar

CRUMBLE

175 g (6 oz) plain flour

55 g (2 oz) fine oats

140 g (5 oz) unsalted butter, chilled

85 g (3 oz) unrefined caster sugar

55 g (2 oz) nibbed almonds

1   Preheat the oven to 170°C/340°F/Gas 3–4.

2   Trim the rhubarb and cut into 2 cm (¾ in) pieces. Put into a bowl with the ginger dice, syrup and sugar, and mix together. Pour into a deep pie dish.

3   For the crumble, mix the flour and oats in another bowl. Cut the cold butter into small pieces and rub into the flour mixture until the texture is somewhat sandy. Add the sugar and mix well, then add the almonds.

4   Pour half the crumble mixture on top of the rhubarb and pat down. Now pour the rest on top and leave sitting loosely.

5   Bake in the preheated oven for about 45 minutes. Take out and leave to sit for 5 minutes. Serve with clotted cream (or custard if you like, see p. 86).

☞   You can of course make a plainer crumble. Use 115 g (4 oz) each of cold unsalted butter, cut into dice, and unrefined demerara sugar, and 225 g (8 oz) plain flour. Make and use as above.

Summer Pudding

The British pudding tradition is long established, but the word 'pudding' is most commonly associated with cooked and hot – suet puds, baked batter, pastry and milk puds. Summer pudding, however, is a later invention, and although the fruit is heated slightly to render the juices, it is basically uncooked and it is served cold. The concept of fruit encased in bread rather than pastry came into being in the eighteenth century, created for patients not permitted the richness of pastry. For some time it was actually known as hydropathic pudding, after the sanatoria where the selfsame patients were being treated. It makes for one of the best summer Sunday lunch desserts ever.

SERVES 4–6

900 g (2 lb) mixed summer fruits (blackberries, raspberries, bilberries, redcurrants, blackcurrants)	115 g (4 oz) unrefined caster sugar 1 cinnamon stick	juice of 1 lemon approx. 450 g (1 lb) day-old, medium sliced bread

1   Clean the fruit and put into a pan. Add the sugar, cinnamon stick and lemon juice, bring up to the boil and simmer gently for 5 minutes.

2   Gently strain off the fruit – a colander works well – and keep the fruit to one side. Reduce the juices by half by boiling, then allow to cool.

3   Take the crusts off the bread and cut a circle from each slice to fit the bottom of four to six ramekin dishes. Cut the same number of circles for the tops as well. Cut the rest of the bread into wedges to fit the walls of the ramekins. It is important that there are no gaps in the bread: to overlap is better.

4   Dip the circles for the base into the reduced juices, and then put into the ramekins. Dip the bread for the sides into the juice and place around the sides. Fill the ramekins with the fruit, then lay the second circle on top. Put a piece of greaseproof paper on top and a light weight on top of that in turn to press it down. Refrigerate overnight.

5   Turn out and serve with clotted cream and a pool of the juice.

☞ For an exciting alternative, use brioche loaf instead of ordinary bread (which also works extraordinarily well in bread and butter pudding, as in the recipe on p. 96).

☞ You could also, of course, make one large pudding in a large basin.

Mother's Day Lunch

You could have an afternoon tea to celebrate Mothering Sunday, or a lunch or dinner. I have chosen a lunch, which could be followed by a tea, at which you would serve the classic Mothering Sunday simnel cake.

Mothering Sunday is the British name for the day celebrated every year on the fourth Sunday in Lent. Mother's Day is the American name for a day celebrated in the States, Canada, Australia, New Zealand and most other countries on the second Sunday in May. They have different origins, although the sentiments are nowadays very similar.

Many historians claim that the earliest predecessor of the British Mothering Sunday was the ancient pagan spring festival dedicated to mother goddesses. If true, as other pagan festivals were taken over to become Christmas and Easter, so it could be that Mothering Sunday was adopted by the Church to become a day on which you were obliged to visit your 'mother' church once a year. The day could have metamorphosed to one on which children working away from home were given the day off to visit their mother.

For, in the very early days, it was quite common for children, some as young as ten, to leave home to work in service. Allowed one day off per year, they would travel home, with a present for their mother. Some girls would make a simnel cake, to show off their recently acquired baking skills. (It being Lent, the cake would probably last until Easter, and it is often served now as an Easter cake.) Today children send cards to their mothers, and I remember when I was young that the local florists would make up little posies of violets that children could afford to buy.

Mother's Day in America has more recent origins, the 1880s and early 1900s. One lady wanted to have the Church dedicate a day to mothers; another began a campaign for a national holiday, to acknowledge the care and love mothers represented. The American government eventually approved the idea in 1914, and since then it has become increasingly commercialised, both there and here.

We used to look after my mother on this day, and that's what we should all do. Going to a restaurant would be the best way of ensuring that your mother didn't do any work, but if you choose to cook at home, make sure everyone else prepares, cooks, serves and washes up. The golden rule is to leave the kitchen as you found it...

Salad of Scallops with Bacon

The combination of scallops and bacon crops up in Scottish, English and Manx cooking, one of those wonderful anomalies of flavour balance, which is similar to oysters and bacon and the Welsh trout cooked with bacon. I've taken it a little into the present time by presenting it in a salad, which would be perfect for a light Mother's Day lunch starter or main course (depending on numbers).

Scallops are one of our most delicious shellfish, native to the cold waters of western Scotland and around the Isle of Man (where there has apparently been a scallop fishery for some 3,000 years). Giant or king scallops are the largest, the queens or queenies being much smaller (and, if used instead, you will need six to seven – or even more – instead of three per person).

SERVES 4

12 large scallops in the shell

5 tbsp olive oil

salt and freshly ground black pepper

6 rashers smoked back bacon

6 spring onions, chopped

1 tbsp grain mustard

2 tbsp white wine vinegar

2 tbsp groundnut oil

1 tbsp each of chopped fresh parsley, chives and chervil

TO SERVE

mixed salad leaves (more or less, depending on whether for a starter or main course)

1 Trim the scallops, using the white muscle meat only for this dish.

2 Heat 1 tbsp of the olive oil in a solid flat-bottomed frying pan, and sear the scallops until golden brown, a minute or two only. Turn over just to sear, season and then take out and keep warm.

3 Meanwhile, trim the bacon and cut into thin strips. Sauté and colour these in the frying pan that the scallops were cooked in. Add the chopped spring onion and sauté until coloured, and then put both bacon and onion into a large bowl.

4 Mix the mustard and vinegar well in a bowl or jar, then add the remaining olive oil, the groundnut oil, herbs and some seasoning. Take some of the dressing and toss with the salad leaves then place these in the middle of four plates.

5 Add the remaining dressing to the bacon and onion. Balance the three scallops per person on each mound of salad leaves, and then spoon the bacon, onion and dressing over and around.

Roast Leg of Pork with Mustard, Gherkins and Cider

Wild pigs – or wild boars as they are more commonly known – once ran free in British forests and were hunted by royalty. But pigs, easy to tame, have been domesticated for thousands of years, and in the Middle Ages, most country people, rich and poor, would have kept at least one pig. This would forage in woodlands, accept scraps and household waste and generally cause little trouble – and then in the autumn it would provide fresh meat for roasting, and sausages, hams, bacon, black puddings and salted joints for the winter. The pig was probably the most useful animal for, as the saying goes, you could eat everything but the squeak.

The sauce is less usual perhaps, but the flavour of the three traditionally British ingredients – mustard, gherkins and cider – is magnificent. It's not often that you can cook a whole leg of pork, so it's ideal for a family gathering such as Mother's Day. It's cooked long and slow – go for a nice walk, or to church – and while I was writing this recipe, in November, I was salivating, thinking of the tender flesh and the crisp crackling. I might even have this for Christmas lunch.

SERVES 8–10

1 x 4.5 kg (10 lb) leg of pork	1 onion, peeled and finely chopped	1 tbsp English mustard
salt and freshly ground black pepper	300 ml (10 fl oz) cider	115 g (4 oz) gherkins, finely chopped
groundnut oil	300 ml (10 fl oz) chicken stock	1 tbsp chopped fresh parsley

1 Preheat the oven to 140°C/275°F/Gas 1.

2 Score the rind on the pork, using a Stanley knife, but do not cut *too* deeply through the fat – you could always ask the butcher to do this. Quickly pour boiling water over the rind to scald it, then dry off. Rub with salt then brush off the excess.

3 Put the oil into a roasting tray, followed by the leg of pork, then roll the joint in the oil to cover, and roast in the low preheated oven for about 4 hours. (You could be preparing everything else for the Mother's Day lunch in the meantime, or just relaxing!)

4 When cooked, remove the leg from the tray and allow to rest for 20 minutes on the side. Keep it somewhere warm – usually above the oven is the right place.

5 Pour off most of the fat from the roasting tray (keep for another use). Add the onions to the fat left in the tray and sweat for about 3 minutes, do not colour. Add the cider and boil to reduce by half.

6 Pour the potential gravy into a clean pan, add the stock and reduce by half. Whisk in the mustard, chopped gherkins and parsley and season.

7 Slice the pork, divide up the crackling, and serve with the gravy.

☞ I read a piece written in French the other day, which said that at the turn of the last century, the French thought that the most valuable possession of the culinary English was their dripping. I agree. Save every last bit of the fat from the pork. Use the fat for cooking roast potatoes, and the bits at the bottom will make great dripping on toast.

Marmalade Bread and Butter Pudding

The use of bread is a consistent theme in the British pudding tradition. Think of apple charlotte, queen of puddings, fruit crumbles and summer pudding, but bread and butter pudding, here with a Scottish marmalade flavouring, must be one of the best known and loved. It's the same concept as *pain perdu*, which became our French toast, a way of using up slightly stale bread. Brioche, which is a French sweet bread, may not be very British, but it does make the most delicious bread and butter pudding (as does the Italian *panettone*).

SERVES 4–6

---

115 g (4 oz) unsalted butter, softened, plus extra for greasing

1 loaf brioche bread

6 tbsp *Marmalade* (see p. 26)

300 ml (10 fl oz) milk

300 ml (10 fl oz) double cream

1 vanilla pod, split

6 egg yolks

2 whole eggs

140 g (5 oz) caster sugar

TO SERVE

8 oranges, cut into segments, for a salad

---

1 Butter the base and sides of a 1.2 litre (2 pint) pie dish.

2 Slice the bread, and butter the slices on one side. Arrange half of the slices in the pie dish, slightly overlapping. Spread the marmalade over, then put on a second layer of bread slices, butter-side up, overlapping.

3 Meanwhile put the milk and cream in a medium pan, and scrape in the vanilla seeds. Add the pod as well, and heat gently to infuse.

4 Mix the egg yolks, whole eggs and sugar together in a large bowl or jug. Pour the warm milk over the egg mixture, then strain this over the bread in the pie dish. Allow to stand for 30 minutes.

5 Preheat the oven to 160°C/325°F/Gas 3.

6 Put the pie dish in a roasting tray filled with enough hot water to come halfway up the pie dish. Bake in the preheated oven for 30–40 minutes.

7 Remove from the oven and serve with an orange salad.

☛ For a grown-up version, add some whisky, about 2 tbsp, after the marmalade.

Simnel Cake

The original medieval simnels were biscuits which had to be boiled before they were baked. By the late seventeenth century, the name had transferred to a rich fruit cake which, traditionally, servant girls would make to take home to their mothers on Mothering Sunday. It may be typical in its fruit content, but the cake differs in its use of almond paste, or marzipan. A circle of marzipan is baked in the middle of the cake, and then the top is covered with another circle. On top, around the edges, are arranged eleven small marzipan balls which symbolise Christ's eleven faithful disciples. Small wonder, then, that it has become the norm at Easter as well.

You don't see simnel cakes all that often and you would find them in a baker's, not in the supermarket. I hadn't made one of these for ages, but it is a very good cake, and eats well at any time. It would be good for Christmas too.

MAKES I CAKE

225 g (8 oz) unsalted butter
225 g (8 oz) caster sugar
finely grated rind of 1 lemon
4 eggs
350 g (12 oz) plain flour
¾ tsp baking powder
55 g (2 oz) ground almonds
1 tsp freshly grated nutmeg
1 tsp ground cinnamon

350 g (12 oz) sultanas
115 g (4 oz) chopped mixed peel
25 g (1 oz) black treacle
a pinch of salt

TOPPING AND FILLING

450 g (1 lb) marzipan
55 g (2 oz) apricot jam
1 egg yolk
icing sugar, to dust

1   Preheat the oven to 170°C/340°F/Gas 3–4. Grease a 20 cm (8 in) round cake tin, and line it with greaseproof paper.

2   In a large bowl, cream the butter and sugar together with the lemon rind. In another bowl, whisk the eggs until light and frothy, then add these slowly to the butter mixture, stirring all the time.

3   Into yet another bowl, sieve the flour and baking powder together then mix in the ground almonds. Stir this carefully into the egg and butter mix. Add all the rest of the ingredients and stir carefully together.

4   Put half of the mixture into the prepared tin. Roll out half of the marzipan into a 20 cm (8 in) circle and put carefully on top of the cake mixture. Add the rest of the mixture and level the top.

5   Bake the cake in the preheated oven for 2–2½ hours, covering the top with paper or foil if getting too brown. Take out and cool on a wire rack, still in the tin. Remove from the tin when cold.

6   Roll out the rest of the marzipan to a circle to fit the top of the cake. Keep the trimmings of marzipan. Make eleven small balls with these.

7   Warm the jam gently in a small pan, and brush over the top of the cake. Put the marzipan circle on top and push down. Place the marzipan balls on top of the cake, around the edges.

8   Beat the egg yolk and brush this over the top of the marzipan on the cake. Colour under a preheated grill.

9   Shake icing sugar over to serve.

Given the vagaries of the British weather, it seems surprising that the idea of eating outside as pleasure ever took hold of our imaginations. However, eating outdoors, or at least outside one's home, has always been part of our heritage: agricultural workers would take something to eat with them in the fields; fishermen would have food with them, to eat on a riverbank or at sea; miners would take their pasties down into the bowels of the earth in Cornwall. The latter is hardly the open air, I agree, and indeed all of these meals would have been taken in a work break, not for leisure. Nature was there to be worked and controlled, and there was no time to sit back, look at and enjoy it.

It was mainly in the nineteenth century that we began to think of eating in the countryside for pleasure. Some scholars have suggested that William Wordsworth, the great Romantic poet, may have had an influence on the concept of picnicking, long before the word itself was actually coined. He and his sister, Dorothy, would organise tramps into the Cumbrian countryside, with fellow poets such as Samuel Coleridge, and upon reaching a suitably picturesque spot, would have a simple afternoon meal in the open air.

The word 'picnic' itself began in a different way. Coming probably from the French, and meaning a miscellany or hotch-potch, a picnic gradually came to mean a party to which all the guests contributed part of the provisions, but not necessarily out of doors. Only later did it become firmly associated with al fresco eating parties which, by 1802, were all the rage.

I love picnics, and they can be as simple or as posh as one likes. I would enjoy a picnic at Henley, at Glyndebourne or Ascot, but I also like just going with friends to a favourite spot in the country and sitting under the trees on a rare, sunny English afternoon. And picnics are actually so easy nowadays, with hampers, chill boxes etc. However, wherever you are going, the prime need is for the food to be portable, and strong enough (or well enough packed) to be able to survive the journey. Pastry-wrapped foods already have their own natural packing, and there are a few ideas here. Cold meats that can be sliced *in situ* (don't forget the cutlery) are useful, and you must have plenty of salads and savoury garnishes to go with them. I haven't suggested any sweet things here, but there are plenty of other ideas elsewhere. Fruit is the ideal picnic fare, and if it's soft fruit (as it might be, picnics are summer affairs), it's best accompanied by some cream.

Barbecues are much more recent in the British eating canon, coming probably from our cousins who enjoy rather more consistent weather – the Americans, Australians and South Africans. Barbecues are usually more home-based, where you have an outdoor means of cooking in place, and you invite friends round. Foods are cooked over charcoal – usually by men, for some reason – and salads are produced from the kitchen. We have probably known about the delights of barbecuing foods for less than fifty years in the UK, but it too would have been part of our far distant past, from when in prehistoric times we discovered fire. I like barbecues because there are no rules, nothing is set in stone. If something isn't ready, it's not ready, so you just have to relax and have a good time!

4 Picnics & Barbecues

Artichoke Flan

Globe artichokes (which are members of the thistle family) were known in Elizabethan times, and were included, along with potatoes and skirrets (an ancient Chinese vegetable, which produces a bundle of swollen roots that are tender, floury and sweet), in rich pies – obviously along with the usual dried fruits and spices. This flan here is less fancy, but it is delicious, and would be good for a picnic, so long as you pack it well.

SERVES 6

---

225 g (8 oz) *Savoury Shortcrust Pastry* (see p. 58)

8 cooked artichoke hearts

175 g (6 oz) spring onions, chopped

1 tsp chopped fresh parsley

juice of 1 lemon

25 g (1 oz) butter

25 g (1 oz) plain flour

300 ml (10 fl oz) single cream

salt and freshly ground black pepper

a pinch of freshly grated nutmeg

3 egg yolks

---

1. Preheat the oven to 190°C/375°F/Gas 5.

2. Line a 15 cm (6 in) floured flan ring, sitting on a baking sheet, with three-quarters of the pastry. (You could make in a flan dish as well.) Cover the remaining pastry with a damp cloth or clingfilm so that it doesn't dry out.

3. Slice the artichoke hearts and lay in the bottom of the pastry case. Sprinkle with the spring onions, parsley and then the lemon juice.

4. For the binding sauce, heat the butter in a medium pan, mix in the flour then cook for a few minutes, but do not colour. Slowly beat in the cream and mix to ensure no lumps. Take off the heat and pass through a sieve. Leave to cool.

5. When the sauce is cool, season with salt, pepper and nutmeg and beat in two of the egg yolks. Pour over the artichokes in the pastry case.

6. Roll out the rest of the pastry to fit the top of the flan ring. Brush the lip of the pastry in the flan ring with water, put the top on, seal the pastry and decorate if you like with pastry trimmings. Brush the pastry all over with the remaining egg yolk, beaten, and decorate with the back of a fork (see p. 58).

7. Bake in the preheated oven for 30 minutes. Turn the heat down to 160°C/325°F/Gas 3, and cook for a further 15 minutes. Allow to cool.

☞ This is delicious hot, served for lunch along with a nicely dressed green salad.

☞ Artichokes take a lot of work, so you might consider using canned artichokes, which are very good. You'll need more than eight, though.

Mustard Pickle

SERVES
ABOUT 20

I gave a recipe in *A Yorkshire Lad* for a home-made pork pie, and I could have repeated it here, but there are so many good pork pies that you can buy now. What they always need, though, is a sharp accompaniment, and this mustard pickle is just the ticket. It only lasts a couple of days, though.

1 cauliflower	55 g (2 oz) salt	25 g (1 oz) dry English mustard powder
1 cucumber	1.2 litres (2 pints) white vinegar	15 g (½ oz) turmeric
450 g (1 lb) pears (or apples), cored and peeled	1 fresh red chilli	20 g (¾ oz) plain flour
2 onions, peeled	115 g (4 oz) caster sugar	
	1 tbsp ground ginger	

1 Cut the cauliflower, cucumber, pears and onions into small pieces, and put in a bowl. Sprinkle with salt, and leave for about 2–3 hours.

2 Put the vinegar on to boil with the chilli, then remove the chilli using a slotted spoon.

3 Drain the vegetables, then rinse off the salt. Drain well, and place in the hot vinegar. Cook at a simmer for about 15 minutes.

4 Remove the vegetables from the vinegar using a slotted spoon, and purée in a food processor. Return to the vinegar in the pan.

5 Mix the sugar, ginger, mustard, turmeric and flour together with 2 tbsp water, then mix into the vegetable purée. Stir and cook until the mixture thickens, about 2–3 minutes maximum, really when it comes up to the boil.

6 Leave to cool, then store for 48 hours in the fridge, in a bowl covered with clingfilm.

Mutton Ham

SERVES 8

Mutton is having a great revival, thanks to HRH The Prince of Wales and the Academy of Culinary Arts. It's a great tasting meat, and there are lots of fabulous dishes you can prepare with it. Mutton has a strength of flavour lamb lacks, and I love to eat this 'ham' with pickles or chutneys (the one opposite would be good) and buttered sourdough bread.

1 x 1.3 kg (3 lb) leg of mutton

2 garlic cloves, peeled and crushed

chicken stock

2 celery stalks

1 large onion

2 carrots

MARINADE

900 g (2 lb) Maldon sea salt

1 bunch fresh thyme

1 bunch fresh oregano

2 bay leaves

6 garlic cloves, peeled and crushed

10 cloves

1 tbsp black peppercorns, crushed

1 tbsp chilli flakes

1 tsp cumin seeds

finely grated zest of 2 oranges

1 bottle Bordeaux style red wine

2 tbsp Cognac

1 Trim all the fat off the leg of mutton. Take off the aitch bone and then tunnel bone to take out the thigh bone (any good butcher would do this for you). Push the crushed garlic cloves into the space left by the bone and tie the leg with one piece of string, holding the open end together.

2 Mix the salt and all the spices, herbs and flavourings with the wine and Cognac, and put into a plastic tray, just big enough to hold the meat. Submerge the leg in this, and keep in the fridge for a week, turning over regularly.

3 Take out of the marinade, and dry well. Take off the string then wrap in two layers of muslin. Tie with string on the outside to keep the shape. Have enough string to be able to hang the leg, and do so in a clean, cool place, preferably with a through current of air, for two to three days.

4 When ready to cook, take off the muslin and trim any discoloured areas (the blood causes this, there's nothing wrong with the meat). Put into a large pan, cover with chicken stock, and add the celery, onion and carrots. Bring to the boil, turn down to a simmer, and cook for about 1½ hours. This will depend on the width of the leg. Test with a skewer by piercing through the leg in the thickest part, and then checking to make sure the meat is hot in the middle. Drain and serve hot, or leave to go cold.

5 To serve, hold the bone end, and slice, across the meat, with a good sharp carving knife, fairly thinly.

Cucumber and Mustard Salad

SERVES 4

Salads are the backbone of summer eating, and picnic eating, and this is classically British, using cucumbers, lettuce, sherry and mustard, with the slightly alien element of chilli. I thought of this as a side salad, but if it becomes a main, bulk it up with more lettuce.

2 cucumbers

1 red onion, peeled

1 small red chilli

1 tbsp white wine vinegar

2 tbsp dry sherry

grated rind of 1 lemon

juice of ½ lemon

1 tbsp grain mustard

salt and freshly ground black pepper

1 little gem lettuce

1 tbsp olive oil

a few chive stalks

1   Peel and slice the cucumbers and put into a bowl. Slice the red onion finely and add to the bowl. Remove the seeds from the chilli, and finely chop the flesh. Add to the cucumber with the vinegar, sherry, lemon rind and juice and the mustard, and mix well.

2   Leave to marinate for 15 minutes.

3   Drain off any excess liquid. Season, then serve on top of well-washed crisp little gem lettuce leaves. Drizzle with olive oil, and decorate with chives.

☞ If you liked, you could halve the cucumber lengthwise and, using a teaspoon, scrape out all the seeds. Then slice the cucumber into half-moons.

Chicken and Pork Brawn

Brawn would have been made throughout the centuries, a hangover from when householders kept their own pigs. Any parts of the pig that might not be used in another way (as ham or bacon or sausages) would be put in the brawn, which originally consisted of small pieces of brined pork. Here the pork is fresh – with refrigeration, we don't have the same necessity nowadays to preserve meat – and I have added a boiling fowl (you can still get these, from good butchers and poulterers). The jellied stock is classic, and you must serve this with strong-tasting relishes (see my pickled veg recipe on p. 112) and, an absolute must, some English mustard.

SERVES 8–10

2 pig's trotters	2 leeks
2 pork shanks	1.2 litres (2 pints) dry cider
½ nutmeg, freshly grated	1 x 1.3 kg (3 lb) boiling fowl
5 cloves	2 tbsp chopped fresh parsley
12 black peppercorns	4 hard-boiled eggs, shelled and chopped
2 garlic cloves	1 tbsp cider vinegar
2 bay leaves	½ tsp ground allspice
2 carrots	salt and freshly ground black pepper

☞ Pig's trotters can be found in good butcher's (you may have to order them). The same goes for pork shanks (which is the same cut as veal *ossobuco* and beef shin). Boiling fowl too is not seen much, but your good butcher or poulterer will be able to get you one. If you can only find chicken, cook this for just 1½ hours.

☞ Most bought brawns will have loads more jelly than there is here. This one contains more meat than jelly.

1   Split the trotters lengthways, and put with the pork shanks into a large pot. Pour in enough water to cover and bring gently to the boil. Drain off the water, refresh the meats in cold water and put into a clean pan.

2   Add the nutmeg, cloves, peppercorns, garlic, bay leaves, carrots, leeks and cider. Add enough water to well cover the ingredients and bring up to the boil. Simmer, uncovered, for an hour.

3   Add the boiling fowl and enough water to keep everything covered. Simmer slowly for a further 3 hours. Take out the meats as they cook: test frequently for tenderness between your thumb and forefinger (don't burn yourself). When removed from the stock, put to one side.

4   When all the meats are cooked and removed, carefully strain the stock through a fine sieve. Put the liquid back on the heat and gently simmer to reduce its volume by about half.

5   Very carefully strip the meat of all bone and gristle and other nasty bits. With a sharp knife, carefully chop the meats into small dice and put into a bowl. Add the chopped parsley, chopped eggs, vinegar and allspice, and mix well. Check the seasoning.

6   Line a 30 cm (12 in) terrine mould with clingfilm and fill with the meat mixture. Press down.

7   Check the stock for salt. Pour the stock over the meat and leave to cool. Refrigerate overnight to set.

8   To serve, slice into medium slices, and serve with *Pickled Vegetables* (see p. 112).

Chicken, Bacon and Olive Club Sandwich

The Earl of Sandwich, in the early eighteenth century, was hungry but did not want to leave the gaming table, so he had them bring him meat between two pieces of bread. Thus was a British stalwart born. The club sandwich, however, is American, first mentioned in print in 1903. It is usually served as toasted bread, in three layers, with chicken or turkey, tomato, lettuce and mayonnaise. It began in a gentleman's club, thus its name, but some commentators say it should be two layers only, to match the two-decker 'club' cars then travelling on the US railroads.

James Beard, a great American chef and food writer, said of the club: 'It is one of the great sandwiches of all time and has swept its way around the world after an American beginning... Nowadays practically everyone uses turkey and there's a vast difference between turkey and chicken where sandwiches are concerned.' I agree, and my preference is definitely for roast chicken. This is, however, another variation on the theme.

SERVES 4

115g (4oz) good large green olives, pitted	salt and freshly ground black pepper	4 iceberg lettuce leaves
55g (2oz) unsalted butter	2 tomatoes	1 tbsp mayonnaise
2 roasted chicken breasts	1 tsp balsamic vinegar	12 rashers streaky bacon
		12 slices sourdough bread

1 Chop the olives finely and mix with the unsalted butter. Slice the chicken and season with salt and pepper.

2 Slice the tomatoes. Put on a plate, season and then sprinkle with balsamic vinegar. Shred the lettuce, then season and mix with the mayonnaise.

3 Cook the streaky bacon until crisp, and lightly toast the bread.

4 For each sandwich place two slices of bread on the table top (eight altogether). Spread each with the butter and olive mixture. On four of the slices, put some lettuce with three slices of bacon on top. On the other four lay the sliced tomatoes and then the sliced chicken breasts. Lift the latter on top of the lettuce and bacon slices. Put the remaining four 'nude' slices of toast on top, and hold together with cocktail sticks.

5 Serve with optional extra olives, or fries for a really substantial meal.

Pickled Vegetables

Hardly pickled vegetables as our ancestors would have known them, but they taste wonderful, especially with the brawn on p. 108, and with any cold meats. Cook them separately in the pickling liquid and serve separately – or you can mix them. This amount of pickling liquid will only do one of the veg at a time, rather than all three together. They are not meant to last, so don't attempt to store them in your larder. They are pickled for flavour, not for keeping, but are perfect to take on a picnic.

MAKES ABOUT
675 G (1½ LB)

1 large cauliflower/	**PICKLING LIQUID**	2 tbsp white wine vinegar
675 g (1½ lb) leeks/	300 ml (10 fl oz) water	8 coriander seeds
675 g (1½ lb) carrots	2 tbsp olive oil	6 black peppercorns
	½ bay leaf	a few parsley stalks

1   Break the cauliflower into small florets that will easily fit in a large jar. Wash the leeks well, and cut into 4 cm (1½ in) lengths. Peel the carrots, and cut into quarters lengthwise then into 4 cm (1½ in) lengths.

2   Blanch the cauliflower florets, leeks and carrots separately in boiling water.

3   Drain and refresh in cold water, then cook in the pickling liquid until cooked, about 10–15 minutes roughly.

4   Leave to cool in the liquor, then refrigerate overnight. Eat as soon as you can, but they will keep in the fridge for up to a week.

Country Pork Salad

This slightly reminds me of the French *rillettes*, thoroughly and gently cooked pork which is then shredded and mixed with fat. Here, I have used a reduction of the cooking liquor instead of the fat, which makes it very much more healthy. It's just a variation on the sort of thing that might once have been taken on a picnic, some cold pork and a salad – but it is, of course, vastly superior!

SERVES 8–10

1 x 900g (2lb) piece shoulder of pork

1 onion, peeled and chopped

1 sprig fresh thyme

1 sprig fresh rosemary

½ garlic bulb

salt and freshly ground black pepper

150ml (5floz) chicken stock

150ml (5floz) dry white wine

SALAD AND DRESSING

2 red apples, cored

2 celery sticks, trimmed

12 radishes, trimmed

175g (6oz) baby spinach leaves, washed

1 tsp grain mustard

2 tbsp cider vinegar

8 tbsp olive oil

1   Preheat the oven to 150°C/300°F/Gas 2.

2   Choose a roasting tray into which the pork will comfortably fit. Put the chopped onion, thyme, rosemary and garlic into the tray, and lay the pork on top. Season with pepper, and pour the stock and wine around the pork.

3   Put into the preheated oven, and cook for about 2½–3 hours. If it dries out, add some water. When fully cooked, take out and leave to rest for 15 minutes. Strain the cooking liquor into a bowl and keep warm.

4   Cut the apples and celery into even-sized batons. Cut the radishes into small batons. Mix these together with the spinach leaves in a bowl, and season.

5   In another bowl mix the mustard with the vinegar. Add the oil and season, then mix with the salad ingredients in the bowl.

6   While the pork is still warm, shred with two forks. Put into a bowl and mix with some of the cooking juices. Taste for seasoning.

7   Mix some of the pork with the salad and put on to a plate. Spoon some more pork on top and serve.

☛   If preparing this for eating at home, it eats well with a poached egg on top, and also with toast (and gherkins). It's a great thing to have as a standby in the fridge – but if you can get it back to room temperature before serving, so much the better.

Pear and Walnut Salad

SERVES 4

This is a perfect salad for a late summer picnic or barbecue, with both pears and walnuts coming into season. It is made extra special by the addition of the blue cheese, but this is optional. I would always use a Yorkshire blue, but you can of course use an alternative blue.

115 g (4 oz) baby rocket leaves

85 g (3 oz) walnut pieces

2 tbsp walnut oil

2 tbsp groundnut oil

juice of ½ lemon

2 pears

salt and freshly ground black pepper

55 g (2 oz) Yorkshire blue cheese or Roquefort (optional)

1   Wash the rocket leaves and dry them. Pick off any larger stems, and put the leaves into a salad bowl.

2   Chop the walnut pieces and, in another bowl, mix with the oils and lemon juice.

3   Cut the pears in half lengthwise and remove the stem and pips. Cut into thin slices, and add these to the dressing and nuts. Season with salt and pepper.

4   When ready to serve, mix the pears and dressing into the leaves in the salad bowl. Toss carefully and divide between individual serving plates.

5   If cheese is needed, just crumble it over the top.

Game Pie

Game was once the most plentiful fresh meat available in Britain, until royal laws were passed and it became an offence for the ordinary man to snare a rabbit or game bird for the family pot. Because the birds obtained (whether legally or by poaching) were often older, they would be encased in suet and steamed for hours as a pudding, or braised first and then covered with a pastry crust as a pie.

Pigeon pie is a speciality of Yorkshire, where young pigeons are cooked with chunks of steak, bacon and hard-boiled eggs under pastry. I've added partridges here as well – in fact you could substitute virtually anything, pheasant or rabbit, for instance – and the quail's eggs are a nice modern Turner touch.

SERVES 4

---

225 g (8 oz) puff pastry

1 egg yolk, mixed with a little water, to glaze

FILLING

55 g (2 oz) unsalted butter

4 smoked bacon rashers, chopped into 5 mm (¼ in) strips

2 shallots, peeled and chopped

4 pigeon breasts

4 partridge breasts

salt and freshly ground black pepper

2 tbsp chopped fresh parsley

8 quail's eggs, hard-boiled and shelled

1 tsp Worcestershire sauce

150 ml (5 fl oz) chicken stock

---

1 Melt half the butter in a frying pan and cook the bacon for 2 minutes to colour. Add the finely chopped shallot, cook for a few minutes to soften then remove both from the pan using a slotted spoon. Put to one side.

2 Melt the remaining butter in the same pan to mix with the bacon fat. Remove the skin from the pigeon and partridge breasts, then seal and colour the flesh in the hot fat. Season and leave to cool.

3 Put a third of the bacon mixture in the bottom of a 1.2 litre (2 pint) pie dish. Lay the pigeon breasts on top and season again. Sprinkle with half of the remaining bacon mixture and half the parsley. Lay the quails' eggs on top along with the partridge breasts, then season. Sprinkle with the remaining bacon mixture and parsley.

4 Mix the Worcestershire sauce with the stock and pour gently over the ingredients in the pie dish.

5 Preheat the oven to 220°C/425°F/Gas 7.

6   Roll out the puff pastry and cut to make a strip that will fit around the edges of the pie dish, and a large piece to fit the top. Dampen the edges of the dish and lay a thin strip of puff pastry around. Seal to the dish. Dampen the edges of the pastry shape and arrange on top of the strip around the pie dish edges. Crimp the edges to seal. Brush all over the pastry with egg wash, and decorate with a fork. Cut a hole in the centre for the steam to escape.

7   Bake the pie in the preheated oven for 20 minutes and then reduce the temperature to 180°C/350°F/Gas 4. Cook for a further 40 minutes or so, covering the pastry with foil if it seems to be getting too brown. Serve hot.

☛ Breasts of game birds are now available from supermarkets, but if you buy or acquire the birds whole, cut the breasts off to use in the pie, and use the skins and carcasses to make a wonderful game stock.

Bacon and Egg Pie

Egg and bacon together are a traditional British combination – in a breakfast fry-up or in a salad – and their relationship in a pie is classic. Most pies would be made with a *Hot Water Crust Pastry* (see p. 168), but here I have stuck to my Yorkshire roots, and made it in a pie plate with shortcrust. Cover with clingfilm, and transport to your picnic spot on the plate.

SERVES 6–8

450 g (1 lb) *Savoury Shortcrust Pastry* (see p. 58)

1 egg, for egg wash

FILLING

2 tbsp grain mustard

350 g (12 oz) smoked bacon, cut into strips and pan-fried until crisp

8 eggs

150 ml (5 fl oz) double cream

juice of ½ lemon

salt and freshly ground black pepper

1   Preheat the oven to 200°C/400°F/Gas 6.

2   Cut the pastry in half. Mould each half into a ball shape. Cover one with a damp cloth. Roll the other out to fit an 18 cm (7 in) pie plate, which you have oiled or buttered. Place the pastry on the plate.

3   Brush the pastry over with mustard. Sprinkle the crisp bacon strips on top of the mustard.

4   Beat two of the eggs in a bowl, then add and mix in the cream and lemon juice. Gently pour over the bacon. If you can, using a wooden spoon, make six indentations in the bacon layer. Carefully and evenly break the remaining eggs on top of the cream mix, trying to place the yolks into the indentations. Season with salt and pepper.

5   Roll out the rest of the pastry into a similarly sized round, and gently place on top of the pie mix. Seal and pinch the edges together. Brush the top with the egg wash, and decorate with the back of a fork (see p. 58).

6   Bake in the preheated oven for 15 minutes, then turn the temperature down to 180°C/350°F/Gas 4. Bake for about a further 30 minutes until cooked.

7   Leave to cool, and take to the picnic on the plate. Cut into wedges to serve.

Butcher's Mixed Grill

This is perfect food for a barbecue, but I haven't been too specific about timings. You know how you like your steak and cutlets done, and you will have to judge by eye when the vegetables are ready. In one sense it doesn't matter about timings, as you don't have to serve everything together: start with sausages, say, and then serve the steaks when they're ready. The whole thing is very meaty, but you can serve some salads as well; there are a couple that are appropriate here in this chapter, but just a selection of nicely dressed green leaves would be good.

SERVES 4

vegetable oil

4 good sausages

4 bacon rashers

2 tomatoes, halved

4 medium field mushrooms

4 black pudding slices

4 x 85 g (3 oz) beef fillet steaks

4 lamb cutlets

4 x 55 g (2 oz) pork fillet medallions

4 lamb's kidneys, opened up, sinews out (use a wooden cocktail stick to keep whole)

salt and freshly ground black pepper

PARSLEY BUTTER

85 g (3 oz) unsalted butter

juice of ¼ lemon

1 tsp chopped fresh parsley

1   Make the parsley butter first. Simply mix the ingredients together well, and season to taste with salt and pepper. Roll into a fat sausage, wrap in clingfilm and put in the fridge to chill.

2   Have the barbecue ready and raring to go, or preheat your kitchen grill.

3   Lightly brush all the ingredients with a little oil. Put the sausages to grill first, and slowly cook until they are nearly done.

4   Then put the bacon, tomatoes and mushrooms on to cook; only you can judge when they are nearly done. Remove all these from the barbecue or grill and keep warm.

5   Next grill the black pudding, then the steaks, lamb cutlets, pork medallions and kidneys. Again timing depends on the heat of the barbecue or grill. Try to keep the beef and lamb pink.

6   When all are cooked, season well, and arrange on a central platter. Put slices of parsley butter on the kidneys. Allow everyone to help themselves.

☛ I often put my sausages in the oven for 10 minutes and then finish them as above on the grill – this way they tend not to burn and are cooked all the way through.

Cornish Pasties

Variations of this idea – ingredients wrapped in pastry to make individual pies – occur all over Europe, but perhaps the nearest to the most famous one, that of Cornwall, are the Forfar Bridie, from the east of Scotland, and the Lancashire Foot. There are all sorts of legends surrounding the quintessential pasty: it is real only if it is dropped down a Cornish tin mine and the pastry doesn't break; that it is unlucky to take a pasty aboard a ship. In Cornwall, the pasty is occasionally called Tiddy Oggy (a local name for potato).

The basic recipe can also be varied in a number of ways. You could use any meat as a filling, and you could use vegetables alone (common when money for the costly meat was scarce). Whatever and however, the pasty is the ultimate portable food, as handy now for a picnic as it once was for the miner to take into the bowels of the earth or the farmer into the field.

MAKES 12

SHORTCRUST PASTRY

450 g (1 lb) plain flour

a pinch of salt

225 g (8 oz) lard

55 g (2 oz) unsalted butter

approx. 150 ml (5 fl oz) water

2 eggs, beaten with a little water, for egg wash

FILLING

450 g (1 lb) topside beef

1 medium onion

225 g (8 oz) potatoes

55 g (2 oz) carrots

55 g (2 oz) turnip

salt and freshly ground black pepper

1 tbsp chopped parsley

Worcestershire sauce

Tabasco sauce

---

1   To make the pastry, sift the flour and salt into a bowl. Chop the lard and butter straight from the fridge into small cubes, then rub into the flour until like breadcrumbs. Add enough water to make the ingredients come together to a dough, then clingfilm and rest for 30 minutes.

2   Preheat the oven to 200°C/400°F/Gas 6.

3   To make the filling, trim the meat of all fat and gristle, cut into small dice then put into a bowl. Peel and finely chop the onion. Peel and cut the potatoes, carrots and turnip into 1 cm (½ in) dice, and add to the bowl along with the onion. Mix well, then season with salt and pepper, and add the parsley and a splash each of the sauces.

4 Cut the pastry into four pieces and roll each of them out thinly. Cut into circles of 15 cm (6 in) in diameter. Brush the edges of each pastry circle with egg wash, then pile a quarter of the filling into the middle of each. Spread in a line across the centre of the pastry. Fold the pastry over and up to make a seal on top of the filling. Using your thumb and forefinger, crimp the edges in a wavy fashion. Brush with egg wash and make a hole in the top for the steam to escape.

5 Put on a baking sheet and bake in the preheated oven for 30 minutes then reduce the oven temperature to 180°C/350°F/Gas 4 and continue to cook for a further 20 minutes. Serve hot or cold.

☛ You could use rough puff or *Hot Water Crust Pastry* (see p. 168) instead of the shortcrust. This shortcrust uses more lard than the other savoury shortcrust in the book: this was traditional, giving more flavour.

☛ If adapting this recipe to make a vegetarian pasty, use a vegetarian shortening for the pastry instead of the lard.

Skuets

Skuets are simply skewers. Prehistoric man would have pierced and cooked his pieces of meat on pointed twigs. (It is a measure of how far we have come that there's now a vogue for skewering foods on pointed rosemary sticks – although that is mainly for the aroma!) Later we would have used metal, and it is said that one of 300 cooks at the court of Richard II took the idea a little further, and served pieces of meat on little silver skewers, surrounding other dishes of meats, or as a savoury. We rarely use silver nowadays, tending more towards stainless steel, but the idea is not bad: a couple of little skewers of grilled meat, fish or chicken would be a perfect savoury to serve, perhaps, after a Father's Day meal (see p. 127).

SERVES 4

---

450 g (1 lb) pork fillet
175 g (6 oz) lamb's kidneys
1 tsp ground coriander

¼ tsp ground ginger
½ tsp freshly grated nutmeg
1 garlic clove, peeled and crushed
juice of ½ lemon

olive oil
salt and freshly ground black pepper

---

1   Cut the pork into 2 cm (1 in) dice. Trim the kidneys, remove the skin and core, and cut into pieces the same size as the pork. Put into a bowl.

2   Add all the remaining ingredients, plus 1 tbsp oil and some salt and pepper. Mix well together, and leave to marinate for 4 hours.

3   Preheat your grill.

4   Divide the meats evenly between skewers. Brush the meat with more oil and grill for 4–5 minutes, or until it's done to your liking, turning frequently.

☞ I think veal kidney is the best, but it is very expensive, and quite difficult to find, so lamb's is fine.

☞ If you are going to cook on wooden skewers, remember to soak them in cold water for some time in advance, which will prevent them catching fire. When grilling food on rosemary twigs, I always cover the ends with foil for the same reason, although I have seen many a burnt offering in other restaurants.

Rib-eye Steak and Radish Relish

The rib-eye steak is a cut much appreciated by the meat-loving Americans, and has become popular in Britain only fairly recently, probably because we preferred to cook our ribs on the bone as roast beef. The steak has all the qualities of sirloin or porterhouse – tender, juicy, well marbled – it's just a bit bigger! It's closer to the muscle which means it has more fat, and therefore is more tasty. In fact there is often an eye of fat in the middle of the steak (when it is closer to the shoulder).

SERVES 4

4 x 225g (8oz) rib-eye steaks	**RADISH RELISH**	I fresh red chilli, seeded
groundnut oil	350g (12oz) red radishes, trimmed	I tsp mustard seeds
salt and freshly ground black pepper	115g (4oz) shallots	150ml (5floz) white wine vinegar
25g (I oz) unsalted butter	I tsp salt	I tbsp chopped fresh parsley
	I tsp caster sugar	I tbsp olive oil

1   Cut the radishes in half, then slice thinly and put in a bowl. Peel the shallots, cut in half through the root and remove the root. Slice thinly, then put into the bowl with the radishes and mix well. Sprinkle with the salt and sugar and leave to stand for 2 hours. Drain well.

2   Chop the red chilli, add to the mustard seeds and white wine vinegar in a small pan, and bring up to the boil. Pour over the shallot and radish mixture, and leave to stand for another 2 hours.

3   Drain the liquid from the radishes, then season them and add the parsley and oil. Set to one side.

4   Preheat the barbecue or grill.

5   Rub the steaks with a little oil, season and put on the hot grill. Cook to medium-rare (see below), take off and leave to rest.

6   Brush with melted butter, re-season and serve with the radish pickle and a dressed green salad.

☞ Take the meat out of the fridge well in advance. Keep at normal room temperature for a couple of hours beforehand so that the middle of the meat is not too cold when you start to cook.

☞ Meat can always be put back on the barbecue if not quite cooked enough, so I would always tend to stay on the underdone side. If you have a good intense heat, rare will take a minute on each side. You will need 2 minutes a side for medium-rare.

BBQ Spare Ribs

No one needs an introduction to barbecue spare ribs. They definitely come from America, but the original influence might have been Chinese, perhaps introduced to the States by the Chinese who came in to work on the railways. This is undeniably Chinese in its use of flavourings and spices, and I hope it becomes a favourite. My pet hate with spare ribs is when they are underdone and chewy, no matter how good in flavour. This method allows you to cook them a little in advance, and by boiling them one tends to get a more tender finished product. These are quite moreish.

SERVES 4 (WITH OTHER DISHES)

	MARINADE	2 tbsp dry sherry
1.3 kg (3 lb) pork spare ribs, in sheets	1 tsp black peppercorns	1 tbsp cider wine vinegar
1 chicken stock cube	8 tbsp hoisin sauce	1 tbsp Worcestershire sauce
1 onion	1 ½ tbsp clear honey	1 tbsp soy sauce
1 carrot	3 garlic cloves, peeled and crushed	1 tsp five-spice powder
1 leek		

1   Start the ribs the day before. Cut the sheets of ribs into three or four rib sections. Put a large pan of water on to boil and add the stock cube and cleaned vegetables. Put the ribs in and boil for 20 minutes. Drain when done (do not throw the stock away).

2   Meanwhile put the peppercorns into a hot dry wok until they start to release their aroma. Take out and grind to a powder. Put into a bowl with the rest of the marinade ingredients.

3   Mix the ribs into the marinade and stir well. Leave overnight in a cool place.

4   On the day, preheat the oven to 220°C/425°F/Gas 7, and fire up your barbecue.

5   Put the ribs on to a rack over a roasting tray, and bake in the preheated oven for 15 minutes. Take out and put on to the barbecue to colour and finish.

☞ If you cook your spare ribs totally on the barbecue, you risk burning them because of the sugar content. That's why I suggest boiling and baking them first. And don't throw the rib-boiling stock away: this will have plenty of flavour from the meat and veg, and can be used as the basis for a soup or sauce.

☞ Always eat spare ribs in your fingers, never with a knife and fork. Lamb spare ribs can be eaten in the same way, but you may need to change the marinade for something less sweet.

☞ If you don't feel like getting out the barbie, then just bake in the oven and baste regularly with glaze.

Stuffed Herrings

I love herrings, and snap them up whenever I see them – they are best in the spring, summer and autumn. I sometimes cook them in the Scottish way, with mustard and a coating of oatmeal, and I am very keen on the baked herring on p. 153, served with fennel and potatoes. Here the additional flavour is all coming from the inside, from a stuffing with onion, garlic, walnuts, breadcrumbs – and, yes, mustard again! The fish can be cooked on the barbecue and eaten hot, or they are delicious cold, when they can be taken on a picnic.

SERVES 4

4 herrings

I tbsp horseradish sauce

2 tbsp olive oil

salt and freshly ground black pepper

STUFFING

55 g (2 oz) unsalted butter

I small onion, peeled and finely chopped

I garlic clove, peeled and crushed

55 g (2 oz) fresh brown breadcrumbs

55 g (2 oz) walnut pieces, chopped

finely grated rind and juice of I lemon

I tbsp grain mustard

I tbsp each of chopped fresh parsley and chives

1 Preheat the barbecue, or preheat the oven to 200°C/400°F/Gas 6 if cooking in the kitchen.

2 Make sure the herrings are boned from the stomach side, cleaned, heads and tails off.

3 To make the stuffing, melt the butter in a small pan, add the onion and garlic, and sweat for about 3 minutes, but do not colour. Take off the heat and mix in the breadcrumbs, walnuts, lemon rind and juice, mustard and the herbs. Season well.

4 Lay the herrings on a roasting tray and brush inside with horseradish. Fill the fish with the stuffing, close, and sprinkle the skin with oil and some salt and pepper.

5 Grill on the barbecue for about 4–5 minutes on each side, carefully turning over or, if you are not grilling outside, pan-fry the fish for about 2 minutes on each side, then finish in the preheated oven for about 8 minutes.

☛ Serve hot at a barbecue, with salads. Leave to go cold for a picnic, and serve with a yoghurt sauce (simply mix together good natural yoghurt with chopped mint and parsley and some lemon juice to taste).

Father's Day

Father's Day is a spin-off from American practice and, rather like Mother's Day, has become very commercialised. Unlike Mothering Sunday, the festival celebrating fathers has only truly been around since the beginning of the twentieth century. It is said that in 1909 a dutiful married daughter from Spokane, Washington, while attending a Mother's Day church service, thought that fathers should be honoured in the same way. It wasn't until 1972 that President Nixon declared that Father's Day would be celebrated annually on the third Sunday in June.

In Britain, we followed suit, and we too celebrate that same day – but perhaps a little less enthusiastically. Although he was a typical working-class Yorkshireman, and never liked a fuss, we always gave my dad a card on Father's Day. Nothing much more than that, although on looking back it seems every day was his day as far as Mum was concerned, for she treated him like a god.

On Father's Day in June, so far as food is concerned, you could have a picnic or barbecue, or a lunch or dinner. I was trying to think of what fathers might like, and came up with a food that has always been associated with men: the 'savoury'. (My dad loved things like this, and I have followed suit.) By Victorian times this small savoury dish had become firmly established as a course towards the end of the meal, before the dessert, and I think it is a uniquely British invention. Thought of as digestive, it is a fair assumption too that men might have wanted something to nibble on while finishing off the main-course wines.

The savoury course nowadays has been somewhat superseded by the cheese course which, like the savoury, is properly served before the dessert. I think, though, that the time is right to start thinking about savouries again. For instance, we could offer a savoury in place of a sweet, not as well as (we're certainly doing that with cheese). Although I admit to a sweet tooth, sometimes a savoury flavour, usually that of cheese, is just what I fancy at the end of a meal. Cheese on toast is a huge favourite, and you can play around with ideas (see p. 148 too). Scrambled eggs, mushrooms, tomatoes etc can also be served on toast (see pp. 14 and 15), and some little skewers of meat, perhaps grilled plain or devilled, could be a possibility as well (see p. 122). Although a good and tasty mouthful at the end of a meal, most savouries, including those offered here, could also be served as a canapé, a starter or a light lunch.

Scotch Woodcock

This classic after-dinner savoury, the most popular in Victorian times apparently, is basically fancy scrambled eggs on toast. I believe it still appears on the menus of many gentlemen's clubs. The only thing I can see to ally the game bird with the savoury is that both are served on toast. The name of the recipe may also be a snide reference to the parsimony of the Scots (Yorkshiremen stripped of their generosity, as an old joke has it), who might serve scrambled eggs instead of woodcock, the most expensive of the game birds. Florence White, in *Good Things in England,* quoted that Scotch woodcock 'is much approved by men'.

SERVES 4

---

4 eggs

4 egg yolks

300 ml (10 fl oz) single cream

salt and freshly ground black pepper

55 g (2 oz) unsalted butter

4 slices sliced bread

12 anchovy fillets

1 tbsp capers, rinsed

4 fresh parsley leaves

1 Beat the eggs, egg yolks and cream together, then season with salt and pepper. Use 25 g (1 oz) of the butter to scramble this mixture (see p. 15).

2 Toast the bread, then butter the slices. Use a round cutter to cut out a large circle from each slice of toast.

3 Load the toast circles with the scrambled eggs. Criss-cross with the anchovy fillets and sprinkle with the capers. Garnish with parsley, and serve immediately.

☛ Many recipes advocate mashing the anchovy with the butter and spreading it on the toast before topping with the scrambled egg. Or you could use some minced ham mixed with mustard and butter. It's the spiciness you want.

☛ Don't waste the remnants of buttered toast – eat them!

Brown Shrimp Rarebit

Welsh rarebit is perhaps the classic savoury, but there are many variations, using different types of bread or cheese. You can mix the cheese topping with other ingredients, such as smoked haddock or prawns, but my favourites are these small brown shrimps from Morecambe Bay, crowned with a mature Cheddar topping. A nice mouthful with which to down the last of the red wine...

SERVES 4

175 g (6 oz) cooked brown shrimps, shelled

1 tbsp chopped fresh parsley

salt and freshly ground black pepper

125 ml (4 fl oz) double cream

1 tbsp beer

1 tsp English mustard

a splash of Worcestershire sauce

225 g (8 oz) mature Cheddar, grated

2 egg yolks

8 slices good bread

1   Preheat the oven to 160°C/325°F/Gas 3, and preheat the grill if using instead of a toaster.

2   Mix the shrimps and parsley in a bowl, season and put to one side.

3   Put the double cream in a small pan, and boil until it thickens, a few minutes. Add the beer, mustard and Worcestershire sauce, and re-boil to thicken, another minute or so. Take off the heat, and stir in the cheese and egg yolks. Add half of this mix to the shrimps.

4   Toast the bread on both sides and cut into circles with a 5 cm (2 in) round cutter. Mould the shrimp mix on top of the toast. Pour the remaining rarebit mixture over and put in the preheated oven for 5–7 minutes to heat through and glaze.

Angels on Horseback

Who would have thought this favourite Victorian savoury could be successful, but the sea tang of the oyster with the saltiness of the bacon makes for a perfect marriage. (Incidentally, a scallop cooked in the same way is called an 'archangel'.)

SERVES 4

12 rashers streaky bacon

12 large oysters, shelled and cleaned

½ lemon

freshly ground black pepper

a little lard or olive oil, if necessary

4 slices thick white or brown bread

25 g (1 oz) unsalted butter

4 sprigs fresh parsley or dill

1   Take the rashers of bacon and stretch out using the back of a large knife so that they are thinner and more elongated than before. Lay out on a chopping board.

2   Meanwhile, take the cleaned oysters, squeeze over the lemon juice and sprinkle on some black pepper.

3   Wrap each oyster with a rasher of bacon and then secure three per person on a wooden skewer (which has been soaked in water if they are to be grilled). Grill until the bacon crisps and the oysters are just cooked. An alternative is to fry them in lard or oil until just cooked.

4   Toast the bread, butter the slices, and cut into your preferred shape. Lay an oyster skewer on each piece of toast and garnish with a sprig of parsley or dill. Serve immediately.

Devils on Horseback

We have 'angels' and 'devils' because of colour, I presume – the white of the oysters and the black of the prunes. But why 'horseback', I cannot fathom. The best I have come up with is the shape and colour of the saddle on a black stallion. Whatever the reason for the name, devils on horseback are almost as delicious as angels, the sweetness of the prunes a good contrast with the salty bacon.

SERVES 4

12 large prunes

55 g (2 oz) unsalted butter

12 rashers streaky bacon

a little lard or olive oil, if necessary

4 slices thick white or brown bread

4 sprigs fresh parsley or dill

1   Stone the prunes, then fry in a frying pan in half the butter. Drain.

2   Stretch the bacon rashers as in the previous recipe, then wrap them round the stoned prunes.

3   Skewer, cook and serve in exactly the same way as the angels on horseback.

Some hot devils and angels, ready to eat

High tea, like afternoon tea and the savoury course (see pp. 32 and 127), is a meal unique to Great Britain. It would have come into being around the time that lunch was becoming part of the daily meal structure (see p. 54). The upper classes began to partake of this new-fangled lunch in the early afternoon, and to take their dinner much later, in the early evening – often, so far as the ladies were concerned, after an afternoon tea. The working classes, however, still ate their 'dinner' at midday, and then they had what came to be called 'high tea' (as opposed to afternoon tea) from around five to seven in the evening. Because people were either working on the land or in the industrialised towns, the fare for high tea would often be something that could have been cooking slowly all day, such as a stew or boiled suet pudding (good in winter), or something that could be prepared very quickly, once they came home, such as cold meat and pickles in the summer, or grilled kippers, chops or bacon. Eggs would have featured often, as would cheese, bread, toast and butter, and there would be a sweet or some baked goods to follow. All washed down with lots of tea.

It was a substantial meal, and it still survives in many households, where people call their evening meal 'tea'. (At home, we had a tea after school, neither 'high' nor 'low', and my dad would have his cooked meal later. As we grew older, we would sit down and have something to eat with him occasionally.) Many regional specialities in Wales, northern England and Scotland owe their continued existence to 'high tea' – things like potted meats, fish pastes and pies – and the British baking tradition itself might not have survived if housewives and mothers had not continued baking oatcakes, muffins, buns, tarts and pies to feed their families. There is a good selection of dishes here suitable for high teas, mainly savoury I admit, but there are many sweet choices in the other chapters, particularly Afternoon Tea (see p. 32), which would be perfect high tea fare.

Supper is a funny one, although it is always the last meal of the day. The French verb 'souper', to sup, gives us 'soup', ' sup' and 'supper' – and indeed the 'sop', the soaked bread that traditionally bulked out the broth in the British soup bowl. In the old days a supper seems to have been a light meal taken just before going to bed, by all classes, some hours after either tea or dinner. Now supper has several meanings. It can be an informal family meal, primarily amongst the middle classes, that you might have earlier in the evening than a formal dinner (7.00pm, say, as opposed to 8.30). You might also have a supper instead of a dinner when you have eaten a heavy lunch earlier on in the day.

So lightness and informality seem to be the order of the day, which is no bad thing when you are just about to go to bed. However, think about fish suppers, Burns suppers, buffet suppers, pot-luck suppers etc, all adding an extra dimension, in this case social, to the basic concept. There are plenty of recipes here that would be suitable for supper, and indeed elsewhere.

And, incidentally, the myth about eating late at night being bad for digestion, for sleep and for calories has recently been debunked. So supper on...

Braised Duck with Peas

Ducks from Aylesbury were becoming popular in the London markets of the eighteenth century, and in many cookery books thereafter (although some say it's a Roman or Elizabethan idea) they were boiled with turnips. I remember at The Savoy we used to cook our duck with turnips too, along with olives and cream. However, peas are traditional with ducklings as well – possibly because they are in season at about the same time of year – and that too became a popular braising combination. Lettuce was often added, which is a French touch, and indeed some old cookbooks describe the dish as '*à la française*', in the French fashion.

Some recipes add cream to the peas and then purée them for a sauce, but I don't think this is necessary. The simple step of braising them and the lettuce in with the duck gives amazing flavour.

SERVES 4

---

2 x 1.1 kg (2½ lb) ducks, with giblets

600 ml (1 pint) duck or chicken stock

85 g (3 oz) unsalted butter

225 g (8 oz) bacon in the piece, cut into stubby strips (lardons) of about 5 x 5 mm x 2.5 cm (¼ x ¼ x 1 in)

175 g (6 oz) small button onions (12 plus), peeled

salt and freshly ground black pepper

1 round lettuce, shredded at the last minute

450 g (1 lb) frozen peas

1 tbsp each of chopped fresh sage, mint and parsley

---

1   Take the giblets out of the ducks. Put the giblets into the stock and leave to gently simmer for 30 minutes.

2   Preheat the oven to 160°C/325°F/Gas 3.

3   Melt 25 g (1 oz) of the butter in a casserole dish large enough to hold both ducks. Add the bacon lardons and button onions and gently colour on all sides. When nicely coloured, take out and keep on one side.

4   Prick the ducks all over with a fork, and rub with a little salt. Colour all over in the same dish as the lardons and onions, then take out of the dish. Drain off all the fat and put the ducks back in the dish.

5   Strain the stock into the dish containing the ducks, bring to the boil and cover with the lid. Put into the preheated oven and cook for 1½ hours.

6   Add the button onions and lardons, and braise for a further 15 minutes.

7   Take the ducks out and allow to rest, keeping them warm.

8 Remove excess fat from the juices in the dish, then add the shredded lettuce, peas and herbs. Simmer to reduce this sauce by a third. Correct the seasoning and consistency, then swirl in the remaining butter.

9 Carve the ducks and put on a flat dish. Pour the sauce over and serve immediately.

Oatcakes, Liver, Onions and Yoghurt

Oatcakes such as those used in this recipe are delicious with cheese, or for breakfast, but were once the staple diet of many a Scot. In the eighteenth and nineteenth centuries, a Scottish university mid-term holiday was known as 'Meal Monday', allowing the student time to go home and stock up on oatmeal, the source of his porridge, brose and oatcakes while he was away. I've added a bit of protein here, which would have been a rarity for a Scots student. However, lamb's liver is in my opinion the best-value liver, so long as it's fresh. It's not often appreciated, but it's good for you and certainly good for students.

SERVES 4

225 g (8 oz) onions, peeled

150 ml (5 fl oz) water

55 g (2 oz) unsalted butter

salt and freshly ground black pepper

115 g (4 oz) Greek-style yoghurt

450 g (1 lb) fresh lamb's liver

a little olive oil

1 tbsp chopped chives

TO SERVE

1 recipe *Oatcakes* (see opposite)

1   Slice the onions thinly and put into a pan with the water, butter and some salt and pepper. Cook to evaporate the water then fry in the residual butter to colour, about 5 minutes. Remove from the heat.

2   Put a little onion on each of the oatcakes, then mix the rest of the onions with the yoghurt.

3   Slice the liver into four slices and rub with the oil. Cook in a hot griddle pan for my preferred time, 2 minutes, then turn over, season and cook on for another 2 minutes. You can cook it for longer if you like. Chop into 1 cm (½ in) strips.

4   Add the chopped liver to the onions on the oatcakes and then serve with the onion and yoghurt mixture.

Oatcakes

Oatcakes were made all over the country, particularly in the areas where oats flourished – upland Wales, Yorkshire and northwards, and in Scotland. Most were simple amalgams of oatmeal, fat and water as here, some were raised by baking powder, and a few from Derbyshire, Staffordshire and Yorkshire were raised by yeast, making them more like thin drop scones or pikelets than the crisp biscuits we mostly associate the name with.

MAKES 4–6

115 g (4 oz) fine oatmeal	1 tbsp melted lard
a pinch of salt	4 tbsp hot water

1   Mix the oatmeal with the salt in a bowl, then add the melted lard and water. Mix to bind together.

2   Roll out on the work surface to 3 mm (⅛ in) thick, using extra oatmeal dusted on the work surface. Cut into 7.5 cm (3 in) diameter rounds.

3   Heat a heavy frying pan or griddle, then cook the oatcakes on one side for 2–3 minutes in the pan, with no fat. Turn over and cook again for a few seconds. Remove the pan from the heat. The residual heat of the pan will finish the second side off.

4   Take out of the pan and keep warm in a clean tea towel. If not using straightaway, cool thoroughly and store in an airtight tin.

Bacon and Potato Omelette

An omelette may not appear to be very British, the name of course being French, but the idea of omelettes has been with us for a long time, since about the sixteenth century. The name derives from the Latin word for a thin plate, *lamella*, and may be how early 'amulets' (as we knew them here) were cooked, as thin as a pancake. With bacon and potato mixed into the egg mixture, the dish becomes more like a Spanish *tortilla* or Italian *frittata* (and see also p. 17).

SERVES 4

---

1 tsp vegetable oil

6 bacon rashers, 3 streaky, 3 back, all rinded

175 g (6 oz) cooked potatoes

1 tbsp chopped fresh parsley

10 eggs

salt and freshly ground black pepper

140 g (5 oz) unsalted butter, 25 g (1 oz) melted

---

1   Warm the oil in a frying pan, not the omelette pan. Cut the bacon into thin strips and add to the pan. Colour and fry well, but do not brown the oil. Remove the bacon strips from the fat using a slotted spoon, and keep to one side in a bowl.

2   Cut the potatoes into roughly 5 mm (¼ in) dice. Put into the bacon oil in the pan and gently colour to a golden brown. Remove from the fat with a slotted spoon, and add to the bacon, along with the parsley.

3   In another bowl, beat the eggs together with some salt and pepper.

4   Heat a 20 cm (8 in) omelette pan and add 25 g (1 oz) of the butter. Melt this, but do not brown. Pour in a quarter of the beaten egg, and add a quarter of the bacon mix. Cook quickly, moving the mixture with a fork until lightly set. Remove from the heat.

5   Half fold the cooked mix away from yourself, then tap the pan so that the furthermost piece folds back over to you. Tip out on to a plate and re-shape gently. Brush with the remaining, melted, butter and serve.

6   Make three more omelettes in the same way. Or you could, as described on p. 17, make one big omelette and cut it into four wedges.

Baked Eggs with Asparagus

The Romans were apparently very fond of asparagus, and perhaps, like so many other foodstuffs, they were responsible for its introduction to Britain. It has always been a vegetable for the rich rather than the poor, as an asparagus bed takes up so much garden space – and only produces a result for less than two months per year. I have combined the food for the rich with the food for the poor here: asparagus with a baked egg. A perfect combination, which would be delicious for breakfast as well, perhaps even for a starter.

Asparagus is always greeted with great acclaim when it arrives in May/June. I think English asparagus is the best in the world.

SERVES 4

55 g (2 oz) unsalted butter

salt and freshly ground black pepper

8 asparagus spears, prepared as on p. 244

1 shallot, peeled and finely chopped

8 eggs

4 tbsp double cream

1 Preheat the oven to 180°C/350°F/Gas 4. Prepare a baking tray with a piece of cardboard or a folded tea towel in the base (a bain-marie). Grease eight cocotte moulds or small ramekins with butter and season them.

2 Cook the asparagus in a tall pan (if you have one), boiling salted water just up to the tips. Test to see if cooked after about 5 minutes (but depending on thickness). When cooked, the spears will just have a little 'give' about 5 cm (2 in) down from the top when pierced with the tip of a sharp knife.

3 Remove and drain the spears. Cut off the tips of the spears, to a size to fit inside the chosen dishes. Keep these tips to one side.

4 Chop the rest of the asparagus spears into fine dice and mix with the chopped shallot. Season well, and sprinkle a good portion into each dish.

5 Break an egg into each dish, and put the dishes into the prepared baking tray. Pour boiling water into the tray to reach halfway up the dishes.

6 Bake in the preheated oven until just soft in the middle, about 8 minutes. Remove from the oven.

7 Lay an asparagus tip on top of each egg dish. Heat the cream briefly, and spoon over the asparagus to serve.

Suffolk Bacon and Sausage Fraze

Also known as 'fraise' and 'froise' (sounds a bit French, doesn't it?), this old Suffolk recipe is a cross between an omelette and a pancake, because of its use of both eggs and flour. Originally, as far back as the fifteenth century, the term referred to foods fried in a batter underneath the spit-roasting meat: *Toad in the Hole* (see p. 158), which is sausages cooked in a Yorkshire pudding batter, is a type of fraze.

SERVES 4

3 eggs
25 g (1 oz) plain flour
150 ml (5 fl oz) single cream
salt and freshly ground black pepper
55 g (2 oz) unsalted butter

2 cooked sausages
4 slices streaky bacon, rinded
½ medium onion, peeled and finely chopped
1 tbsp chopped fresh parsley

1   Mix the eggs, flour and cream well together, season with salt and pepper, and put to one side.

2   Melt half the butter in a non-stick frying pan. Cut the sausages into slices and the bacon into strips. Add both to the pan, and fry for a few minutes. Add the onions and gently fry for a further 5–6 minutes.

3   Turn the mixture into a bowl, and mix in the parsley. Add half of this mixture to the egg mixture.

4   Melt the rest of the butter, add the egg mixture and cook, stirring frequently. When set, after about 2–3 minutes, leave untouched for a few minutes to allow the base to colour.

5   Turn the fraze out of the pan, using a plate and inverting it. Sprinkle the rest of the sausage mixture into the base of the pan. Slide the fraze back into the pan, with the uncooked side now on the base of the pan, on top of the sausage mixture. Cook on for about another 3 minutes to brown all over.

6   Slide the fraze on to a large plate, quarter and serve immediately.

☛ You could vary the content of the fraze – using Suffolk ham perhaps with some spring onions and blanched asparagus spears.

Bubble and Squeak

When I was a child, we always had plenty of cooked potato and cabbage left over after a meal so that we could make bubble and squeak, a classic dish for leftovers. Here, though, I describe how you might do it from scratch. Serve with cold meat, a chutney such as piccalilli and/or brown sauce – and my dad used to serve it with runny fried eggs on top in his café. My own personal favourite accompaniment is black pudding.

The name 'bubble and squeak' is said to come from the noise the dish makes as it cooks, and it was originally a way of utilising leftover meat, made with meat and cabbage only. The potato addition and the gradual loss of the meat made it more like the Irish colcannon.

SERVES 4–6

675 g (1½ lb) medium baking potatoes, scrubbed

55 g (2 oz) bacon or duck fat

450 g (1 lb) Savoy cabbage, cored, finely shredded and cooked until tender

salt and freshly ground black pepper

1   Preheat the oven to 180°C/350°F/Gas 4, and bake the potatoes until tender, about an hour. Take out and leave to cool.

2   Melt the fat in an ovenproof frying pan and add the potato flesh scraped out from the potato skins. Leave until it starts to colour. Crush with a fork, but leave some lumps in.

3   Add the cooked cabbage, season with salt and pepper, and fry well. Keep moving in the pan.

4   When the bottom is coloured, put the pan in the preheated oven for 15 minutes.

☞ You can add other ingredients to the basic mix if you like – onions, carrots or peas, say – and you could used mashed instead of baked potato if you had that left over, or sliced Brussels sprouts instead of the cabbage.

☞ You could shape the mixture into little cakes before frying, but why bother? It's the taste that counts – and the choice of fat is *vital*.

Cauliflower and Wensleydale Fritters

I've always been a sucker for anything fried, especially with cheese, and so I've had to add cauliflower here, just to make it a little more healthy. Cauliflower cheese is one of my all-time favourite dishes anyway. Although I'd probably eat these with my fingers, it would perhaps be a knife and fork job for most people, but then that's what high tea is all about.

MAKES ABOUT
24 PIECES

I small cauliflower

salt and freshly ground black pepper

vegetable oil, for deep-frying

FRITTER BATTER

115 g (4 oz) plain flour, plus extra to dust

I egg, separated

2 tbsp olive oil

150 ml (5 fl oz) cold water

55 g (2 oz) Wensleydale cheese, grated

---

1   Separate the cauliflower into large florets, then cook in boiling salted water until just underdone, about 8–9 minutes. Remove from the heat, drain and refresh under cold running water. Drain and dry and cut each floret in half.

2   To start the batter, sieve the flour and a pinch of salt into a bowl. Add the egg yolk, olive oil and most of the water, and stir well to a smooth batter. Add only enough of the remaining water to get a creamy consistency, then leave to rest for at least 30–60 minutes.

3   Heat the oil to cook (see below and p. 13).

4   Whisk the egg white until stiff. Add the grated cheese to the batter and carefully fold in the whisked egg white.

5   Dust the cauliflower pieces with some extra flour and drop a few at a time into the batter. Pick out a piece at a time, let excess batter drain off, and drop carefully into the hot oil. Fry for a minute or so, turning once. Drain quickly on kitchen paper, and serve immediately.

☞ When deep-frying, the oil will be ready when, if you put in a little cube of bread, it visibly turns brown in under a minute while you are watching.

Cheese and Onion Muffins

This typical British yeast batter cake is so versatile, and can be served at breakfast time, for tea, for high tea, or a snack, perhaps, when the children come home from school. The ingredients that go into it can be varied almost endlessly too.

MAKES 8–10

175g (6oz) onions, peeled
55g (2oz) unsalted butter
150ml (5floz) chicken stock
115g (4oz) Lancashire cheese, grated

plain flour, to dust
unsalted butter, to serve
BASIC MUFFIN DOUGH
15g (½oz) fresh yeast

300ml (10floz) milk, at blood temperature
450g (1lb) strong white flour
¾ tsp salt

1   Cut the peeled onions in half through the root, then take off the root. Lay flat side on the board, then cut very thinly from top to tail into shreds.

2   Put the onions into a medium frying pan with the butter. Gently fry to colour, then add the stock. Cook to soften the onions and reduce the liquor, about 5 minutes. Remove from the pan and leave to cool. Drain.

3   To make the muffin dough, mix the yeast and warm milk in a bowl, sprinkle a little flour on top and leave in a warm place for about 15 minutes until it begins to froth up. Sift the flour and salt into a bowl, make a well in the centre and mix in the yeast liquid. Knead the dough on a lightly floured surface for about 15 minutes until it is 'clear' – i.e. it sticks together in one ball.

4   Add the grated cheese and the cooled onion to the dough, and knead for about 15 minutes. Put the dough into a floured bowl, cover with a clean tea towel and put into a warm place for about 45 minutes, until doubled in size.

5   On a lightly floured surface, roll the dough out to 1 cm (½ in) thick, then rest for 10 minutes, keeping it covered with a clean cloth.

6   Cut into 6 cm (2½ in) circles and put on a floured baking sheet. Dust lightly with flour. Allow space between the muffins, cover and leave in a warm place to double in size, about 30 minutes.

7   Cook the muffins on a preheated griddle, griddle pan or frying pan for about 8 minutes per side.

8   To eat, split using your thumbs, put cold butter in the middle, and sandwich!

Bacon and Onion Buns

Buns are basically small loaves, for individual consumption, and are usually sweet, full of dried fruit rather like the original cake mixtures (think of Chelsea buns and hot cross buns). Although the Scots have their plain baps, they take the sweetened bun idea much further, with their rich Hogmanay *Black Bun,* which is dried fruit and spice encased in pastry (see p. 226). But I have chosen to take the bun back to the basic bread concept, and added a few bits and pieces to give flavour and texture. In this day and age, you can eat them at any time you like, perhaps with a fish dish, or as a snack; or if there are any left over, cut in half, toast and spread with cold butter.

MAKES 16

---

115 g (4 oz) onions, peeled

25 g (1 oz) unsalted butter

2–3 tbsp water

225 g (8 oz) smoked back bacon, rinded

1 tbsp chopped parsley

BUN DOUGH

450 g (1 lb) strong plain flour

25 g (1 oz) fresh yeast

25 g (1 oz) caster sugar

150 ml (5 fl oz) milk

2 eggs, beaten

115 g (4 oz) unsalted butter, melted

150 ml (5 fl oz) warm water

plain flour, for dusting

salt and freshly ground black pepper

TO FINISH

1 egg, beaten, for egg wash

sesame seeds (optional)

---

1   Slice the onions and fry in the butter to colour, about 3 minutes. Add the water and cook until the water disappears. Continue to cook and fry to colour the onions, a few minutes more.

2   Cut the bacon into thin strips, then add to the onions and cook to colour the strips, about 2–3 minutes. Stir in the parsley, then remove from the heat and leave to cool.

3   To start the bun dough, sieve the flour into a warm bowl. Dissolve the yeast and sugar with a little of the milk. Make a well in the flour and add the yeast mixture. Sprinkle the top of the liquid with a little of the flour, then cover with a clean tea towel and leave in a warm place until the mixture froths up.

4   Add the beaten eggs, melted butter and enough of the remaining liquids, mixed together, needed to make a soft dough.

5   Knead on a lightly floured board until smooth and no longer sticky. Put into a floured bowl, cover with a clean tea towel and put in a warm place to double in size, about 45 minutes.

6　Preheat the oven to 230°C/450°F/Gas 8. Grease a baking sheet.

7　Add the bacon and onion mix and some salt and pepper to the dough, and knead together. Divide into sixteen equal pieces. Mould each into a ball shape, and put on the greased baking sheet with space between each. Cover with a clean tea towel and leave in a warm place until doubled in size, about 30 minutes.

8　Brush each bun with egg wash and sprinkle with sesame seeds if you like. Bake in the preheated oven for 15–20 minutes.

☞　For a different presentation, try putting six buns around a baking tin and one in the centre, allowing them to touch when proving and baking.

Onion Toast

We love things on toast in this country, and cheese on toast or Welsh rarebit are tea-time and snack necessities. Welsh rarebit, as many of you might know, is one of my all-time favourite dishes, and this is a different interpretation of the theme, combining cheese and melting white onions. This is a sophisticated adaptation of one of my dad's favourite tea-time dishes.

SERVES 4

225 g (8 oz) white onions, peeled and sliced

I tsp olive oil

85 g (3 oz) unsalted butter

6 slices sourdough bread

6 slices mature Lancashire/Wensleydale cheese

I tbsp mustard (your choice)

1 Preheat the oven to 200°C/400°F/Gas 6.

2 Slowly cook the onions in oil and 25 g (1 oz) of the butter until very brown, about half an hour.

3 Toast the bread, then butter it well on one side with the remaining butter. Spread this buttered side with the onions.

4 Spread each piece of cheese with a little mustard, then put the cheese, mustard-side down, on top of the onions.

5 Bake in the preheated oven for about 5 minutes, just until the cheese melts. Cut in half and serve.

☛ This also works extremely well with goat's cheese, but it mustn't be too sharp.

Prawn Cocktail Cakes

This recipe combines a basic prawn cocktail mix with mashed potato to make a typically British fishcake – but one with a difference. They would be delicious for breakfast or a snack as well as for a high tea or supper, and if you made them small enough they would do well as a canapé. I was on a show called *Daily Cook's Challenge,* which Antony Worrall Thompson was presenting. The person I was working with loved prawn cocktail, so I invented these little cakes. When AWT was tasting them in the judging section, I could virtually hear his mind working, 'Must put these on the menu next week...'

SERVES 4

4 jacket potatoes, baked

175 g (6 oz) cooked prawns, peeled and chopped

1 garlic clove, peeled and crushed

3 tbsp mayonnaise

1 tbsp tomato ketchup

1 tsp horseradish sauce

a splash of Worcestershire sauce

2 tbsp chopped parsley

salt and freshly ground black pepper

plain flour

2 eggs, beaten, for egg wash

white breadcrumbs

vegetable oil and unsalted butter, for
   shallow-frying

1   Scrape the potato flesh out of the skins into a bowl. Add the chopped prawns, garlic, mayonnaise, ketchup, horseradish, Worcestershire and parsley. Season to taste with salt and pepper, and mix well.

2   Shape into cakes of about 5 cm (2 in) in diameter: you could have eight to ten. Have the flour, egg and crumbs on separate plates. Season the flour. Dip the cakes carefully into flour first, then the egg, then the crumbs.

3   Heat a little oil in a frying pan, and add a knob of butter. Shallow-fry the cakes in the hot fat on one side for about 2 minutes, then turn over and cook gently on the other side until completely hot in the middle. Or you could put them into the oven at about 200°C/400°F/Gas 6 for 5 minutes after browning the first side. Drain on absorbent paper.

4   Serve hot. These are delicious on wilted spinach.

☛   Never throw away the skins of baked potatoes, they can be transformed into a delicious snack. Deep-fry them and serve them with soured cream (very now), or bake them in the oven as above with some butter and grated cheese for about 10 minutes.

Sardines and Tomatoes on Toast

Sardines on toast is the sort of thing you might expect to have as an after-dinner savoury, or snack, and it would usually be made with canned sardines. Here, however, I have taken the idea a step further, and used fresh sardines, mixing some of the flesh into a tasty tomato spread, and serving the remaining fish on top of the toast and its spread. It's good!

SERVES 4

6 fresh sardines

olive oil

25 g (1 oz) unsalted butter

1 shallot, peeled and finely chopped

½ garlic clove, peeled and crushed

4 tomatoes, skinned (see below), seeded and chopped

a splash of Worcestershire sauce

salt and freshly ground black pepper

TO SERVE

4 slices wholemeal toasting bread

55 g (2 oz) unsalted butter

1   Clean the sardines and remove all the ribcage bones. Cut the heads off, and open out as in the photo. Brush the sardines with olive oil, season and place under a preheated grill for 3–4 minutes on each side.

2   Meanwhile melt the butter and sweat the shallot and garlic for a few minutes, but do not colour. Add the chopped tomatoes and season with Worcestershire sauce and salt and pepper. Cook until the liquid evaporates, about 5 minutes.

3   When the sardines are cooked, skin and flake two of them and mix into the tomato mixture. Meanwhile keep the rest of the sardines warm.

4   Toast the bread on both sides then cut each into a long finger shape of about 10 x 5 cm (4 x 2 in), cutting off the crusts, and trimming off the corners equally to give an eight-sided piece.

5   Butter the pieces of toast, then pile with the sardine and tomato spread. Lay an opened-out sardine on each. Put under the grill quickly, just to warm things through, and serve.

☛ Skin and seed the tomatoes first. Put the whole tomatoes in a bowl, and make a tiny nick in the skin of each with a sharp knife. Pour boiling water over, and leave for a minute. Drain, and the skins should pull off easily, starting at your little nick. Cut the tomatoes in half, and spoon out the seeds and liquid.

☛ You could also add a splash of balsamic vinegar to the tomato mix.

☛ Adding a little tomato dressing makes this dish look special.

Fish and Chips

The fish and chips my dad cooked at his café were adequate, but as life's gone on, I've had some fantastic fish and chips. It may seem strange that a man who's experienced all that I've experienced gastronomically can eulogise about fish and chips more than anything, but they're part of that eating past that always stays with you. I love finger food, and I'm more than happy to eat fish and chips without a knife and fork. And it is as street food that fish and chips started. Apparently London street vendors and stalls in around the 1850s would sell fried cod or flounder with an accompanying baked potato. Later the potato was chipped and fried (perhaps a Belgian influence?) and a Great British tradition was born.

SERVES 4

---

675 g (1 ½ lb) King Edward potatoes

sunflower oil, for deep-frying

4 x 225 g (8 oz) boned and skinned haddock fillets

BATTER

115 g (4 oz) plain flour, plus extra for dusting

½ tsp salt

2 tbsp malt vinegar

85 ml (3 fl oz) ice-cold water

---

1   To make the batter, put the flour in a bowl with the salt. Whisk in the vinegar and water and leave to rest.

2   Peel and cut the potatoes evenly into long chip shapes, 5 mm (¼ in) square in thickness. Dry them well. Meanwhile gently heat the oil in a heavy-based frying pan to 150°C/300°F. Slowly cook the chips in the oil to allow them to cook through but not colour as yet, about 8 minutes. Take out and drain.

3   Increase the heat of the oil to 200°C/400°F, and remove the wire basket from the hot oil if you used one; this is not necessary for the fish.

4   Dip the fish fillets in the batter, allowing excess to drip off quickly, then drop into the pan of hot oil. Allow the fish to sink to the bottom; it will start to float as it sets and cooks. When it is a deep golden brown, take out, drain on kitchen paper and keep hot.

5   Let the fat reheat, and put the chips into the wire basket and into the oil. Cook until crisp and golden brown. Take out, drain, and serve immediately with the fish.

☛   I personally prefer cod, but make sure it comes from sustainable stocks.

Herrings with Roasted Fennel and Saffron Potatoes

Herrings used to be a major part of the economy of the east coast of Britain, but sadly they have been over-fished and stocks are in decline. They are also closely associated with Scotland, where they are usually cooked in oats and served with a mustard sauce. Here I have used breadcrumbs instead of oats, and have mixed mustard into the coating.

SERVES 4

---

4 fresh herrings	**ROASTED FENNEL**
2 tbsp English mustard	2 fennel bulbs
groundnut oil	25 g (1 oz) unsalted butter
a pinch of cayenne pepper	**SAFFRON POTATOES**
salt and freshly ground black pepper	450 g (1 lb) new potatoes, cleaned
55 g (2 oz) fresh white breadcrumbs	55 g (2 oz) unsalted butter
55 g (2 oz) clarified butter (see p. 29)	10 saffron strands

---

1   Preheat the oven to 180°C/350°F/Gas 4.

2   Scale, de-fin and clean the herrings thoroughly on the outside. Take out the guts and remove the head. Wash the fish inside and out, and pat dry then make two incisions on both sides at the thickest part.

3   Mix the mustard, a tsp of oil, the cayenne pepper and a pinch of salt. Brush the herring with this mix, then dip the herring in the breadcrumbs. Put the fish in a suitable dish. Melt the clarified butter and sprinkle over the fish. Bake in the preheated oven for about 10–12 minutes.

4   Meanwhile cook the fennel in boiling salted water for 10 minutes then take out and cool. Slice the fennel bulbs into four slices each through the root. Heat 1 tbsp of the oil in a small roasting tray, then add the butter and fennel, and roast in the preheated oven until nicely coloured, about 15 minutes. Remove from the oven, drain and season.

5   At the same time boil the new potatoes until almost cooked, about 15–20 minutes. When ready melt the butter with a tbsp of water and add the saffron. Add the potatoes, and heat to reduce the water a little. Season.

6   To serve, arrange the fennel on the plates, with a herring on top and potatoes around. Spoon over the rest of the saffron butter.

Devilled Whitebait

Whitebait, the fry of herrings and sprats, are said to be so called because they are 'white' and were used as bait to catch larger fish. They once shoaled so prolifically on the coasts and estuaries of Essex and Kent that fisheries grew up around them. They were caught in the Thames as well, and wealthy Londoners used to travel downriver for whitebait dinners at Greenwich. Whitebait used to be a big seller at Simpson's in the Strand, and I think they make a very tasty mid-table nibble for people to share.

The whitebait fishery in Britain is discouraged now because of the effect on mature fish stocks, but frozen fish are brought in from abroad. Let the fish defrost and drain well in a colander before cooking.

SERVES 4

450 g (1 lb) whitebait

55 g (2 oz) plain flour

salt and freshly ground black pepper

cayenne pepper

a neutral oil (like sunflower), for deep-frying

juice of 1 lemon

1 If using fresh whitebait, wash carefully then dry.

2 Season the flour with salt, pepper and 1 tsp cayenne, then sprinkle over the fish and carefully shake off the excess.

3 Heat the oil to 190°C/375°F. Drop the whitebait into the oil, in batches, until nice and crisp, and golden brown. Turn frequently, using a slotted spoon or spider.

4 When cooked, remove from the oil with a slotted spoon, and drain on kitchen paper. Sprinkle with cayenne and squeeze a little lemon juice over. Serve quickly.

Cheese-filled Sausage Meatballs on Spicy Tomato Sauce

Meatballs are probably more continental than British, but with such a strong sausage/faggot/olive/pudding tradition, we may have rolled our meat into little balls as well. The tomato has been around for a long time, although we didn't take to it for some centuries after it had been introduced. We cooked it to death, and preserved it as chutney and sauce, but apparently didn't eat it raw until the twentieth century. We like it now, though, allying tomato sauce with that most British of dishes, fish and chips.

I think this is a nice supper dish, probably best in the autumn months, when it's just starting to get a bit chilly at night. It's another of those great dishes which, although it's probably already in someone else's repertoire, I happened to come up with on one of my TV shows.

SERVES 4

---

450 g (1 lb) pork sausagemeat

a splash each of Worcestershire and Tabasco sauces

6 bacon rashers

225 g (8 oz) fresh white breadcrumbs

115 g (4 oz) Wensleydale cheese, cut into 12 cubes

115 g (4 oz) plain flour

2 eggs, beaten

a little groundnut oil

SPICY TOMATO SAUCE

55 g (2 oz) unsalted butter

1 onion, peeled and finely chopped

1 garlic clove, peeled and crushed

a sprinkle of chilli flakes (to taste)

1 x 400 g can chopped tomatoes

150 ml (5 fl oz) chicken stock

1 tsp chopped fresh oregano

6 tomatoes, skinned and seeded (see p. 150)

salt and freshly ground black pepper

☞ If you don't want to fry them, you could put them straight into the oven, but I find the caramelisation and colour of the pan-frying makes the whole thing much more appetising. If you don't eat pork, then lamb or beef mince can be used. I have found that the better the meat (and the more expensive it is), the better the meatballs.

☞ This tomato sauce is very useful served in tandem with quite a number of other recipes in the book. If you don't like it spicy, simply leave out the chilli.

1 Preheat the oven to 200°C/400°F/Gas 6.

2 Start the tomato sauce first (or well in advance and just reheat at the last minute). Melt the butter in a medium pan, add the onion and garlic and sweat for 2 minutes, do not colour. Add the chilli flakes, canned chopped tomatoes, chicken stock and oregano, and slowly cook until it reaches a thick pouring consistency. Chop the fresh tomatoes and add to the sauce, then check the seasoning. Leave to one side.

3 Meanwhile, mix the sausagemeat in a bowl with the two seasoning sauces, and leave to rest.

4 Cook the bacon on a baking sheet in the preheated oven until well done. Take out, cool and chop finely. Mix with the breadcrumbs. Keep the bacon fat on the sheet.

5 Divide the meat mix into twelve even-sized pieces and mould into balls. Push a piece of cheese into the centre of each, and re-shape to seal in the cheese. Roll each ball in the flour, shaking off any excess, then roll through the beaten egg and finally through the bacon breadcrumbs. Roll and shape nicely.

6 Fry in shallow oil to colour lightly.

7 Place on the bacon-greased baking sheet and bake in the preheated oven for about 10–15 minutes. Take out, and put the meatballs into the hot tomato sauce. Allow to sit for 5 minutes, then serve, sprinkled with chopped parsley if you like.

Toad in the Hole

Most traditional British batter puddings started off by being cooked in a dish under the spit-roasting meat (see *Suffolk Fraze* on p.141). Often they would include some meat, a convenient way of stretching small amounts of protein. Toad in the hole is usually now made with sausages – the Yorkshire beef ones are particularly good – but originally it would have been pieces of leftover meat or, rather posher, pieces of raw rump or fillet steak, or lamb chops.

SERVES 4

Yorkshire Pudding batter (see p.73)
55 g (2 oz) beef dripping or lard
12 pork sausages

1 Make the batter as described on p.73, and leave to rest.

2 Preheat the oven to 200°C/400°F/Gas 6.

3 Heat the dripping or lard in a suitably sized ovenproof pan or roasting tray, and colour the sausages on top of the stove. Put the pan into the preheated oven and cook for 10 minutes.

4 Whisk up the batter, and then immediately pour into the tray and return to the oven. Close the door quickly and bake for 25 minutes. Turn the pan round and cook on for another 10 minutes. Serve immediately.

Glamorgan Sausages

Made from cheese, leeks or onions and breadcrumbs, this is more a savoury, meat-free rissole than a sausage, and it can be cooked in either shape. It is attributed to South Wales, where of course there has always been a strong cheese-cooking tradition (think of Welsh rarebit), but similar mixtures exist elsewhere. As a cheese lover, I like these very much, but especially since Franco Taruschio (then of the Walnut Tree in Abergavenny) cooked some superb examples at Turner's one St David's Day. And he's an Italian!

SERVES 4

---

140 g (5 oz) Caerphilly cheese

175 g (6 oz) fresh white breadcrumbs

55 g (2 oz) young leeks or spring onions, finely chopped

1 tbsp chopped fresh chives

½ tsp dried thyme

a pinch of dry English mustard powder

salt and freshly ground black pepper

2 egg yolks

1 egg, beaten

lard, for frying

---

1 Preheat the oven to 200°0C/400°F/Gas 6.

2 Grate the cheese and mix in a bowl with 115 g (4 oz) of the breadcrumbs. Add the chopped leek or spring onion, chives, thyme, mustard, salt and pepper and egg yolks, and mix well together.

3 Divide the mix into eight, and roll each piece into a sausage shape. Dip the sausages into the beaten egg, and then coat with the remaining breadcrumbs.

4 Fry the sausages in a little lard, until they become golden brown on the outside. Finish them in the preheated oven for 3–4 minutes.

☞ If I were going to serve these as a main course, I would accompany them with a rustic, spicy tomato sauce (see p. 156).

☞ You could also make the mixture into tiny patties and cook to serve as canapés or *amuse-gueules*.

☞ As it stands, this is a great dish for vegetarians, but you could cater for meat-eaters too by adding a dice of smoked bacon, ham or cooked sausage to the basic mixture.

☞ If for vegetarians, fry it in vegetable oil rather than lard.

Bakewell Tart

Bakewell tart was originally known as Bakewell pudding and still is in parts of Derbyshire. There are several stories about its origins, but most must be apocryphal as it has long been known in its present form – a pastry case with a jam lining and an almond 'cake' topping. This almond mixture is known as 'frangipane' in the business, and I always wondered what the connection between it and the flower, frangipani, was. It seems a trifle tenuous, but the almond mix was supposedly named after an Italian aristocrat, Frangipani, who invented a perfume, probably using red jasmine, or frangipani, for the gloves of Louis XIII.

SERVES 8

PASTRY

175 g (6 oz) plain flour

a pinch of salt

25 g (1 oz) unrefined caster sugar

finely grated zest of 1 orange and 1 lemon

55 g (2 oz) cold unsalted butter, diced

25 g (1 oz) cold lard, diced

2 egg yolks, beaten

about 2 tbsp ice-cold water to mix

FILLING AND TOPPING

55 g (2 oz) raspberry jam

3 eggs

115 g (4 oz) unrefined caster sugar

115 g (4 oz) unsalted butter, melted

115 g (4 oz) ground almonds

25 g (1 oz) icing sugar, mixed with a little water to a thin icing

1 To make the pastry, sift the flour and salt into a bowl and add the sugar and citrus zest. Rub the butter and lard into the flour until the texture resembles breadcrumbs. Add the egg yolks. Mix to a dough, using the water if necessary, and form into a ball. If you have time, chill, wrapped in clingfilm, for about 20 minutes.

2 Meanwhile, preheat the oven to 180°C/350°F/Gas 4.

3 Roll the pastry out to a round to fit a 25 cm (10 in) flan ring on a baking sheet, and place in the ring. Cut off any excess pastry, and crimp the edges.

4 Warm the jam and then, if you like (it's the correct way), press it through a fine sieve to get rid of the seeds. Spread over the base of the tart.

5 Meanwhile, beat the eggs and sugar together, and slowly fold in the melted butter and the almonds. Pour carefully into the pastry-lined flan ring.

6 Bake in the preheated oven until set, about 35 minutes. Take out and cool.

7 Pour the icing into the centre of the tart and, using a palette knife, spread it as thinly as possible. Leave to set.

Rhubarb Plate Pie

Rhubarb is grown in East Ardsley in Yorkshire, near where I come from. Farms in an area bordered by the cities of Leeds, Wakefield and Bradford are known as the 'Rhubarb Triangle'. The rhubarb is grown in warm sheds, without any light, which blanches it and makes it sweeter. I like rhubarb baked, poached, jammed and made into a crumble or fool. This baking in a plate pie – which means that the pie is made on an old enamel plate – is very much a phenomenon of the north of England, I think.

SERVES 4

55 g (2 oz) unsalted butter, melted

450 g (1 lb) young rhubarb, peeled

finely chopped peel of 1 orange, blanched for a few minutes

½ tsp chopped fresh root ginger

115 g (4 oz) caster sugar

egg wash (2 medium egg yolks and a little water)

icing sugar, to dust

SHORTCRUST PASTRY

175 g (6 oz) plain flour, plus extra for dusting

a pinch of salt

85 g (3 oz) unsalted butter

25 g (1 oz) lard

about 2 tbsp water

1 Make the pastry first, as described on p. 58. Wrap in clingfilm and leave to chill for at least 30 minutes.

2 Preheat the oven to 240°C/475°F/Gas 9. Divide the pastry in half and roll out one-half into a 25 cm (10 in) circle on a floured board. Brush a 25 cm (10 in) pie plate with melted butter, lay the rolled pastry on it, and trim around the edges. Brush with more melted butter.

3 Cut the rhubarb into 2.5–5 cm (1–2 in) sticks, wash and shake nearly dry, then put into the middle of the plate. Sprinkle with the orange peel and ginger, then the caster sugar to taste (depending on the sourness of the rhubarb).

4 Roll out the other half of the pastry to cover the top and cut a 5 cm (2 in) circle out of the middle. Wet the edges of the base pastry with egg wash, then lay the second piece on top. Push the edges together to seal. Trim and decorate the edges by pinching with a thumb and finger. Brush the top with egg wash and sprinkle with icing sugar.

5 Bake in the preheated oven for 10 minutes, then for a further 20 minutes at 220°C/425°F/Gas 7 to cook the fruit through completely. When cooked, sprinkle with icing sugar and serve with clotted cream or crème Chantilly (whipped cream, with sugar and vanilla seeds).

Burns Night Supper

Robert Burns is Scotland's best-known and -loved poet, and Burns Suppers have been held in his honour for over 200 years. And not just in Scotland, but all over the world. In Russia, for instance, Burns societies flourish from Volgograd to Vladivostok, and a Burns Supper has even been held in the Kremlin. He's probably better known there than he is now in his native Scotland!

Born in 1759, Rabbie Burns died very young, on 25 January 1796, and a group of his friends were instrumental in founding a Burns Night ritual, on that very same night, a few years after his death. And virtual ritual it is too, for the suppers adhere to the same structure year after year. An address from the chairperson is followed by the haggis being piped in, someone reciting the Burns poem 'To a Haggis', and then the haggis being cut open and dispersed among the diners. There are usually readings and songs following the meal, and I have fond and hazy memories of an evening when our Scottish host thought it a good idea that everyone should read a stanza from 'Tam o'Shanter': we were mostly English, one was from Tennessee, another from Barbados, and we stumbled, to a man, over the incomprehensible dialect Scots words. But it's a great evening, crowned always by the singing of 'Auld Lang Syne'.

So far as the food is concerned, I am a great fan of haggis. Once, on *Daily Cook's Challenge*, I had to prepare a dish with haggis, a problem set by John Stapleton, the GMTV presenter. We used a McSween haggis (the best, a great texture), and cooked it fairly traditionally. I'm glad to say I beat my competitor's version, and was even more pleased when, after the programme was finished, the camera crew enthusiastically polished it off. I also cooked for friends of Sir Alex Ferguson last year. For a late Burns Night, I did haggis; the next day at a premature St George's Day dinner, I served Somerset beef. Although I love haggis, on that occasion I have to say I thought the beef was better.

I'm also very keen on the mashed potato and swede that traditionally go with the haggis, and other Scottish soups and savoury delights that can be found at this time of year (and Hogmanay, or New Year). Both Burns and I enjoyed the whisky: he appreciated one of his many loves among the 'rigs o' barley', and was known to have supped much on the water of life, the fruit of John Barleycorn. And what other country can boast of a national bard who has written an ode to a pudding and a mouse?

Scotch Broth

Also known as barley broth, this soup is simple, but very satisfying, its only necessities being some lamb, barley and vegetables. Barley has become very fashionable nowadays, and many rated restaurants serve barley 'risottos' or 'pilaffs', but it was a staple in Scotland from very early times, as indeed it was throughout much of the northern hemisphere. It has a good flavour and texture, and here it thickens the broth.

Apparently the famous and acerbic English writer, Dr Johnson, was not too fond of Scotland despite the Gaelic origins of his companion, James Boswell, but did actually approve of Scotch broth! It would be a perfect warmer on a cold January Burns Night, and a great supper dish. It's one of those soups that gets better with time, when made correctly.

SERVES 4

675 g (1½ lb) scrag end or shoulder of lamb, cut into large pieces

55 g (2 oz) good pearl barley

1.7 litres (3 pints) cold water

1 *bouquet garni* (parsley, thyme, bay leaf, black peppercorns)

1 medium onion, peeled and finely diced

2 leeks, cleaned and finely diced

2 carrots, trimmed and finely diced

4 celery stalks, finely diced

1 small white turnip, scrubbed and finely diced

85 g (3 oz) shredded cabbage

salt and freshly ground black pepper

1 tbsp chopped fresh parsley

1   Trim the lamb of excess fat.

2   Put the barley into a large saucepan and add the water, then the lamb. Bring up to the boil and put in the *bouquet garni*. Cover with a lid, but use a wooden spoon to make sure the lid doesn't close properly, and simmer for about 1½ hours, taking off the scum regularly. (If you don't use a spoon, it'll boil over and make an awful mess on the top of your stove.) Stir occasionally as well to make sure the barley doesn't stick.

3   Add the onion, leek, carrot, celery and turnip to the pan, and simmer for about 10 minutes. Take out the meat and dice it.

4   Put the meat back into the pan with the shredded cabbage. Cook for 5–10 minutes more. Check the seasoning, add the parsley and serve.

Bashed Neeps

'Bashed neeps' (mashed *swede*, rather than turnip) and 'champit tatties' (mashed potatoes) are the classic accompaniments for the haggis eaten by the Scots on Burns Night (and indeed on Hogmanay, New Year's Eve). Haggis is perhaps the greatest surviving example of the traditional British boiled pudding: a mixture of grain, offal and herbs wrapped in the stomach bag of an animal. A nip of malt with the haggis (sometimes actually *on* it) is mandatory! My dad loved that.

The lightly spiced vegetable purée is also delicious with roast meats such as beef (see p. 73).

SERVES 6–8

675 g (1 ½ lb) swede, peeled and cut into even pieces	2 tbsp double cream
salt and freshly ground black pepper	¼ tsp ground cinnamon
85 g (3 oz) unsalted butter	juice of ½ lemon

1   Plunge the swede pieces into boiling salted water, bring back to the boil, and cook until tender. Drain and put back into the pan.

2   Mash with a potato masher until smooth, then add the butter, cream, cinnamon and lemon juice. Season to taste and serve.

☛   It mixes well with other root vegetable purées of potato, parsnip, turnip, carrot etc.

Scotch Eggs

These sausagemeat-wrapped eggs, served for breakfast or as a snack or high-tea dish in Scotland, stood alone, I thought, with no obviously similar dishes existing in other cuisines. Some sources have suggested, however, that there is an association with the Indian Moghul 'kofta', which consists of pounded spiced meat wrapped round savoury fillings, sometimes eggs. How the idea came to Scotland, no one seems to know, but it could be something to do with men returning from service in India during the days of the Raj. Another cold dish that would be good on a Burns Night supper table, and to take on a picnic.

MAKES 6

6 hard-boiled eggs (8–10 minutes)	115 g (4 oz) boiled ham, very finely chopped
55 g (2 oz) plain flour	2 eggs, beaten
salt and freshly ground black pepper	115 g (4 oz) fresh white breadcrumbs
350 g (12 oz) sausagemeat	vegetable oil, for deep-frying

1 Shell the eggs and dry in a clean cloth. Season the flour with salt and pepper. Dip the eggs in this and shake off the excess.

2 Mix the sausagemeat and ham together, and split this mixture into six even parts. Flatten out in your hands to make a meat coating for each egg. Cover each egg with a portion of this mixture, pressing well at the joins to seal.

3 Dip the coated eggs into the seasoned flour again, and shake off the excess. Dip into the beaten egg and finally into the breadcrumbs to coat completely.

4 Re-shape at this stage, and put into the fridge for 10 minutes.

5 Deep-fry in moderately hot fat – 160°C/325°F – for about 10 minutes, turning as they cook. Take out, drain well and serve hot or cold.

☞ Try making the recipe with hard-boiled quail's eggs. Very fiddly, but great for a canapé.

☞ Many recipes use only sausagemeat, but the addition of ham is occasionally found. Try Parma ham, an interesting substitute for boiled ham. You could also spice things up by adding some chopped fresh herbs or spices to the mixture.

☞ You could use chicken meat instead of the sausagemeat. If you mince it and then beat it in the bowl, the flesh becomes elastic and will then wrap easily around the egg.

☞ Be careful not to overcook as the sausagemeat will split. If necessary finish cooking in the oven at about 160°C/325°F/Gas 3.

Mutton Pies

Large and small pies made with mutton or lamb have been popular since the Middle Ages. At first, like so many meat dishes of the time, they would have been quite sweet, mixed with dried fruit, sugar and sweet spices; later they became more savoury. There are lots of such pies in the north of England (perhaps *the* pie centre of the country) and in Scotland. North of the border they use minced, spiced mutton; in places like Northumberland the meat is chunkier, as here. But both are made with a hot water crust pastry, as is the famous British pork pie.

Apparently Dr Johnson admired mutton pies (as well as Scotch broth), and so did Queen Victoria and King George V, who both served them at Balmoral and Buckingham Palace receptions. Fine fare indeed, and perfect for a Burns Night spread.

MAKES 4

25 g (1 oz) unsalted butter	a little vegetable oil	HOT WATER CRUST PASTRY
1 red onion, peeled and finely chopped	300 ml (10 fl oz) lamb stock	350 g (12 oz) plain flour
1 tsp chopped fresh rosemary	salt and freshly ground black pepper	a pinch of salt
115 g (4 oz) mushrooms, finely chopped	1 tsp freshly grated nutmeg	150 ml (5 fl oz) water
450 g (1 lb) shoulder of lamb, off the bone, trimmed and cut into 5 mm (¼ in) pieces	1 tsp *fécule* (potato flour) or cornflour, slaked in 1 tbsp cold stock	115 g (4 oz) white lard
		1 egg yolk
		1 egg, mixed with a little water, to glaze

☛ Pies such as this are very portable, good for picnics. You could make them in smaller moulds if you liked.

☛ Note that I haven't asked you to use the pastry in the traditional way, persuading it up around the sides of a jam jar or similar to get the shape. Very hands on and complicated!

☛ If you want to buy them, be careful. I have been to fairs and such like in Scotland where the mutton pies were very sludgy.

1 Make the filling first. Melt the butter and sweat the onion and rosemary without colouring for a few minutes. Add the mushrooms and cook for 3 minutes.

2 Put the meat in a frying pan, and pan-fry in the oil to colour well on all sides. Drain the meat and add to the onion mixture along with half the lamb stock and season with salt, pepper and nutmeg. Cover and cook for 30 minutes on top of the stove, then allow to cool.

3 Meanwhile, preheat the oven to 190°C/375°F/Gas 5.

4 For the pastry, sift the flour and salt into a bowl. Bring the water up to boiling in a medium pan, take off the heat, add the lard and allow it to melt. Add the flour and beat well to amalgamate, then knead until smooth. Stir in the egg yolk and keep warm. Try to work quickly.

5 To use, roll out and cut into rounds to fit patty tins or muffin moulds of about 10 cm (4 in) in diameter. Keep the leftover pastry covered and warm; you need it for the lids.

6 Spoon the cold filling into the pie cases. Roll out the rest of the pastry and cut out the correct lid shapes. Moisten the edges of the pie cases and put the lids on top, pressing to make a seal. Make a hole in the middle, and brush the tops with mixed egg and water to glaze.

7 Bake in the preheated oven for 45 minutes, until the pastry is crisp and golden. Remove from the tins immediately.

8 Mix the slaked *fécule* or cornflour with the remaining lamb stock. Bring to the boil gently, stirring, until thickened (this is what chefs call a 'thickened stock').

9 When the pies come out of the oven, re-cut the holes in the top, and carefully pour some hot thickened stock into each pie. Serve hot or cold.

In the autumn, there are two very British celebrations, Hallowe'en on 31 October, and Bonfire Night or Guy Fawkes Night on 5 November. Culturally and historically, their origins are different but they have come to share certain characteristics.

The word 'Hallowe'en' is derived from All Hallows Eve, the night before All Hallows or All Saints Day ('hallow' is an old word for saint). 1 November, All Saints Day, is a major Catholic festival, followed on the 2nd by All Souls Day. These Christian festivals fall at the same time as an ancient pagan Celtic festival known as Samhain, and concepts from both philosophies have become intertwined, superstition competing with religious belief.

Samhain was in essence the start of a new year, marking the end of 'the season of the sun' and the beginning of 'the season of darkness and cold'. The Celts believed that, on that particular night, the barriers between this world and the spirit world were weaker, and a central belief of the current Scottish Hallowe'en is that it is the night the spirits can leave their graves: think of Burns' 'Tam o' Shanter'. Add to this mix the two Christian days, on which the dead were remembered, and you have a potent recipe for the pot-pourri of superstition that Hallowe'en has become.

At Samhain, the pagan Celts would make huge bonfires, and dance around them, creating enough noise to keep any evil spirits away, which is not a million miles from how we celebrate on the 5th today. Although 5 November commemorates an actual moment in history – when Guy Fawkes and other Catholic plotters tried to blow up King James I and the Houses of Parliament – it has always been marked by bonfires, and this must surely be more than a coincidence.

Bonfire Night has remained stalwartly British, and we burn effigies of Guy Fawkes and let off fireworks. Hallowe'en, however, introduced to the States by immigrants, has been hijacked by the Americans, and returned to us in the last 25 years as a plastic, highly commercialised Fright Night of over-consumption. (Apparently Hallowe'en has become the sixth most profitable celebratory event of the American year.) Today's children in this country go 'trick or treating' now, as they do in America, and don't expect to do anything at all (we used to sing, recite or dance) to earn their swag-bags of candy.

I remember going 'chumping' with my mates, which was looking for wood for our bonfire. If that meant taking wood off someone else's bonfire, we did (and there was no gang warfare then). I have many happy memories of, scarf on, wandering around from fire to fire (the local Scout group used to do a good job), the heat on my face, the pungent smoke. No such luck for our children now, because in the interests of health and safety everything has become antiseptic, and to see any sort of firework you have to stand three miles away!

At this time of year, we need warm foods, carbohydrate foods, foods that stick to your ribs. If you are eating outside while watching fireworks, you need a good traditional hot soup. I also like simple stews and pies, toasted breads with good toppings, and would even consider offering a pizza (which may be Italian, but some say is nothing but a piece of bread dough with a topping). Some rich puds are the order of the day too, and you could perhaps try a piece of parkin for afters. Parkin is traditional in my home county on 5 November, because Guy Fawkes came from Yorkshire...

Chunky Tomato Soup

Soup is one of the most traditional of dishes on the British culinary scene, and local 'pot' vegetables were used in the beginning, perhaps with a little grain or, when they were lucky, some meat. When tomatoes gradually came to be accepted, some two centuries or so after they had been introduced from the New World, they were pounded to make soups or acid sauces of ketchups, rarely served raw! We are very keen on tomato soup in this country, usually from a can, but this is a delicious alternative, great on a cold October or November night.

I wish I could get people back to making soup. The mentality is that it's too easy to buy them (in packets, jars or cans). But if you made the slight effort to get into the soup-making mode, it is much easier than you think – and it's healthy and thrifty.

SERVES 4

---

55 g (2 oz) unsalted butter

115 g (4 oz) each of carrots, peeled onion and celery, finely chopped

2 garlic cloves, peeled and finely chopped

675 g (1 ½ lb) tomatoes, roughly chopped

basil stalks (see garnish)

a handful of fresh parsley stalks

1 tbsp chopped fresh thyme

a pinch of unrefined caster sugar

salt and freshly ground black pepper

1.2 litres (2 pints) chicken stock

150 ml (5 fl oz) single cream

GARNISH

10 tomatoes, skinned and seeded (use skins and seeds in the soup, so do this first)

a splash of olive oil

a bunch of fresh basil, chopped (use the stalks in the soup)

1 garlic clove, peeled and chopped

---

1 Melt the butter in a large pan, and sweat the finely chopped carrot, onion and celery together. Do not colour. After 3 minutes, add the garlic, the skins and seeds of the garnish tomatoes, and the chopped tomatoes, along with the basil stalks, parsley stalks, thyme, sugar and some salt and pepper to taste. Stew gently for about 10 minutes.

2 When almost all of the liquid has disappeared, add the chicken stock, and cook gently for a further 20 minutes. Pass the soup and vegetables through a sieve.

3 Put back into a clean pan and bring back to the boil. Add the cream and check the seasoning.

4 Chop the skinned garnish tomatoes into neat dice. Warm them in the splash of oil with the basil and garlic. Pour into the soup and serve, with a swirl of cream if desired.

Green Pea and Ham Soup

The traditional English pea soup was made with dried peas, and its greeny-brown colour was so similar to the dense smog that dominated London in the winter (until as late as the 1960s), that the smog became known as a 'pea-souper'. In *Bleak House*, Dickens referred to the fog as the 'London Particular', and the name has been used for both fog and soup ever since.

There are so many versions of pea soup that to say one is the definitive classical recipe is practically impossible. Soup made from tinned peas is my least favourite but, if made from dried, fresh or a mixture, can work well. The following, however, is the one I like best. It will always remind me of the time Bob Holness came on *Ready Steady Cook*, and I made him some pea soup. This allowed the lovable Fern Britton to utter these immortal lines, 'Can I have a "P" please, Bob?'

SERVES 8

85 g (3oz) unsalted butter	85 g (3 oz) plain flour	3.4 litres (6 pints) water
1 large onion, peeled and finely diced	300 ml (10 fl oz) double cream	2 carrots, trimmed
900 g (2 lb) frozen peas	salt and freshly ground black pepper	2 onions, peeled
1 small bunch fresh mint, tied together	HAM STOCK	1 head celery, washed
	1 ham hock, about 900 g (2 lb) in weight	12 black peppercorns
		1 bay leaf

☞ It's not always easy to buy ham hocks these days, except from good butchers. You could use gammon instead (or bacon rinds tied up in muslin, for flavour). Use some boiled ham with peas in the soup at the end.

☞ A pea soup is not traditionally served with ham in it, but this addition makes for a much more 'gutsy' dish.

☞ This soup is often served with toasted bread triangles, but I prefer it with croûtons, i.e. fried bread dice.

☞ Pea soup is great chilled with perhaps extra cream and chopped mint. The French serve stewed lettuce and baby onions with their pea soup.

1   To start the stock, soak the hock for 12 hours in enough cold water to cover.

2   Drain off the soaking water, and cover the ham hock with the measured cold water. Bring to the boil and skim off any scum, then add the carrots, onions and celery, all whole. Leave to simmer gently for about 20 minutes, then add the peppercorns and bay leaf. Gently simmer for a further 1½–2 hours, until the ham is cooked through. Watch it carefully: you don't want the liquid to reduce too much. Strain off the soup – you will need 1.7 litres (3 pints). Put the ham to one side and discard the vegetables and flavourings.

3   Melt the butter in a heavy-bottomed pan, and add the finely diced onion and half the frozen peas. Add the mint, and put the lid on the pan. Leave to gently stew for 3–5 minutes. At this point add the flour, and stir in carefully, possibly taking the pan off the heat to stop it sticking. Return the pan to the heat, and cook the pea roux for 2 minutes. Do not let it colour.

4   Slowly add the measured hot ham stock to the roux, beating well with a wooden spoon after each addition to get rid of any lumps of flour. When the stock is all added, make sure that the bottom of the pan is clear of everything. Leave to simmer for 20 minutes.

5   Meanwhile, blanch the remaining peas in boiling water for just 2 minutes. Plunge into a bowl of iced water, which will retain the bright green colour.

6   At the same time it is a good idea to take the skin from the ham hock, to take the meat from the bone and to carefully cut the latter into fine dice. Mix this ham with half of the blanched peas and keep to one side.

7   The soup is now cooked so take out the bunch of mint and put the remaining blanched peas (not those with the ham) into the soup. Liquidise the soup, and then I like to push it through a fine sieve or chinois (conical strainer).

8   When all is through, re-boil the soup gently, adding the double cream, and season as necessary. Put the reserved peas and ham into the soup, and serve immediately.

Sausage and Bean Stew

This is not meant to be a take on *cassoulet*, the French meat, sausage and bean stew. For a start there's no meat and no garlic (my mum used to make this, and she had never tasted garlic!), and there are no finishing breadcrumbs (although quite a good idea). Nothing could be more basic or warming than this combination of the good British sausage with beans. But not the baked beans you might expect: instead I have included a mixture of green beans and pulses, which is interesting, and much more healthy. Just the job for a dish to eat with a fork while you are watching Guy Fawkes burn on the bonfire.

SERVES 4

---

2 tbsp olive oil

1 shallot, peeled and finely chopped

1 garlic clove, peeled and crushed

6 tomatoes, cut into tiny dice

1 tsp chopped fresh oregano

115 g (4oz) cooked haricot beans

115 g (4oz) cooked broad beans (at this time of year, they would be frozen)

115 g (4oz) cooked French beans

115 g (4oz) cooked runner beans

12 good pork sausages

salt and freshly ground black pepper

1 tsp chopped fresh chives

---

1 Preheat the oven to 180°C/350°F/Gas 4.

2 Heat 1 tbsp oil in a largish pan, add the chopped shallot and garlic and sweat for 5 minutes, do not colour. Add the tomatoes and oregano and cook for 5 minutes.

3 Add the haricot beans and broad beans. Cut the French beans and runner beans into 1 cm (½ in) pieces at an angle, and add to the other beans.

4 Meanwhile cook the sausages in the remaining oil until cooked, about 10–12 minutes. Then take off, cool and cut into 1 cm (½ in) pieces at an angle. Add to the beans and season well.

5 Bake in the preheated oven for 15 minutes, uncovered. Take out, stir in the chives and serve.

Hot Brisket and Tomato Stew

SERVES
ABOUT 10

This is basically boiled salt beef, but without the dumplings (the salt here for flavour rather than preserving). It's very medieval in the use of so many spices, and it is a classic example of the many boiled beef dishes in the British culinary canon. Boiled meat has a texture and flavour that is its own and we shouldn't dismiss it as less interesting than roast.

1 x 1.8 kg (4 lb) piece brisket of beef, no bone, trimmed

1.2 litres (2 pints) chicken stock

2 onions, skin on

2 carrots

1 x 400 g can tomatoes

1 tsp fresh oregano

salt and freshly ground black pepper

6 tomatoes, cut into eighths

2 tbsp young centre celery leaves

SPICE MIX

115 g (4 oz) Maldon sea salt

25 g (1 oz) black peppercorns

6 cloves

25 g (1 oz) allspice berries

1 star anise

½ tsp freshly grated nutmeg

1   In a coffee grinder (or spice mill) grind the spice mix ingredients to as near powdery as you can. Rub into the meat on all sides, then put in a cool place, lightly cover, and leave to rest for 48 hours.

2   On the day of cooking, wash off the spices and put the brisket into a pan of cold water to cover. Bring up to the boil. When the water boils, take the meat out and throw away the water.

3   Wash the pot out and put the brisket back in it. Pour the chicken stock in and then add enough fresh cold water to cover the meat well. Bring up to the boil then leave to simmer gently for 2 hours, uncovered.

4   After 2 hours, add the onions and carrots and continue to cook for about another 2 hours. If it gets too dry, top up with water. When cooked, after 4 hours altogether, turn the heat off and leave the meat in the stock to cool.

5   Take out one of the onions, remove the skin and mash the onion. Put into another smaller pan with the canned tomatoes and the oregano. Season with salt and pepper, and leave to cook slowly for about 10 minutes. Add the fresh tomato pieces, and if necessary a little strained stock, and cook for 5 minutes.

6   Slice the brisket, arrange in a dish and put the stewed tomatoes over. Chop the celery leaves and sprinkle over at the last minute. Serve with piccalilli or just loads of black pepper.

Cauliflower Cheese

Cauliflowers, which belong to the cabbage family, were developed by the Arabs, and in the eighteenth century in Britain were highly regarded vegetables, suitable for the best treatment, being buttered, coated with a rich white sauce and sprinkled with cheese. It's thought of more now as a supper or high tea dish, on a par with macaroni cheese, but cooked well, it can be great. My grandma wouldn't recognise the modern additions of Parmesan and breadcrumbs, but they bring both flavour and texture. See also my more sophisticated take on the dish on p.144.

SERVES 4

1 large cauliflower	1 tbsp fresh white breadcrumbs	150 ml (5 fl oz) milk
salt and freshly ground black pepper	CHEESE SAUCE	a dash of Tabasco sauce
55 g (2 oz) Parmesan, freshly grated	40 g (1½ oz) unsalted butter	1 tsp Dijon mustard
	40 g (1½ oz) plain flour	175 g (6 oz) Lancashire cheese, grated
	300 ml (10 fl oz) double cream	

1 Preheat the oven to 180°C/350°F/Gas 4.

2 Cut the cauliflower into even-sized florets. Plunge these into boiling salted water and cook until tender, then drain (keep the water).

3 Meanwhile, for the cheese sauce, melt the butter in a medium pan, add the flour and cook for 2 minutes, stirring to avoid lumps. Add the cream and bring back to the boil, still stirring. Add the milk, whisk in and take from the heat. Add the Tabasco and mustard and stir in well, along with the cheese. Season. If the sauce is a little thick, add 2 tbsp of the cauliflower water.

4 Arrange the cooked florets of cauliflower in a dish, if possible built to look like a whole cauliflower. Gently pour the sauce over.

5 Sprinkle with the Parmesan and breadcrumbs and bake in the preheated oven for 15 minutes until brown on top. Serve immediately.

☛ A tendency these days is to undercook cauliflower for this dish. But, although you don't want it to be a mush or purée, it should be soft enough to be able to spoon out easily (and soft enough for your grandma to eat without her teeth!).

☛ Another way of cooking the cauli would be to gouge out the centre stalk, leaving the vegetable whole with a hole in the middle. Cook it for a little longer to ensure the inside parts are cooked.

Partridge Pie

Wild birds were very popular centuries ago, often representing the only fresh meat that could be found in winter, and there was also such a variety: wild pigeon (other than those kept in dovecotes), quail, grouse, mallards, cygnets, blackbird, thrush... Partridge is my favourite game bird, as it has such a distinct flavour, but not overpowering; it's got good flesh; it's a nice size; and they are still quite plentiful. Delicious roasted too, but here I have cooked it in a pie with steak and ham.

SERVES 4

1½ recipes *Savoury Shortcrust Pastry* (see p.58)	25 g (1 oz) plain flour	12 button onions, peeled
1 egg, for egg wash	salt and freshly ground black pepper	175 g (6 oz) boiled ham
FILLING	2 tbsp groundnut oil	300 ml (10 fl oz) chicken stock
2 partridges	175 g (6 oz) rump steak	1 tsp Worcestershire sauce
		2 tbsp chopped fresh parsley

1   Preheat the oven to 200°C/400°F/Gas 6.

2   Cut the partridge up into breasts and legs. Put the flour on a plate, season with salt and pepper, and coat the partridge pieces with this.

3   Heat 1 tbsp oil in a large frying pan and colour the partridge joints all over, for about 2–3 minutes. Season and put into a 1.2 litre (2 pint) pie dish.

4   Clean out the partridge pan, and heat the remaining oil in it. Cut the rump steak into 1 cm (½ in) dice and sear quickly in the oil. Add the peeled button onions and colour lightly for a few minutes, then season. Put the steak and onions into the pie dish.

5   Cut the ham into 1 cm (½ in) wide strips and sprinkle over the meats in the dish. Pour over the stock with the Worcestershire sauce and parsley.

6   Roll out the pastry to a shape just slightly larger than the top of the pie dish. Cut a thin strip from round the edges and put this round the rim of the dish. Moisten this with water, and then lay the rolled-out pastry on top. Crimp and seal the edges. Brush with egg wash and make a hole in the centre for the steam to escape.

7   Bake for 20 minutes in the preheated oven, then turn the temperature down to 170°C/340°F/Gas 3–4 and continue baking for a further hour. Serve with buttered cabbage.

Cornish Caudle Chicken Pie

A 'caudle' was a warm, thin, spiced gruel made with wine and sugar which was given to invalids and women after childbirth. But the caudle in the chicken pie that has become famous in Cornwall is a mixture of eggs and cream that is poured into the pie near the end of the cooking time. This sets everything together, and tastes very good.

SERVES 4

225 g (8 oz) puff pastry

2 eggs

150 ml (5 fl oz) soured cream

FILLING

25 g (1 oz) unsalted butter

1 tsp groundnut oil

1 onion, peeled and sliced

1 x 1.3 kg (3 lb) roasting chicken

salt and freshly ground black pepper

1 tbsp chopped fresh parsley

6 spring onions, shredded

150 ml (5 fl oz) single cream

1　Preheat the oven to 200°C/400°F/Gas 6.

2　Melt the butter in a medium pan, and add the oil. Add the sliced onion and gently colour, not too much, for about 3–4 minutes. Remove the onion from the pan and put into a 1.2 litre (2 pint) pie dish.

3　Chop the chicken into eight pieces, four white meat and four dark meat, and add to the oil and butter. Gently colour for about 3–4 minutes, and then lay on top of the onions in the pie dish. Season.

4　Throw away the excess fat from the pan, then put the parsley, shredded spring onions and single cream into it, and bring up to the boil. Simmer for 2 minutes then pour over the chicken.

5　Cover the pie dish with foil, and put into the preheated oven for 30 minutes. Take out and leave to cool.

6　Roll out the pastry on a lightly floured board to slightly larger than the shape of the pie dish. Cut a strip all round, and lay this on the rim of the pie dish. Moisten with water, and lay the pastry shape on top. Crimp and seal, then make a hole in the middle for steam to escape. Mix the eggs and soured cream together and brush some of it over the top of the pastry.

7　Bake for 10 minutes, then reduce to 180°C/350°F/Gas 4. Pour the remaining soured cream and egg mixture through the hole in the pastry into the pie. Shake slightly to allow even distribution. Bake for a further 15 minutes.

8　Remove the pie from the oven, leave to stand for 5 minutes, then serve.

Sausage and Tomato Pizza

Pizza, as we all know, is an Italian invention, but it could so easily have been invented here, as we have always used bread as a base for other things – all our cheeses and savouries on toast, for instance – and we once used hardened or baked slices of bread as plates. Pizza is a bread dough, but baked with toppings, and although definitely not British, we have adopted it so enthusiastically that it could almost be called a modern British dish. Once you get the hang of making the dough, it'll be a 'piece of cake' to knock up an almost instant pizza for a snack or light lunch.

To be thick or thin, that is the question. This one is thinnish, and I think the Americans were responsible for making the Italian base thicker. And be sensible with the topping. Here we have good British sausage – not a pineapple chunk or piece of chicken tikka korma in sight!

MAKES 4 x 30 CM (12 IN) PIZZAS

PIZZA BASES
850 g (1 lb 14 oz) strong white flour

2 tsp salt

15 g (½ oz) fresh yeast

600 ml (1 pint) tepid water

plain flour, for dusting

55 g (2 oz) semolina, for dusting

TOPPING
1 tbsp olive oil

1 shallot, peeled and finely sliced

1 garlic clove, peeled and crushed

450 g (1 lb) canned tomatoes

salt and freshly ground black pepper

150 ml (5 fl oz) extra virgin olive oil

225 g (8 oz) mozzarella cheese

12 cooked pork sausages

55 g (2 oz) Parmesan, freshly grated

4 spring onions, sliced

1 Make the topping first. Heat the oil in a medium frying pan, add the shallot and garlic and soften for about 5 minutes, do not colour. Pass the canned tomatoes through a fine sieve into the pan with the garlic and shallot. Cook to reduce to a semi-sticky consistency, which will take about 15 minutes. Season and leave to cool.

2 To start the bases, sieve the flour and salt into a bowl. Dissolve the yeast in the tepid water and slowly add to the flour to make a dough. Add carefully in order to get a dough that is not too sticky. If necessary, add a little more flour.

3 Shape into a ball, put into a lightly floured bowl, cover with a clean cloth and leave for 5 minutes.

4 Knead the dough by hand on a lightly floured board for 10 minutes. Split it into four equal parts and shape into balls. Put on a floured tray, cover with a damp cloth, and leave in a warm place to prove for 30 minutes.

5   Sprinkle some more flour on the table and spread each piece of dough, using your fingers, into a circle about 30 cm (12 in) in diameter, as even as possible, and with a slightly thicker border. Sprinkle a baking tray with semolina and lay the bases on the tray.

6   Preheat the oven to 200°C/400°F/Gas 6.

7   Drizzle a spoonful of oil on to each pizza base. Using the back of a ladle, spread the tomato mixture evenly across the bases to within 1 cm (½ in) of the edges. Cut the mozzarella into slices and divide evenly between the bases. Cut the sausage into 5 mm (¼ in) slices at an angle and scatter over the bases. Sprinkle with Parmesan.

8   Bake in the preheated oven for about 8–10 minutes. Drizzle with oil, sprinkle with the spring onions and serve.

Pickled Cabbage, Mushrooms, Ham and Potatoes

Cabbage and ham are two basic British ingredients, possibly more Irish, and they go extremely well together. Choose the best ham you can find, or perhaps use the mutton ham on p. 105. Cabbage is much maligned, as it is so sulphurously smelly when cooking. But here I have shredded, blanched and pickled it: it's not a long process, but adds huge depth of flavour – and avoids the smell. This simple dish is perfect for a buffet.

SERVES 4

225 g (8 oz) mushrooms
225 g (8 oz) boiled ham
225 g (8 oz) potatoes
1 tbsp groundnut oil
55 g (2 oz) unsalted butter
1 tbsp chopped fresh parsley

salt and freshly ground black pepper

PICKLED CABBAGE

1 small Savoy cabbage
1 small white onion, peeled
2 tbsp Maldon sea salt

450 ml (15 fl oz) cider vinegar
175 g (6 oz) caster sugar
1 small red chilli, left whole
1 tsp dry English mustard powder
½ tsp turmeric
1 tsp mustard seeds

1 Make the pickled cabbage first. Discard the outside leaves of the cabbage and shred the rest finely, taking care to remove all large pieces of stalk. Shred the onion and mix with the cabbage in a glass bowl. Add the salt and mix well. Add a few ice cubes and cold water and stir to dissolve the salt. Leave for about 2 hours.

2 Drain well, then dry carefully between tea towels, and put into a clean bowl.

3 Bring the remaining pickling ingredients up to the boil in a saucepan, and simmer for 3 minutes. Turn the heat off and leave to cool. When cold pour over the cabbage and stir well. Cover with clingfilm and refrigerate for 48 hours. Drain well to serve (and pick out the chilli).

4 Slice the mushrooms thickly. Cut the ham into 5 mm (¼ in) dice. Peel the potatoes and cut them into the same size dice.

5 Heat the oil in a medium frying pan, add half of the butter, and cook the potato dice until they take some colour and are cooked, about 5 minutes.

6 In another pan, colour the mushrooms in the remaining butter, about 5 minutes, then add the ham dice and season. Mix the potato with the mushrooms and ham, add parsley and serve hot with some cold pickled cabbage.

Sticky Toffee Pudding

Dried fruit boiled in a suet pastry base in a cloth would once have been the most traditional British pudding, such as *Spotted Dick* (overleaf). As ovens became more common, the pastry base became lighter, and here the fruit is mixed with a darkly sweet cake mixture. Francis Coulson and Brian Sack of the Sharrow Bay Hotel in Cumbria were responsible, I think, for reintroducing us to the joys of this pudding.

SERVES 8

175 g (6 oz) medjool dates
115 g (4 oz) dried figs
55 g (2 oz) sultanas
150 ml (5 fl oz) boiling water
finely grated zest of 2 oranges
115 g (4 oz) unsalted butter

175 g (6 oz) unrefined demerara sugar
3 eggs, beaten
140 g (5 oz) self-raising flour
55 g (2 oz) ground almonds
55 g (2 oz) pistachio nuts, chopped

SAUCE
115 g (4 oz) unsalted butter
175 g (6 oz) unrefined demerara sugar
150 ml (5 fl oz) double cream

1 Grease a baking tray about 20 cm (8 in) square, or the same volume, and preheat the oven to 180°C/350°F/Gas 4.

2 Stone the dates and chop them finely with the figs and sultanas. Put them into a bowl and pour the boiling water over. Whisk to a pulp, then add the orange zest.

3 Cream the butter and sugar together, then add the egg. Beat together, then fold in the flour, ground almonds and fruit pulp.

4 Pour the mixture into the prepared baking tray and bake in the preheated oven for 30–40 minutes. To test if cooked, press with your hand: there will be some resistance. Take out when cooked and allow to cool slightly.

5 Cut the cooked cake into shapes. I like round ones, although this means wastage: use a round metal cutter (the leftover bits could possibly be used in one of the other puds in the book). Square means you can use the whole thing!

6 Meanwhile, for the sauce, melt the butter, add the sugar and bring to the boil. Add the double cream and simmer for 5 minutes until lightly thickened.

7 Pour a little sauce over and around the pudding, sprinkle with the chopped pistachios and serve.

Spotted Dick

Perhaps the most infamous of British roly-poly puddings – and not just the cause of many a schoolboy snigger: a few years ago an English health service board was forced to rescind its decision to re-christen the pudding 'Spotted Richard' on hospital menus, with a well-known supermarket chain following suit. It is also known as spotted dog (strictly speaking, when the dried fruit is mixed with the pastry instead of being encased in it) and plum bolster.

SERVES 4–6

225 g (8 oz) plain flour, plus extra for sprinkling	150 ml (5 fl oz) water
15 g (½ oz) baking powder	115 g (4 oz) currants
a pinch of salt	55 g (2 oz) raisins
115 g (4 oz) finely chopped beef suet	finely grated zest of 1 lemon

1   To make the basic suet pastry, sift the flour, baking powder and salt together, then rub in the suet. Add the water and mix to a dough.

2   Roll out to a rectangle 25 x 15 cm (10 x 6 in) and 1 cm (½ in) thick. Sprinkle with the currants and raisins, leaving a border of 1 cm (½ in) round the sides. Press the fruit in and sprinkle with the lemon zest. Paint the borders with water.

3   Turn the two short sides in and seal. Roll up from a long side carefully to keep all the fruit in. Seal when rolled up.

4   Rinse a clean tea towel in boiling water. Sprinkle with flour and shake off the excess. Lay the roll on top of the cloth, fold the cloth over and fix at the ends with string. Steam the cloth-wrapped roll for 1½ hours. Or you could put the pud on a rack in a roasting tray full of water, then cover with foil. Bring to the boil then steam in the oven at 200°C/400°F/Gas 6 for about 2 hours. Top up the water occasionally. Or bake at the above oven temperature, but not in the cloth, brushed with egg wash, for about 1¼ hours.

5   Take out, unwrap while still hot (if necessary), cut into slices and serve with a custard sauce or jam sauce.

Hallowe'en Pumpkins

The cucurbit family, originating from Central and South America, includes various edible fruits which are eaten as both fruit and vegetable: melons and watermelons; cucumbers and gherkins; vegetable marrows and courgettes; and all the pumpkins and squashes. Culinary squashes are divided roughly into two groups, summer and winter. Summer squashes are eaten young and have soft skins (the courgette, for instance); winter squashes, such as the familiar orange pumpkin, have harder skins and therefore can be stored, when their skins harden even more and their seeds mature.

Because pumpkins come from the Americas, they would not have been known in British cooking until after what is known as 'the Columbian exchange', when plants and animals discovered by Christopher Columbus in the New World, in 1492, were introduced to Europe. The Tudors, some 100 years later, knew 'pompion' or pumpkin, which had already been introduced from France. Poor people removed the seeds and pith, stuffed them with apples, and baked them. Wealthy people made them into the rich and sweet pies so typical of the time, and many food historians think that it was a British recipe, taken to America in 1620 by the Pilgrim Fathers on the *Mayflower*, that became the famous American pie. A pumpkin pie was said to have been enjoyed by those early colonists in celebration of their first harvest – pumpkins are harvested in the autumn – and since then Americans bake a pumpkin pie every year on the American national holiday of Thanksgiving (on the third Thursday in November).

Pumpkin in this country went out of fashion some time in the course of the eighteenth century, and didn't re-enter our collective British consciousness until the Americans introduced us to their version of Hallowe'en some 200 years later (see p.170). Along with 'trick or treat' came the pumpkin jack o' lantern, which had previously been carved here from turnips (*much* harder work). It's taken us even longer to come to appreciate the pumpkin in a culinary sense, but now it is immensely fashionable, and pumpkin and squash appear on many a sophisticated restaurant menu. It's probably related to the fact, too, that we can now grow them in this country: they may need flavouring up a bit, but not nearly so much as the marrow we used to cultivate. Try to choose a medium pumpkin, as the bigger ones are often bred for size not flavour, and the flesh can also be too watery to enjoy. Smaller versions will be better, and try not to boil them: baking is the best way to get rid of the inherent wateriness and intensify the sweet and nutty flavour.

Pumpkin Soup

You could make the entire soup with raw pumpkin, but baking the flesh of some of it gives the soup an intense flavour, caramelising the natural sugars. This would be a great soup to serve, perhaps from a mug, while you watch a firework display on Bonfire Night.

SERVES 4

450 g (1 lb) pumpkin flesh

2 tbsp olive oil

salt and freshly ground black pepper

55 g (2 oz) unsalted butter

1 onion, peeled and finely diced

1 garlic clove, peeled and crushed

1.7 litres (3 pints) vegetable stock

115 g (4 oz) potato, peeled and diced

115 g (4 oz) tomato flesh, roughly chopped

a splash of balsamic vinegar

2 tbsp chopped fresh parsley

1 Preheat the oven to 200°C/400°F/Gas 6.

2 Cut the pumpkin into 5 mm (¼ in) dice. Put 115 g (4 oz) of it into a roasting tray with half of the olive oil and seasoning, and roast and colour for about 30 minutes.

3 Meanwhile, put the remaining olive oil and half the butter in a large pan and heat. Add the remaining pumpkin, the diced onion and garlic. Sweat gently for 5 minutes, then add the stock and bring up to the boil. Simmer for 20 minutes until the pumpkin is soft. Put everything in a liquidiser, and blend. Remove to a clean pan.

4 Meanwhile, cut the potato into 5 mm (¼ in) dice and boil in salted water for about 15 minutes. When almost cooked, drain. Colour in the remaining butter for a few minutes, then add to the roasted pumpkin. Season with salt and pepper.

5 Drain the potato and pumpkin mixture and stir in the tomato and balsamic vinegar. Add to the puréed soup along with the parsley, taste for seasoning again, and serve.

Roast Pumpkin

I'm not a great fan of simply roasted pumpkin (although it's better than boiled). So I always add flavourings, and this recipe is quite unusual, with bags of flavour. It uses a sweet spice with honey, along with the savoury tang of soy sauce. It could be eaten without the breadcrumb and cheese topping, and you could vary the flavourings: the Italians do a great chilli and garlic roast pumpkin.

SERVES 6–8 AS AN ACCOMPANIMENT

I small pumpkin, about I kg (2¼ lb)	I tsp light soy sauce
2 tbsp melted unsalted butter	115 g (4 oz) fresh white breadcrumbs
I tbsp runny honey	55 g (2 oz) Cheddar, freshly grated
a pinch of ground allspice	

1 Preheat the oven to 180°C/350°F/Gas 4.

2 Peel the pumpkin, using a sharp knife. If it's easier, cut in half first and then peel it.

3 Cut the pumpkin in half lengthways, and scoop out the seeds and fibres. Cut into wedges lengthways, and put into a roasting tray.

4 Mix the butter, honey, allspice and soy sauce together. Brush over the pumpkin wedges and roast in the preheated oven until tender, about 35 minutes.

5 When almost cooked, transfer to an ovenproof serving dish. Sprinkle with the breadcrumbs then the grated cheese, and finish in the oven turned up to 200°C/400°F/Gas 6 until cooked and coloured, about 5–7 minutes.

☛ In the trade, we peel pumpkins like we would segment an orange. The base is thinly sliced off, so that it sits well, then we carve down in segments from the top, taking wedges of skin off.

Pumpkin Rice

This is an unashamed reworking of an Italian risotto, but it is an excellent way of using up the flesh cut from a pumpkin lantern – and good enough, too, to make from scratch, with a whole pumpkin. Risotto is hardly British, but it has become one of our favourite rice dishes, and we do have a fairly strong rice tradition, especially in the cooking of sweet rice puddings. Actually the texture you want with this dish is much the same, an ambrosial smoothness. Be careful that it doesn't get too stodgy: some restaurants serve risottos in moulds, which I think is completely wrong.

SERVES 4–6

450 g (1 lb) peeled pumpkin flesh

1 garlic clove, peeled and crushed

2 tbsp olive oil

1 sprig fresh thyme

225 g (8 oz) white of leeks, washed and finely shredded

400 g (14 oz) arborio risotto rice

1.7 litres (3 pints) vegetable stock

150 ml (5 fl oz) dry white wine

55 g (2 oz) unsalted butter

115 g (4 oz) Parmesan, freshly grated

1 tbsp double cream

salt and freshly ground black pepper

2 tbsp chopped fresh chives

4 fresh sage leaves, shredded

1   Preheat the oven to 200°C/400°F/Gas 6.

2   Cut the pumpkin flesh into 5 mm (¼ in) dice. Put in a roasting tray and mix with the crushed garlic and 1 tbsp of the olive oil. Add the thyme, and roast in the preheated oven for about 20 minutes. Do not colour too much.

3   Meanwhile heat the remaining olive oil in a large pan, add the shredded leek and sweat for about 3 minutes. Do not colour. Add the rice and stir until the grains are separate and coated with oil.

4   In a separate pan bring the stock to the boil and then keep at a simmer.

5   Put the wine into the rice pan, and stir until it evaporates. Add a ladleful of boiling stock to the rice and stir, allowing the stock to evaporate. Keep adding stock and letting it evaporate in the same way until the rice is almost cooked, about 20 minutes.

6   At this stage add the roast pumpkin and carefully stir in. The rice should now be firm and cooked through, and creamy in texture. Take the pan off the heat, add the butter, Parmesan and double cream, and check for seasoning. Stir in the chopped chives and leave to sit for 5 minutes before serving sprinkled with the sage.

'Christmas comes but once a year, and when it does, it brings good cheer.' So they say, but Christmas brings quite a lot of headaches too: what presents to buy for whom, how much food to buy, and is it your turn to have the grandchildren? I don't know why we worry. It's perhaps lacking a little in the Christian ethos, but it's a good excuse to relax, eat and drink a lot. I have two grandchildren now, and Christmas has come to mean buying toys and then playing with them, which is magic!

Throughout history, there have always been celebrations in December, the time of the winter solstice. The shortest day (on the 21st) marked the rebirth of the sun. In northern Europe the heathen Scandinavians worshipped their gods and feasted for twelve days at this time, from which comes our word 'Yule'. In southern Europe, the Romans celebrated in December, in honour of the god Saturn; they feasted, and gave each other presents. As the word of Christianity spread throughout Europe, the Church appropriated the pagan festivals of the winter solstice, and although precise dates are unknown, 25 December was chosen as the supposed birth day of Jesus.

The decking of trees, houses and rooms with light are also a casting back to more ancient beliefs. The Yule log is probably a remnant of a major fire festival. The gaudily bedecked Christmas tree, although that was much later – Victoria's Prince Albert introducing the idea from Germany in 1841 – is probably a nod to the respect shown by the ancients to evergreens (including holly and ivy) during the winter months.

Christmas food is very traditional as well. The main feature of a Christmas meal has always been a roast bird, but this would once have been swan or peacock or goose. Turkey wasn't introduced to Britain from the Americas until the sixteenth century, but it soon took over: it was large, fleshy, tender and easily fattened. In true British style, it was served with a sharp sauce: when cranberries appeared, probably introduced from America as well, they took over the saucing role from apple and sorrel.

New Year comes a week after Christmas and to the Scots, their Hogmanay is much more important. As 'the bells' sound at midnight, the back door would be opened to let the old year out, the front door opened to let the New Year in. And in would come the 'first foot' or 'first fit', preferably a tall, dark, handsome man (rather than an invading Viking, who would have been short and blond), carrying a lump of coal to ensure your house would be warm through the coming year. Guests would be treated to whisky and black bun, shortbread, sometimes haggis.

For many of us now, this celebratory week has become a four- to five-day holiday from work (or even more, sadly), when we seem to do nothing but eat, drink and sit watching television. It can be exhausting, and it can be bad for you. The key to enjoying the holiday is good planning in advance, to serve meals in smaller portions, and to make good use of any leftovers, which there are bound to be. There are several ideas throughout the book which could use an excess of turkey, or Brussels sprouts, and never forget to make a stock with the turkey bones. Think responsibly at this time – waste is not good.

Brown Windsor Soup

SERVES 8–10

I first encountered this soup when I worked at Simpson's in the Strand (my first job, at the tender age of seventeen). It was popular, along with the infamous *Mulligatawny Soup,* opposite. We made it from tomato soup mixed with mock turtle soup, adding pieces of canned turtle, which has a similar gelatinous texture to calf's feet. It was popular, apparently, at Windsor, thus the name. It takes a long time to make, primarily because of the veal stock, but it is well worth it, as the flavour is wonderful.

55 g (2 oz) beef dripping

1 onion, peeled and sliced

450 g (1 lb) stewing beef, cut into 1 cm (½ in) dice

1 carrot, peeled and diced

1 leek, cleaned and diced

1 celery stick, diced

10 tomatoes, roughly chopped

1 bunch fresh parsley, tied together

55 g (2 oz) long-grain rice

300 ml (10 fl oz) Madeira wine

salt and freshly ground black pepper

VEAL STOCK

2 calf's feet, boned

1.8 kg (4 lb) veal bones, chopped

2.2 litres (4 pints) water

2 carrots

2 onions

225 g (8 oz) leeks

225 g (8 oz) celery

1 *bouquet garni* (fresh parsley stalks, rosemary, thyme, bay leaf)

1 Put all the veal stock ingredients into a large pan. Bring up to the boil and skim off any scum that forms on the surface. Simmer for 2½ hours.

2 Strain off the liquid and retain. Discard everything else except the calf's feet. Trim these. Take the gelatinous surrounds off the feet, and get rid of the bones. Make sure there is no cartilage there, cut the meat into dice and put to one side.

3 To make the soup itself, heat the dripping in a large pan. Add the onions and diced beef and fry to colour, about 5–6 minutes.

4 Add the rest of the vegetables to the meat and onion, with the stock and parsley, and bring up to the boil. Cook at a simmer for an hour.

5 Add the rice and Madeira and simmer for a further hour until the meat is cooked.

6 Take out the bunch of parsley and put the rest of the soup through a liquidiser or food processor. Taste for seasoning.

7 To serve, bring back to the boil, and add the diced calf's feet. Check the seasoning.

Mulligatawny Soup

I also met this soup when I worked at Simpson's, and it was particularly popular with gentlemen of a certain age who had presumably served in India at some time, and learned to love the heat and pepperiness of the cuisine. For the soup and its name are both relics of the Raj, the word 'mulligatawny' coming from two Tamil words meaning 'pepper' and 'water', the nearest thing to soup in India. It was originally a vegetarian sauce apparently, but the British adapted it to include all manner of flavourings and garnishes: the basic pepper water could be served with side bowls of cooked rice, grated coconut, crispy bacon pieces, sliced chillies and hard-boiled eggs. This version here is a little posher, but lacks the extras!

SERVES 4

55 g (2 oz) unsalted butter	2 small onions, peeled and finely chopped	1.2 litres (2 pints) lamb stock
2 chicken thighs	4 tomatoes, seeded and diced (see p.150)	1 tbsp mango chutney, chopped
1 apple, peeled, cored and finely diced	1 tbsp Madras curry powder	4 tbsp cooked basmati rice
		salt and freshly ground black pepper

1   Melt the butter in a saucepan, add the chicken thighs, allow them to colour lightly, then turn down the heat.

2   Add the diced apple and chopped onion to the pan, then the tomato dice. Do not allow the vegetables to colour. Sprinkle the curry powder over and fry carefully to release its flavour. Do not let it burn.

3   Now add the stock and bring up to the boil, lower the heat and simmer for about 40 minutes.

4   Take the chicken out of the soup and remove and discard the bones and skin. Cut the meat into dice and put back into the soup along with the chopped mango chutney. Add the rice, warm through briefly, and check for seasoning. Serve hot.

☞ You could make the soup with coconut milk instead of stock – or half and half – and grind your own spices such as cumin and coriander for curry powder, but you must have some heat – preferably chilli powder or a fresh chilli or two.

☞ Some versions of the recipe use scrag end of lamb instead of the chicken.

☞ It's often easier to put the rice straight into the cups or bowls, then pour the soup on top.

☞ If lamb stock is not available, chicken stock will do.

Potato Dumplings with Wilted Spinach

SERVES 4

The British are famous for dumplings – think of those we serve with boiled beef or stew, the Norfolk dumpling and cloutie dumpling – but these potato dumplings are very obviously a take on the Italian *gnocchi*. If foreign in concept, the ingredients are very British.

900 g (2 lb) potatoes, baked in their jackets

675 g (1 ½ lb) baby spinach

115 g (4 oz) unsalted butter

1 egg

175 g (6 oz) plain flour, plus extra for dusting

½ tsp freshly grated nutmeg

salt and freshly ground black pepper

300 ml (10 fl oz) chunky tomato sauce (see p. 156)

55 g (2 oz) Parmesan, freshly grated

1 Cut open the baked potatoes, scrape out the flesh and pass it through a sieve or a ricer, not a food processor. Weigh 675 g (1 ½ lb) into a bowl.

2 Cook 225 g (8 oz) of the spinach in 25 g (1 oz) of the butter until wilted, a minute or so, then drain well. When cool enough to handle, squeeze out as much liquid as you can from the leaves. Add the cooked spinach to the potato, along with 25 g (1 oz) of the butter, the egg, flour, nutmeg and some salt and pepper. Knead to a soft dough.

3 Using plenty of extra flour, take a quarter of the dough at a time and roll into a sausage shap. 2 cm (¾ in) in diameter on the table, using your hands. Cut into 2.5 cm (1 in) pieces and leave on the table. Use all the dough.

4 Then, using a fork, roll each piece of dough down the prongs to form ridges. (This is traditional in Italy. If you have lots to do, then you can omit this stage, but the dumplings will still taste as good.) If not using straightaway, cover.

5 Heat the sauce and keep warm. Preheat the grill.

6 Have ready a large saucepan full of boiling salted water. Drop a handful of dumplings in, and when they rise to the top, after a few seconds, scoop out, drain and add to the sauce. Repeat until all the dumplings are cooked.

7 Meanwhile melt the remaining butter in a pan, add the remaining spinach, and wilt, another 2 minutes. Season and drain.

8 Put the spinach into the bottom of an ovenproof dish. Pour the dumplings and their sauce over. Sprinkle with Parmesan, and grill for 2 minutes. Serve hot.

Salamagundy

Herb and flower salads were popular in the time of Elizabeth I, and began to be made more elaborately, with cold meats, hard-boiled eggs, anchovies, and other delicacies. These compound salads were first-course dishes, often served for a supper. The name 'salamagundi/y' was first used in the seventeenth century, and was often corrupted to 'Solomongundy' (the connection, if any, with the nursery rhyme of 'Solomon Grundy' escapes me).

It's not seen much today, but the more I play with the idea, I see the opportunity of using leftovers sensibly (not last week's!) to produce an interesting and appetising platter. This is my version. Use some or all of the following simple recipes, and present them individually on plates or, preferably, arranged on a large platter in concentric circles. Make sure everyone sees your arrangement before they dive in!

SERVES 4

Roast Beetroot, Cumin and Chives

450g (1 lb) small beetroots
1 tbsp olive oil
25g (1 oz) unsalted butter
salt and freshly ground black pepper

1 tbsp cumin seeds
1 tbsp chopped fresh chives
1 tsp malt vinegar

1 Cook the beetroots in salted water to cover, until just cooked, about 45–60 minutes, but depending on size. Drain, and when cool enough to handle, remove the skin and cut into quarters.

2 Heat the oil in a small roasting tray and add the butter and beetroot quarters. Colour for a few minutes on top of the stove, then season and bake in the preheated oven for 10 minutes.

3 Remove from the oven, add the cumin seeds and check the seasoning. Drain, mix with the chives, put in a bowl and add the vinegar.

Radish and Apple Salad

175g (6 oz) radishes
2 eating apples
DRESSING
1 tsp grain mustard

2 tbsp cider vinegar
8 tbsp olive oil
2 tbsp chopped fresh parsley
salt and freshly ground black pepper

1 Put the mustard into a bowl. Add the vinegar and stir in, then add the olive oil, parsley, salt and pepper, and mix well.

2 Cut the radishes into circles about 3mm (⅛ in) thick. Add to the dressing. Core the apples and cut into thin batons. Add to the radishes.

3 Mix well and leave all to stand for 10 minutes.

Pickled Herrings with Red Onion

8 fresh herring fillets

150 ml (5 fl oz) white wine vinegar

1 red onion, peeled and shredded

a pinch each of sea salt and caster sugar

1 small sprig fresh thyme

½ garlic clove, peeled and chopped

1 small chilli, chopped

6 black peppercorns

2 tbsp olive oil

1 Scale, trim and bone the fillets if necessary (you could get your fishmonger to do all this). Lay each fillet skin-side up in a non-reactive dish.

2 Pour the vinegar over the herring fillets, and sprinkle with the shredded onion. Add the salt and sugar, thyme, garlic, chilli and peppercorns, and leave to stand for half an hour.

3 Preheat the oven to 180°C/350°F/Gas 4.

4 Bake the herring in the preheated oven for 15 minutes. Take out and leave to cool.

5 Take out the herrings and onions and put into a clean serving bowl. Add the olive oil to the fish liquor, mix and strain over the fish.

Ham and Wensleydale Cheese with Boiled Eggs

225 g (8 oz) boiled ham

115 g (4 oz) Wensleydale cheese

1 tbsp groundnut oil

1 tbsp olive oil

salt and freshly ground black pepper

4 hard-boiled eggs

1 Cut the ham into 1 cm (½ in) wide strips. Cut the cheese into 5 mm (¼ in) dice. Mix together with the oils and some salt and pepper.

2 Peel the eggs, and cut them into quarters.

3 Put the cheese and ham into a serving bowl, and sprinkle with the eggs.

☛ There are no acidic elements here because you should be getting that from other dishes. You can of course add some lemon juice or vinegar if you like.

Spinach Salad

225 g (8 oz) baby spinach

a pinch of freshly grated nutmeg

salt and freshly ground black pepper

LEMON DRESSING

½ tsp Dijon mustard

1 tbsp lemon juice

2 tbsp olive oil

1 Mix all the dressing ingredients together.

2 Put all the salad ingredients in a bowl, and toss with the dressing. Serve.

Chicken Mayonnaise Salad

½ roast chicken, off the bone

2 tbsp mayonnaise

1 tbsp vinaigrette

1 tbsp plain yoghurt

salt and freshly ground black pepper

1 Cut the roast chicken into large dice.

2 Mix the mayonnaise, vinaigrette and yoghurt, and season to taste.

3 Add the chicken to the dressing and mix carefully.

Roast Turkey and all the Trimmings

Thankfully every year I get asked by someone to talk on radio or TV about Christmas meats. Ribs of beef and legs of pork are delicious, as is roast goose. But I am a traditionalist, and I like to have turkey on Christmas Day, even if we have another joint alongside it. Despite the fact that people generally overcook turkey, when treated properly it's a delightful dish. Kelly Bronze turkeys, raised by Paul Kelly, are the best in the country, I think, but you may prefer a white or black or bronze: the choice is yours. When buying turkey, try to buy one that has neither been in a plastic bag, nor frozen.

This is my favourite stuffing, and I have given a number of recipes for the traditional trimmings. Please read and understand how we have cooked the turkey to keep the breast moist; you never want the breast to be dry. I don't mean to be sexist (not me), but it could be useful to have a man around the house to help turn the turkey over...

SERVES 8–10

---

1 x 4.5kg (10lb) turkey

115g (4oz) unsalted butter, softened

½ onion, peeled and finely chopped

675g (1½lb) sausagemeat

225g (8oz) pre-cooked chestnuts, chopped

55g (2oz) white breadcrumbs

1 tbsp chopped fresh parsley

salt and freshly ground black pepper

2 tbsp groundnut oil

GRAVY

1 onion, peeled and finely shredded

300ml (10 floz) chicken stock

1 tbsp chopped fresh parsley

---

1   Preheat the oven to 200°C/400°F/Gas 6.

2   Take out the wishbone from the neck end of the turkey, keeping the skin intact. Release the skin with the forefinger then push about 85g (3oz) of the softened butter underneath, between skin and flesh, on both sides of the bird.

3   Soften the onion in the remaining butter for about 3 minutes, then allow to cool. Add the sausagemeat, chestnuts, breadcrumbs, parsley, salt and pepper to the softened onion, and mix well.

4   Put as much of the stuffing that will fit into the neck cavity and re-shape the turkey, tying it to its original shape. Put any excess stuffing into an ovenproof dish and bake separately, along with the turkey at the lower heat, below, for about an hour.

5   Heat a large roasting tray on top of the stove, and add the oil. Put the turkey into the tray on one leg side, and roast in the preheated oven for 30 minutes.

6   Turn the turkey on to its other leg, and roast for another 30 minutes.

7   Turn the temperature of the oven down to 180°C/350°F/Gas 4. Turn the turkey on to its back, and finish the cooking, about another 30–45 minutes, basting frequently.

8   When cooked, take the turkey out of the oven, and out of the tray, and leave to rest for 20 minutes before carving.

9   Meanwhile, for the gravy, add the shredded onion to the roasting tray, and colour in the fat for 4–5 minutes. Drain off the excess fat (and keep for potatoes). Add the stock to the onion in the tray, and bring to the boil. Pour into a clean pan and boil to reduce by about half or until it tastes really great. Sieve if you like, but it's nice with the onions. Season with salt and pepper, and add the parsley. Keep warm while you carve the turkey.

10 After the turkey has rested for 20 minutes, take out the stuffing and cut into slices. Take off the legs, put to one side, then take off the breasts.

11 Separate the meat and the bones from the legs and carve the dark meat from the thigh. (Keep the drumstick meat for turkey pie.) Put to one side, on a platter, with the stuffing at one side. Carve the breasts into fairly thick pieces and place on top of the dark meat. Pour gravy over and serve.

☞ This is a good place to use a meat thermometer. The one I have says you should go to 65°C in the centre, but I would go to 68. Turkey has a reputation for being dry, but the way to do it is take it out earlier and test. You can't put it back in the oven if it's overdone, but you can if you take it out earlier.

☞ For a leftover turkey hotpot, fry some sliced onions and potatoes, and layer in a round flat pan with cooked turkey, chopped cooked sausages, and little balls of leftover stuffing. Mix some stock with a little Worcestershire sauce, and pour over. Finish with a layer of potatoes. Brush with some oil and butter, season and bake in a hot oven (220°C/425°F/Gas 7) until coloured. Turn down to medium (180°C/350°F/Gas 4) and bake for about 1¼ hours.

☞ For a turkey stir-fry, mix cubes of cooked turkey in a bowl with a little cornflour and vegetable oil. Heat some oil in a wok, add and colour the turkey. Keep warm while you melt some butter and oil, in which you stir-fry some seeded and sliced peppers, sliced mushrooms and sliced shallots. Add a little stock, and season to taste with some dry sherry, white wine vinegar, soy sauce, a splash of Tabasco, and some tomato ketchup. Heat the turkey through in this sauce, and serve with rice.

☞ You could make turkey dumplings, blitzing cooked turkey together with tasty ingredients such as shallots, spring onions, garlic, fresh root ginger, chilli and mushrooms. Check the seasoning, and roll into little balls which you can then colour in some oil. These are good served with cabbage.

Bread Sauce

SERVES 6

A typical British sauce, made from breadcrumbs and spiced milk. It is good with game birds as well.

300 ml (10 fl oz) milk
150 ml (5 fl oz) double cream
1 onion, peeled and stuck with 6 cloves
1 bay leaf

85 g (3 oz) fresh white breadcrumbs
25 g (1 oz) unsalted butter
salt and freshly ground black pepper

1 In a medium pan, bring the milk and cream to the boil with the onion and bay leaf.

2 Take off the heat, remove the onion and bay leaf, add the breadcrumbs and butter, and season with salt and pepper. Pour into a plastic bowl.

3 Leave to stand for 10 minutes, cover with clingfilm and serve when needed. If necessary, reheat in the microwave. Don't be afraid to add a little more milk if the sauce is too thick.

Cranberry Sauce

MAKES 300 ML (10 FL OZ)

The cranberries may be American in origin, but they replace the typical sharp fruit sauce that would have been served with roast birds.

450 g (1 lb) cranberries
100 ml (3 fl oz) water
a squeeze of fresh orange juice

55 g (2 oz) caster sugar
salt and freshly ground black pepper

1 Simmer the cranberries, water, juice and sugar together until soft, about 10–12 minutes, but it depends on how ripe the berries are. Add more water if necessary.

2 Season, and allow to sit and cool a bit before serving.

☛ Serve cold with cold turkey later that day.

Chipolatas and Bacon

What more need I say, sausages and bacon are perfect with the turkey. Traditionally the sausages would be wrapped in bacon, but this is good too. You could reheat them in the microwave.

SERVES 4

8 chipolata sausages
2 rashers back bacon

2 rashers streaky bacon
freshly ground black pepper

1   Cook everything under the grill, about 5 minutes each.

2   When cooked, cut the chipolatas into 1 cm (½ in) pieces, and the bacon rashers into thin strips.

3   Mix the bacon and chipolatas in a dish, season with pepper and serve.

Sage and Onion Stuffing

Birds and rolled pieces of meat have been stuffed with savoury fillings for centuries. Some of the most classic have got a seasonal nicety about them – the chestnut one with the turkey above, for instance. This one would also be perfect with a turkey or goose at Christmas.

SERVES 4–6

2 medium onions, peeled and finely
   chopped
55 g (2 oz) pork dripping (lard will do)
1 tbsp chopped fresh sage

115 g (4 oz) fresh white breadcrumbs
1 egg, beaten
salt and freshly ground black pepper
25 g (1 oz) unsalted butter

1   Preheat the oven to 200°C/400°F/Gas 6.

2   Slowly fry the onion in the lard to soften, but do not colour. Take off the heat and add the sage, breadcrumbs, beaten egg and some salt and pepper.

3   Put in a small buttered ovenproof dish and bake in the preheated oven for 20–30 minutes until well coloured.

☛   I am cooking the stuffing separately here, but you can of course stuff it into a bird. Remember, though, to do so at the neck end, not in the cavity.

Brussels Sprouts with Chestnuts

Brussels sprouts were developed in the Low Countries in the Middle Ages, but did not become popular in Britain until the mid-nineteenth century (and are still not particularly popular in some quarters...). Chestnuts too have been with us forever, although the French and the Italians have always appreciated them rather more in a culinary sense. The combination of the two is fairly recent, I imagine, created probably because both are in season at the same time.

Although now traditional with our Christmas turkey, the vegetable mixture is so good it deserves to be used more often – delicious with roast pork or poultry, for instance.

SERVES 4

225 g (8 oz) chestnuts
350 g (12 oz) Brussels sprouts

salt and freshly ground black pepper
55 g (2 oz) unsalted butter

1   Make a cross with a small sharp knife in the bottom of each chestnut and cook in the preheated oven with the turkey for 20 minutes or until the shells start to split. Cool a little until you can handle them, then peel.

2   Meanwhile, prepare the Brussels. Trim off the outside leaves and put a cross in the stalk of the large ones. Plunge into boiling salted water and cook until just done, which depends on their size. Refresh and drain.

3   Cut the peeled chestnuts and the cooked sprouts in half. Fry in the butter to heat through and brown a little, then season and serve.

☞ You could cook the dish in an interesting alternative way. Blanch, then shred the sprouts before cooking. Stir-fry in butter, add some chopped garlic to taste and the cooked, peeled and crumbled chestnuts. Season and serve.

☞ The best chestnuts are those cooked in a special container over an open fire. To test whether a chestnut is ready, shell one, dip it in salt and eat. You'll soon know. (And be sure to buy more chestnuts than you need if, like me, you are obliged to carry on testing to see whether they are ready.)

☞ To cut the workload down, there are some good pre-cooked vacuum-packed chestnuts – these work extremely well.

Steak Plate Pie

To me, plate pies are a feature of northern England, and I can still see them for sale in shops. My dad used to make them in his transport café, on an enamel or thick porcelain plate (the latter a bit discoloured), but both took good heat. He made pies like this, with mince, but his favourite filling was chicken. A plate pie is certainly easier to serve than many pies: it's a sandwich of two pastries. You just have to make sure that the base pastry is slightly thinner, so that it cooks well. These pies are good for Christmas in that you can make one or more in advance and freeze them.

SERVES 6–8

PASTRY

450 g (1 lb) plain flour, plus extra for dusting

a pinch of salt

225 g (8 oz) lard

85 g (3 oz) unsalted butter

150 ml (5 fl oz) cold water

1 egg, for egg wash

FILLING

55 g (2 oz) lard

450 g (1 lb) minced beef

2 onions, peeled and chopped

2 garlic cloves, peeled and chopped

115 g (4 oz) grated carrot

115 g (4 oz) grated turnip

2 large flat mushrooms, diced

140 g (5 oz) canned tomatoes

1 tbsp Worcestershire sauce

300 ml (10 fl oz) chicken stock

salt and freshly ground black pepper

1   For the pastry, mix the flour and salt in a bowl, and then rub in the lard and 55 g (2 oz) of the butter. Mix until it looks like breadcrumbs, but do not over-mix. Add the water and mix to a dough as quickly as you can, using extra flour if necessary. You want a dough that just sticks together nicely without you pushing it back together. Wrap in clingfilm and put to rest for half an hour.

2   To start the filling, heat the lard in a casserole dish. Sprinkle in the meat and, over quite a high heat, stir to break up the pieces. When the meat has coloured, after about 6 minutes, take out of the pan, and put to one side.

3   Lower the heat and add the onion and garlic to the pan. Sweat, but do not colour, for 2–3 minutes. Add the carrot and turnip, and sweat for 3–4 minutes.

4   Put in the diced mushrooms, tomatoes and Worcestershire sauce, then add the meat and bring up to simmering point. Leave to stew and thicken, uncovered, for about 20 minutes, stirring every now and then.

5   Add the chicken stock and some salt and pepper, and bring up to the boil. Simmer away until cooked, about 45 minutes. Turn the heat up again to evaporate any excess liquor and to concentrate the flavours. Check the seasoning, remove from the heat, and allow to cool.

6   Preheat the oven to 200°C/400°F/Gas 6. Have ready a 25 cm (10 in) metal pie plate.

7   Roll out half of the pastry to the size of the plate. Brush the plate with softened butter. Lay the pastry circle on the plate. Put the cooled filling in (if too much, don't worry, keep for another meal – but make sure the pie is well filled). Egg wash the rim of the pastry circle.

8   Roll out the rest of pastry to a circle big enough to form the top of the pie, and place gently on top of the meat. Seal the edges together, then crimp the edges. Brush the top of the pie with egg wash. Make a hole in the centre to allow steam to escape.

9   Bake the pie in the preheated oven for 10 minutes then turn the temperature down to 180°C/350°F/Gas 4, and cook for a further 30 minutes.

☛   The beef mince mixture above could be served under a coating of mashed potato as a cottage pie. Or you could use cut-up leftovers of roast beef. And don't forget that lamb – minced or leftover roast – can be topped with potato too, for a shepherd's pie.

Roast Pheasant

SERVES 4

Roast pheasant needs to be carefully treated as it can become very dry. I like to take the legs off and just roast the breasts, keeping the legs for a stew or a braise, but this recipe cooks the birds whole in the traditional manner. Pheasants make good braised dishes at the back of the season.

2 hen pheasants

115 g (4 oz) unsalted butter

salt and freshly ground black pepper

6 rashers streaky bacon

1 onion, peeled and quartered

1 tbsp groundnut oil

150 ml (5 fl oz) dry white wine

300 ml (10 fl oz) chicken stock

55 g (2 oz) fresh white breadcrumbs

TO SERVE

Bread Sauce (see p. 204)

game chips

8 chipolata sausages, cooked

1 Preheat the oven to 200°C/400°F/Gas 6. Rub half the butter over the breasts of both birds. Season the birds then lay three rashers of bacon over the breasts of each. Put two onion quarters in the cavity of each pheasant. Tie the legs together with string.

2 Heat the oil in the roasting tray and seal the skin on the legs of the birds. Lay the pheasants in the roasting tray with breasts towards each other, resting on a leg each (if necessary use a piece of potato to support the breasts).

3 Roast for 15 minutes on each leg, then turn the birds on to their backs and take the rashers of bacon off. Turn the oven temperature down to 180°C/350°F/Gas 4, and roast for a further 10 minutes or so until the juices turn clear when the pheasant is held up on the end of a fork.

4 When cooked, take the birds out of the oven and tray, and keep in a warm place, upside down so that the juices flow down into the breasts.

5 Remove a little of the fat from the roasting tray and keep to one side. Take the onion out of the cavities, and put into the roasting tray. Mash the onion, then add the white wine. Reduce this a little by boiling, then add the stock, and reduce by one-third in volume. Strain into a clean pot, bring up to the boil, then remove the excess fat and season.

6 Put the breadcrumbs into a frying pan with the reserved dripping and remaining butter and season. Fry to colour, a few minutes only. Take out and drain.

7 Carve the pheasant and serve with fried breadcrumbs, bread sauce, game chips, cooked chipolatas, and gravy.

Rabbit Pie

Rabbits would once have been a major protein source, as they were prolific in the wild, and not so hemmed in by regulation as other game. A pie, in the British tradition, would have been favourite. Although rabbit is coming back into fashion now – I see plenty of them on sale when I walk through Smithfield to the office in the morning – no restaurant seems to serve rabbit in pies. This is a great old-fashioned dish, and one I remember from my childhood, when we would find rabbits shot by the local farmers left just outside the door. The forcemeat balls are traditional, and add flavour, but you can leave them out if you want.

SERVES 4

350 g (12 oz) puff pastry

FILLING

1 large rabbit, jointed

6 bacon rashers, diced

½ onion, peeled and minced

1 tsp chopped fresh parsley

salt and freshly ground black pepper

¼ tsp freshly grated nutmeg

600 ml (1 pint) chicken stock

115 g (4 oz) minced veal

55 g (2 oz) minced pork

55 g (2 oz) fresh white breadcrumbs

1 tsp chopped fresh thyme

¼ tsp dry English mustard powder

1 egg, beaten

1 tsp groundnut oil

1   Put the joints of rabbit in a suitably sized saucepan. Add the bacon, onion and parsley, and season with salt and pepper and nutmeg. Pour in the chicken stock and bring up to the boil. Cover and simmer for about 30 minutes. Put into a 1.2 litre (2 pint) pie dish and leave to cool.

2   Preheat the oven to 200°C/400°F/Gas 6.

3   Mix the veal, pork, breadcrumbs, thyme and mustard powder. Add a little of the beaten egg, just enough to hold things together (keep the remainder for egg wash), then season with some salt and pepper. Make into eight forcemeat balls. Heat the oil in a small frying pan, and fry the balls to colour only, about 5 minutes. Take out of the pan, drain and put into the pie mix.

4   Roll out the pastry to a shape slightly larger than the shape of the pie dish. Cut a strip from around the edges, and put on the rim of the pie dish. Moisten with water, and then put the pastry shape on the top. Seal and crimp the edges. Brush with egg wash, and make a little hole in the middle to allow steam to escape.

5   Bake in the preheated oven for 20 minutes, then reduce the oven temperature to 180°C/350°F/Gas 4 for another 30 minutes. Serve hot.

Sausage Hotpot

SERVES 4

This is a similar kind of dish to the one on p. 176, but is more of a hotpot. It's got potatoes in it, but the great idea of hotpot is to use up what you have around ('hotch potch'), and often the ingredient that you hadn't thought about and put in turns out to be the star. Over Christmas time, it's quite possible to end up with pre-cooked sausages, and these work just as well. This is simple, uncomplicated, and quick to make – a good taste after rich foods.

I tbsp olive oil

12 pork sausages

115 g (4 oz) smoked bacon

I onion, peeled and finely chopped

2 garlic cloves, peeled and chopped

225 g (8 oz) dried haricot beans, soaked in water overnight

225 g (8 oz) canned chopped tomatoes

225 g (8 oz) carrots, peeled and cut into I cm (½ in) dice

850 ml (1½ pints) chicken stock

salt and freshly ground black pepper

225 g (8 oz) potatoes, peeled and cut into I cm (½ in) dice

2 tbsp chopped fresh parsley

1   Preheat the oven to 180°C/350°F/Gas 4.

2   Heat the olive oil in a casserole, put in the sausages and colour all round, about 4 minutes. Take out and keep to one side.

3   Cut the bacon into large strips and colour in the oil in the casserole, about 3–4 minutes. Add the chopped onion and garlic, and turn down the heat. Add the drained soaked beans, the tomatoes, carrots and stock and bring back to the boil. Season.

4   Add the sausages, put a lid on the casserole, and cook in the preheated oven for 40 minutes.

5   Add the potatoes to the hotpot, stir and put back in the oven with the lid off. Cook for another 20 minutes.

6   When cooked take out, sprinkle with parsley and serve.

☞ Instead of the parsley, you could mix 175 g (6 oz) diced bread croûtons with 2 tbsp chopped fresh parsley and 115 g (4 oz) grated Cheddar cheese and sprinkle over the hotpot when it is cooked.

☞ You can cook this dish in one container then decant into a more table-friendly pot to serve.

☞ I like this hotpot when the liquor is reduced so the meat and vegetables are not too sloppy.

Baked Stuffed Onions

SERVES 4

Sausage and onion make a great combination, and this is a good, old-fashioned baked onion dish. My dad used to make something like it, although he wouldn't have used *chorizo*!

4 large onions	I tbsp olive oil	55 g (2 oz) minced celery
salt and freshly ground black pepper	115 g (4 oz) *chorizo* or spicy sausage	115 g (4 oz) boiled ham, diced
225 g (8 oz) pork sausages	55 g (2 oz) minced carrot	115 g (4 oz) fresh breadcrumbs
		300 ml (10 fl oz) chicken stock

1 Preheat the oven to 200°C/400°F/Gas 6.

2 Peel the onions and then par-boil for 10 minutes in boiling salted water. Cut a slice off the root end and carefully scoop out a good half of the centre of the onion. (Keep this for another dish, you don't need it here – but don't waste it!)

3 Take the meat out of the sausage skins. Heat the oil in a frying pan and add the sausage meat. Chop the *chorizo* finely and add to the sausage meat. Break up this meat with a wooden spoon, and mix well, but do not brown too much, about 4 minutes.

4 Add the minced vegetables and diced ham and some salt and pepper, then cook on a low heat for about 10 minutes. Put to drain in a sieve or colander – you want this stuffing to hold together, and not be too mushy.

5 Fill the onions just to the rim with the stuffing, and sprinkle breadcrumbs on top. Put the onions into a lightly greased ovenproof dish, and pour in enough chicken stock to come 1 cm (½ in) up the onion. (Top up during baking if necessary.)

6 Bake in the preheated oven until cooked, about 20–30 minutes. Serve hot.

Chicken Steak and Roasted Cauliflower

SERVES 4

This may not be traditional, but it is a good combination of two great British ingredients. I invented it for a TV show, one of those in which I had to cook a dish in five minutes. You can take longer, but it's still not too lengthy to prepare. I love the flavours of the roast cauliflower and chicken, and a squeeze of lemon juice will bring them all together at the end.

4 chicken breasts, skin on

2 tsp groundnut oil

140 g (5 oz) unsalted butter

salt and freshly ground black pepper

24 even-sized cauliflower florets

juice of 1 lemon

1 tbsp chopped fresh parsley

½ garlic clove, peeled and crushed

1 Preheat the oven to 200°C/400°F/Gas 6.

2 For added presentation, clean the wing bone. This is done by freeing the meat from the end of the wing bone nearest the bird, and scraping the meat off. However, should you not feel the need for this enhanced presentation, just carry on. Tap the breast a bit flatter, using clingfilm under and on top, and a meat mallet.

3 Heat half of the oil in a frying pan, and add 25 g (1 oz) of the butter. Pan-fry the chicken, skin-side down first, then season. Turn over and cook for about 7 minutes.

4 Meanwhile, cook the cauliflower florets in boiling salted water for 3 minutes, then take out, refresh in cold water and drain well.

5 Heat the remaining oil in a small roasting tray, add 25 g (1 oz) of the butter and the cauliflower, and roast in the preheated oven for about 6 minutes, turning frequently.

6 Season and drain the cauliflower, then arrange the florets in the middle of the hot serving plates. Put the chicken steaks on top and season with pepper.

7 Working quickly, heat the remaining butter to golden brown. Take off the heat, add the lemon juice, parsley and garlic, and spoon over the chicken to serve.

Pork Faggots

Faggots were made to use up the bits and pieces of offal and meat left over after the pig was killed. They are the British version of the French *crépinettes* or the Cypriot *sheftalia,* as the sausage mixture is wrapped in caul fat (as all sausages were once wrapped in animal entrails). It's amazing to think how many pork products we use over Christmas – the bacon, sausages, ham, roasting pork, lard etc.

I grew up with dishes like this. Walking back from school, I could easily pop into the butcher's and get a warm pork faggot to eat in my hand. Everyone has their own way of making faggots – this is mine.

SERVES 4

---

350 g (12 oz) pig's liver

115 g (4 oz) belly pork

55 g (2 oz) shoulder of pork meat

1 tsp vegetable oil

1 onion, peeled and finely chopped

1 garlic clove, peeled and crushed

1 tbsp mixed chopped fresh herbs (parsley, chives, chervil)

freshly grated nutmeg

salt and freshly ground black pepper

1 egg, lightly beaten

55 g (2 oz) fresh white breadcrumbs

225 g (8 oz) pig's caul, soaked (see below)

450 ml (15 fl oz) rich meat stock

---

1   Take off the skin membrane, remove blood vessels and finely chop or mince the liver, then the belly pork and pork meat. Put into a saucepan with the onion and garlic, and stew slowly for about 30 minutes with the lid on. Do not colour.

2   Preheat the oven to 180°C/350°F/Gas 4.

3   Strain off the fat, and put the meat mixture into a bowl. Add the herbs, nutmeg and some salt and pepper, then stir in the beaten egg. Add enough breadcrumbs to make an easy-to-handle mixture.

4   Divide the mixture into 55 g (2 oz) pieces and wrap each in as little caul as possible to hold together. Shape into balls and put into an earthenware dish in which the little balls will fit closely together.

5   Pour enough stock over to come halfway up the faggots. Bake for about 45 minutes, until brown on top. Regular basting will help with the colour.

☞ This recipe needs pork caul which is the inner lining of a pig's stomach. You probably need to order this from a farm shop or local butcher. When you get it, it needs soaking in water until it becomes easy to handle. Drain well, and use sparingly; it's very stretchy.

Quick Pease Pudding

My dad would not forgive me for this recipe, but sometimes we need to move with the times. He was a traditionalist: he used to soak marrowfat peas overnight in water with added bicarbonate of soda, then wash the water off and cook the peas to soft for a couple of hours. This recipe, on the other hand, is very quick indeed (the benefit of the freezing age), but it is important to plunge the peas into salted water and then refresh, as this maintains the colour. The pudding will be traditionally perfect with the faggots opposite.

SERVES 4

Close your eyes, Dad, they'll taste great!

450g (1 lb) frozen peas

salt and freshly ground black pepper

55g (2oz) unsalted butter

a splash of malt vinegar

1 Plunge the peas into boiling salted water. Bring to the boil and cook for 2–3 minutes. Take out and put into cold water to refresh. Drain.

2 Melt the butter in a medium pan, add about 280g (10oz) of the peas, and mash slightly. Add the rest of the peas, stir in and heat.

3 Season with salt, pepper and vinegar and serve.

Christmas Pudding

Christmas cake, mince pies and Christmas pudding are all part of the same tradition: rich mixtures of dried fruit cooked for festive occasions. Christmas puddings were one of the first things I learned to cook when I was at Simpson's in the Strand. Working with Sam Costa, the pint-sized pastry chef, we would make the puddings in September: the mixes would be stored in huge plastic dustbins in the cool room. The smell as the mixture matured was fantastic – you could almost get drunk on it!

You don't need to make your puddings three months in advance, although they do get better as they mature. This recipe is for a light pudding, as I don't really like them made with molasses, treacle or stout. It is delicious with the rum sauce opposite, my favourite.

SERVES 8

175 g (6 oz) beef suet

55 g (2 oz) self-raising flour

55 g (2 oz) fresh white breadcrumbs

115 g (4 oz) each of chopped dried figs and chopped pitted prunes

175 g (6 oz) raisins

55 g (2 oz) each of chopped mixed peel and chopped semi-dried apricots

25 g (1 oz) ground almonds

115 g (4 oz) soft brown unrefined sugar

finely grated rind of 1 orange

finely grated rind of 1 lemon

1 tsp ground mixed spice

55 g (2 oz) each of grated peeled and cored apple and grated peeled carrot

1 tbsp golden syrup (see p. 46)

2 tbsp brandy

1 egg, beaten

a pinch of salt

55 g (2 oz) unsalted butter, to grease

TO SERVE

55 g (2 oz) caster sugar

3 tbsp brandy

1   Chop the suet finely if fresh, and put in a large bowl. Add the flour, breadcrumbs and dried fruit, chopped where necessary. Mix in the ground almonds, sugar, orange and lemon rind and the spice. Add the grated apple and carrot, the syrup, brandy, egg and salt. Mix well.

2   When all the ingredients are in, leave to stand, covered, for 24 hours.

3   Butter a 1.2 litre (2 pint) pudding bowl. Spoon in the pudding mixture. Cover the pudding with buttered greaseproof paper: put a pleat in the middle of this to allow for expansion during cooking. Then cover with a cloth and tie.

4   Put the pudding in a steamer (or on an upturned saucer in a saucepan), and steam for 6 hours. Make sure the steamer does not boil dry. Top up with water if necessary.

5   After 6 hours, take the pudding out and leave to cool. When cold take off the paper and cloth, and wrap in clean paper. Store away in a cool place: this pudding could be stored for a year without a problem.

6   To serve, steam again for about 2 hours. Unwrap and put on a Christmas plate. Get someone to turn the lights down or out.

7   Sprinkle the pudding with the sugar and I tbsp of the brandy. Heat a metal ladle and take away from the heat. Carefully and quickly pour the remaining 2 tbsp brandy into the ladle. Put the ladle over the flame or ignite with a match, then pour over the pudding. Take into the darkened dining room, and parade the pudding before cutting into it!

☛   Fanny Cradock is said to have added vodka to the brandy, as it stayed alight longer...

Rum Sauce

Many people would serve a brandy or rum butter with Christmas pudding, and this is very traditional: we have always eaten a lot of butter in this country. But basic butter sauces are also very common, and are generally known as 'English sauces'. This is a cross between a butter sauce and a custard, the latter known in France as *crème anglaise*!

SERVES 6–8

55 g (2 oz) unsalted butter
55 g (2 oz) plain flour
55 g (2 oz) caster sugar
450 ml (15 fl oz) double cream

150 ml (5 fl oz) milk
I vanilla pod, split
150 ml (5 fl oz) dark rum

I   Melt the butter in a pan, and stir in the flour, mixing well.

2   Bring the sugar, cream, milk, vanilla pod and seeds up to the boil in a separate pan. Add slowly to the butter and flour roux, and beat well to avoid lumps.

3   Add the rum and strain into a clean pan (keep the vanilla pod for another use). Bring up to the boil and serve with the Christmas pudding.

Cakes for the Festive Season

Traditional Christmas cakes, puddings and mince pies are direct echoes of the celebratory pottages and puddings of earlier centuries. The earliest pudding – which was a cake in essence – was a mixture of suet or bone-marrow, flour, dried fruits, spices and sugar. This would have been stuffed into an animal gut and boiled in water. That is basically what our current Christmas pudding is, although we tend to steam it now. Traditionally the pudding is made on Stir-up Sunday, the Sunday before Advent, which will allow the pud time to mature for Christmas. Everyone lends a hand with the stirring, making a wish as they do so. I remember the old silver sixpences, wrapped in greaseproof, as the highlight of my granny's puddings in the old days; somehow a silver 10p piece isn't quite the same.

Enthusiasm for the mixture of sweet and savoury is reflected par excellence in the original mincemeat: once it was actually made with meat, and preserved with sugar and spices. I love mince pies, and sometimes lift up the lid and pop in a knob of brandy or rum butter. They say you should eat a mince pie on each one of the twelve days of Christmas, preferably in a different house each time, to ensure twelve good months in the year to come. I'd be happy to do that.

Christmas cake, a rich fruit cake, echoes the same theme and a fruit cake, iced or not, is served traditionally at Christmas, weddings, high days and holidays. I haven't given you a separate recipe for a cake here – the one on p. 43 would be good – but I do tell you how I decorate a Christmas cake.

Once the Christmas festivities are over, the next celebration is New Year or Hogmanay, and the Scots make another dried fruit concoction for the occasion. Black bun is not a cake, but a tart really, with dried fruit and nothing much else enclosed in pastry. It is served to the first-footers who come through the door after the New Year bells.

And Twelfth Night, or 6 January, was once an integral and highly celebrated part of the whole Christmas feast. Although we still bake a traditional Twelfth Night cake, what we generally do on that day is take down the Christmas decorations and dismantle the tree...

Baking is an art that, sadly, seems to have fallen out of fashion. Children – boys included – should be taught how to bake, although perhaps even their mothers don't now know the basics. Over Christmas and New Year, when everyone is at home, is an ideal time to start baking!

Christmas Cake Decoration

In the chapter on morning coffee and afternoon tea, there is a good, typically British fruit cake, which can serve as a Christmas cake. Once made, and cooled, you can decorate it as below.

1 *Fruit Cake* (see p. 43)	MARZIPAN	ROYAL ICING
115 g (4 oz) apricot jam	450 g (1 lb) ground almonds	450 g (1 lb) icing sugar
	675 g (1½ lb) icing sugar	3 egg whites
	3–4 egg yolks	juice of ¼ lemon
	a splash of vanilla essence	

1   For the marzipan, sieve the almonds and sugar together into a bowl. Add the egg yolks and vanilla essence and mix well. Knead well for about 5 minutes on a work surface dusted with a little extra icing sugar.

2   Warm the apricot jam through in a small pan, then push through a sieve. Brush this over the cake, top and sides.

3   Roll out the marzipan carefully, using more icing sugar to stop it sticking, to a round large enough to cover the whole cake, top and sides. Lay the marzipan on top and carefully, using your hands, seal it to the cake.

4   For the royal icing, mix the icing sugar and egg whites well together with a wooden spoon. Splash with lemon juice and beat in well.

5   Spread the royal icing over the cake. You can decorate it now very simply: just use the back of a spoon to lift the icing up in little peaks. If you want a smooth finish with applied decorations (little trees, Santas etc), leave the icing to set for 24 hours. You could make more icing and practise your piping skills at this stage: if it doesn't work, you can simply smooth the icing over again!

Mincemeat Rolls
with Clotted Cream Custard

Apparently little pies with a filling of *Mincemeat* (see p. 224) were associated with Christmas as long ago as the sixteenth century. They were known as 'minced' or 'shred' pies, referring to the actual meat they once contained. I make them now only for Christmas, but my dad served them throughout the year in his café, often making a single large tart.

Conventional mince pies are made with puff or shortcrust pastry, and baked in Yorkshire pudding or muffin trays. To ring the changes, I have used filo pastry here, and made little Christmas rolls of mincemeat, which are dipped into a vanilla clotted cream custard. The great thing about these is that you can make lots in advance, freeze them individually, then put them into plastic freezer bags. If you have unexpected guests, you can stick them in the oven straight from the freezer, and they'll be ready before your guests have even sat down.

MAKES 12

---

6 sheets filo pastry, approx. 50 x 24 cm (20 x 10 in)

450 g (1 lb) *Mincemeat* (see p. 224)

115 g (4 oz) unsalted butter, melted

icing sugar

ground cinnamon

CLOTTED CREAM CUSTARD

150 ml (5 fl oz) milk

1 vanilla pod, split

2 egg yolks

25 g (1 oz) caster sugar

1 x 140 g tub clotted cream

---

1 Preheat the oven to 190°C/375°F/Gas 5.

2 Lay a sheet of filo pastry on the table, the longer side in front of you, and cut in half, so that you have two fairly square pieces.

3 Place 1 tbsp of the mincemeat across the middle third of one square of the pastry to 1 cm (½ in) from the edge. Brush the remaining pastry lightly with the melted butter.

4 Fold the edge nearest you over the mincemeat to make a cylindrical shape. Fold the edges in so that the pastry is now just a half of the width it started. Lightly brush again with melted butter and fold, rolling away from you into a cigarette/spring-roll shape. Brush the outside with butter and put on a baking sheet. Continue the process until all the pastry has been used. (At this stage they can be frozen.)

5   Bake in the preheated oven for 8–10 minutes. Take out and allow to rest for 5 minutes. Mix some icing sugar and cinnamon, and sift over the top.

6   Meanwhile, for the custard, bring the milk to the boil with the vanilla pod and seeds scraped out.

7   Mix the egg yolks and sugar together well in a bowl. Pour the hot milk into the egg mixture and mix well. Pour back into the pan and heat gently, stirring continuously, until it starts to thicken. Do not boil.

8   Strain the custard into a clean bowl, and when cool beat in the clotted cream. Put into a small bowl.

9   Dip the rolls into the custard to eat.

☞ Small ones make great petits-fours-type bites. Don't worry if the rolls are not all the same size!

☞ You can also use bought mincemeat for ease.

Mincemeat

MAKES ABOUT
450 G (1 LB)

In the Middle Ages, we British used to love sweet meat mixtures, and mincemeat is actually very medieval in flavour. It would once have contained meat – beef, lamb or offal – but the only remnant of that now is the beef suet. However, as late as the 1860s, Francatelli, chef to Queen Victoria, gave four recipes for mincemeat in his *A Plain Cookery Book for the Working Classes*. These were all price based: the cheapest, at 9d, was made with tripe. Hard to believe, but true. Could you imagine this today?

---

115 g (4 oz) chopped beef suet

115 g (4 oz) each of chopped mixed peel, currants, sultanas and raisins

2 apples, peeled, cored and finely diced

175 g (6 oz) unrefined demerara sugar

finely grated zest and juice of 1 lemon and 1 orange

1 tsp ground mixed spice

½ tsp freshly grated nutmeg

75 ml (2½ fl oz) each of rum and brandy

---

1 Make sure that all the chopped items are very finely chopped.

2 Mix all the ingredients together, then put into a bowl. Cover with clingfilm, pushing it on to the surfaces of the mincemeat – you don't want any air to get to it.

3 Allow to stand for a week in the fridge before using. It could last longer, but it's so delicious I don't think it'll get the chance.

☛ Use this mincemeat in things like mincemeat *Roly-poly* (see p. 88), mincemeat cheesecake and the *Mincemeat Rolls* on p. 222.

☛ A less usual way with mincemeat is to stick a little under a turkey or chicken skin before roasting, as you might a flavoured butter. You could spread a little on a pork fillet before wrapping in bacon and cooking. Only use a little, you don't want to overdo it.

Black Bun

SERVES PLENTY
(IT'S SO RICH)

Black bun, once a Twelfth Night cake, is now eaten exclusively at Hogmanay. It is the closest example in Scottish cookery, along with the (Selkirk) bannock, to the traditional rich English fruit cake. I usually take currants out of cake mixes, as I don't like them, but they need to be here. (My dad used to call them rabbit nuts!)

175 g (6 oz) plain flour

1 tsp baking powder

1 tsp ground cinnamon

1 tsp ground ginger

115 g (4 oz) mixed peel

55 g (2 oz) chopped crystallised ginger

175 g (6 oz) nibbed almonds, toasted

115 g (4 oz) unrefined soft brown sugar

225 g (8 oz) currants

900 g (2 lb) raisins

1 egg

4 tbsp buttermilk

2 tbsp malt whisky

PASTRY

280 g (10 oz) plain flour

a pinch of salt

140 g (5 oz) unsalted butter, plus extra for greasing

a splash of water

1 egg, mixed with a little water, for egg wash

1　Mix all the bun ingredients together in recipe order in a large bowl. Cover with clingfilm and put in the fridge overnight.

2　Preheat the oven to 170°C/340°F/Gas 3–4. Grease a 25 cm (10 in) round cake tin.

3　To make the pastry, sift the flour and salt into another bowl, and rub in the cold butter until the texture is like breadcrumbs. Use just enough cold water to make a good dough.

4　Roll out two-thirds of the pastry into a large circle with which you can line the base and sides of the cake tin. Don't try to do anything fancy. If you break it any way, take some of the other pastry to patch up the hole. It needs to be whole to keep the filling in. Put the filling into the pastry case, and flatten carefully on the top with the back of a large moistened spoon.

5　Roll out the rest of the pastry into a 25 cm (10 in) circle. Moisten the top of the sides of the pastry case, then put the circle of pastry on top. Carefully seal the sides to the top. Brush the egg wash over the top lightly. Using a fork, gently pierce the top all over to allow the steam to escape.

6　Bake for an hour, then reduce to 150°C/300°F/Gas 2 and continue baking for a further 1½ hours. Take out and leave to cool in the tin. Remove from the tin, cut into *thin* wedges, and serve.

Twelfth Night Cake

Twelfth Night, or 6 January, was the last day of Christmas, and was often celebrated with feasts, dancing, masques, and general tomfoolery. It was the last day of holiday before the work of the New Year was to begin in earnest. A rich fruit cake, inevitably, formed part of the traditional food, and this used to contain a bean. Whoever found the bean was called 'King of the Bean', and could lord it over people for the remainder of the day – and hopefully have good luck in the coming year.

I have never been very keen on carrot cake, but I have used carrots here, their natural sweetness contributing both to the flavour and the texture of the cake. The crystallised fruit you can buy now is great; you can find much more interesting stuff than I remember from years ago.

MAKES 1 CAKE

225 g (8 oz) unsalted butter	225 g (8 oz) carrots	TOPPING
225 g (8 oz) unrefined caster sugar	225 g (8 oz) raisins	225 g (8 oz) icing sugar
4 eggs	115 g (4 oz) chopped mixed peel	1½ egg whites
2 egg yolks	55 g (2 oz) nibbed almonds	juice of ½ lemon
225 g (8 oz) plain flour, sieved	½ tsp freshly grated nutmeg	crystallised fruit
	2 tbsp Cognac	

1 Preheat the oven to 170°C/340°F/Gas 3–4. Grease and line a 25–30 cm (10–12 in) round cake tin.

2 Cream the butter and sugar together well.

3 Separate the eggs. Whisk up the whites in one bowl until thick, and then whisk up the six yolks. Mix the eggs gently back together, and then gently mix into the butter and sugar mixture.

4 Carefully fold in the sieved flour and then the carrot, fruit, nuts and nutmeg. Blend in the Cognac to give a softish consistency.

5 Pour into the prepared cake tin, level the top, and bake for about 2 hours.

6 Take out and leave to cool in the tin. Remove from the tin, and place on a board.

7 Beat the icing sugar and egg whites together with a wooden spoon, then add the lemon juice and beat until stiff.

8 Pour this carefully over the cake, top and sides, and just before it sets, decorate round the edge with crystallised fruit.

As Christianity spread around the world, it became the norm to appropriate and modify non-Christian festivals partly, presumably, in an attempt to woo disbelievers to the faith, and to make the new religion more acceptable to potential converts. Therefore Easter too, like Christmas, had its origins in pagan practice. The Ancient Saxons would celebrate the passing of winter with a festival in honour of their goddess of spring, Eostre. Spring is a time of rebirth and renewal, which is very much in tune with the Christian belief in the Resurrection.

The date of the Easter festival is variable, but it must be celebrated on the first Sunday after the first full moon on or after the vernal or spring equinox, which falls on 21 March. Easter, therefore, is usually celebrated on a Sunday between 22 March and 25 April. After a penitential month or so of Lent, which begins on Ash Wednesday, a whole week is devoted to the festival, often called 'Holy Week'. It starts with Palm Sunday, and Holy Thursday is the day of the Last Supper. Good Friday is the day on which Jesus was crucified and buried; the day's name is said to come from 'God's Friday' (which has elided to 'good' in much the same way as 'God be with ye' has become 'good-bye'). Easter Sunday marks the Resurrection, on the third day after Jesus's death.

Easter is the highest festival of the Church, but even this is not immune to the commercialisation that has afflicted so many other Christian festivals. Months in advance, the shops are full of expensive Easter eggs made of chocolate, and as a result chocolate eggs seem now to be the most potent symbol of Easter. However, brightly coloured eggs were said to have been used by the ancients to represent the colours of the new spring, and an egg of course was and is an important fertility symbol. The custom of rolling eggs is more Christian, thought to symbolise the rolling away of the stone from the tomb.

Eggs are important as food as well as symbol. That penitential month of Lent was when people were supposed to avoid certain foods (to mirror Christ's forty days' suffering in the wilderness), and one of those foods was eggs. Those who had been without eggs for a month would have been happy to eat them again on Easter Sunday.

Other foods traditionally associated with Easter are simnel cake and hot cross buns. As described on p. 98, simnel cake used to be eaten on the fourth Sunday in Lent, Mothering Sunday, which is halfway through Lent, a time when fasters were allowed to relax and enjoy themselves.

Some people maintain that hot cross buns date back to pagan tradition. But history tells us that many pre-Reformation breads were marked with a cross before baking (to keep evil spirits away). This practice was abandoned in the seventeenth century – thought to be popish – but was retained for the breads baked for Good Friday, when the symbol of the cross had the greatest significance. Hot cross buns are traditionally eaten for breakfast on that day, and their rich fruity taste would have been welcome after the weeks of abstinence.

The Easter holiday is another of those long weekends which requires good planning. Using foods in season is best, and there are a few choices in the following recipes. For me Easter is primarily a time for long walks: it's warmer with spring on the way, and there are always daffodils and bluebells.

Prawn Cocktail

No one seems to be quite sure where and when the infamous prawn cocktail originated, but it appeared on restaurant menus in Britain throughout the 1960s, and can still be found today. It may be an American idea. A combination of shredded lettuce, prawns and, usually, a bottled mayo-based sauce, it has been much maligned but in actual fact, when made correctly, can be wonderful. It makes an ideal Easter-time starter.

SERVES 4

350 g (12 oz) shelled prawns

I little gem lettuce

I tbsp Dijon mustard

I tbsp white wine vinegar

4 tbsp olive oil

salt and freshly ground black pepper

2 tbsp finely chopped cucumber

SAUCE

6 tbsp mayonnaise

2 tbsp good tomato ketchup

I tbsp double cream

I tsp each of brandy and creamed horseradish

juice of ½ lemon

4 drops Tabasco sauce

TO GARNISH

2 tomatoes, seeded and finely diced

I shallot, peeled and finely chopped

I tbsp chopped fresh chives

1 Put the prawns into a bowl. Finely shred the lettuce.

2 Make a vinaigrette with the mustard, vinegar and oil. Season with salt and pepper.

3 Make the sauce by mixing the mayonnaise with the ketchup and cream, then stir in the brandy, horseradish, lemon juice and Tabasco. Check the seasoning.

4 Mix the prawns with I tbsp of the sauce and I tbsp of the vinaigrette.

5 Mix the shredded lettuce with the cucumber, add the remaining vinaigrette and season.

6 Put the lettuce into four glasses, with the prawns on top. Cover lightly with the rest of the sauce.

7 Mix the tomatoes, shallot and chives, sprinkle over the sauce and serve.

Hotch-potch Chicken

'Hotch-potch' is as it sounds, a mixture, and any number of ingredients can be cooked in a stew-soup, such as this. In fact the older name has been corrupted to the better known 'hot-pot', which now means a thick casserole, which this is too! It's also a good example of a recipe that is simply a guide: you can really put in anything you like. The saffron, for instance, doesn't need to be used at all, but I like its taste. With some good bread and butter, this is a meal in itself.

SERVES 4

---

4 large chicken legs, claw bone trimmed	2 garlic cloves, peeled and chopped	225 g (8 oz) potatoes, peeled
2 tbsp olive oil	4 tomatoes, seeded and chopped	225 g (8 oz) carrots, peeled
2 red onions, peeled and sliced	a pinch of saffron strands	salt and freshly ground black pepper
1 bay leaf	150 ml (5 fl oz) white wine	6 spring onions
1 sprig fresh thyme	600 ml (1 pint) chicken stock	

---

1 Heat the olive oil in a suitable casserole, and add the legs, skin-side down. Fry to colour, about 3 minutes, then remove from the pan.

2 Turn down the heat and add the sliced onions. Sweat, do not colour, for about 2 minutes. Add the bay leaf, thyme, garlic, tomato and saffron, turn the heat up and cook for 2 minutes. Add the white wine and reduce by half.

3 Add the stock, bring to the boil and skim. Put the chicken legs in and leave to simmer, uncovered, for about 20 minutes.

4 Meanwhile cut the peeled potatoes and carrots into 1 cm (½ in) dice. Add to the pot, stir and cook gently for 15 minutes. Season to taste.

5 Cut the spring onions into three baton pieces each, add to the pan and cook for about 3–4 minutes.

6 Serve the chicken in a soup plate with plenty of liquor.

☛ This is good served with rice or pasta.

Baked Cauliflower with Gammon

SERVES 4

It wasn't until the eighteenth century that we used cheese as a topping for baked or grilled foods such as macaroni, cardoons and cauliflower. This version, using some gammon steaks, takes the traditional idea just a little further (and see my original *Cauliflower Cheese* on p.178).

280g (10oz) cauliflower	225g (8oz) baby spinach, washed and dried	1 tbsp grain mustard
salt and freshly ground black pepper	freshly grated nutmeg	1 tbsp chopped fresh tarragon
25g (1oz) unsalted butter	4 x 115g (4oz) gammon steaks	115g (4oz) Lancashire cheese, sliced
½ onion, peeled and chopped	150ml (5fl oz) double cream	

1   Preheat the oven to 180°C/350°F/Gas 4, and preheat the grill.

2   Cut the cauliflower into florets. Cook in plenty of boiling salted water for about 5 minutes. You want them to be underdone. Remove from the water, and leave to cool.

3   Melt the butter in a large pan and add the onion. Sweat for a few minutes, then add the spinach and allow to wilt, about 2 minutes. Season with salt, pepper and nutmeg to taste. Drain and pour into a suitable ovenproof dish. Put the cauliflower on top.

4   Trim the rind, if any, off the gammon steaks and snip the fat side at 1 cm (½ in) intervals (to prevent the steaks curling). Grill on hot for a minute on each side, then place on top of the cauliflower.

5   Mix the cream, mustard and tarragon together, and season with salt and pepper. Pour over the meat, then lay the slices of cheese on top. Bake in the preheated oven for 20 minutes. Serve hot.

☛ The recipe can be prepared in advance and, after you come back from your Easter walk, you can pop it in the oven.

☛ I like Lancashire cheese because it is crumbly and slightly acidic in flavour, but any hard cheese will do.

Saddle of Lamb with Glazed Vegetables

In many Christian cultures, Easter is celebrated with the slaughter of a lamb or kid, and lamb has become particularly associated with the festival for us. Traditionally a roast lamb main course was followed by egg custards and cream (the dairy foods given up for Lent). Easter is of course the time when you can see the new lambs in the fields, but I would prefer to eat older lamb such as hogget (over a year old) at this time: they have more flavour, and are slightly bigger. A short saddle means a saddle with the chump end taken off.

SERVES 6

---

1 short saddle of lamb, about 1.8 kg (4 lb) in weight

1 garlic clove, peeled and crushed

1 tbsp chopped fresh parsley

salt and freshly ground black pepper

GLAZED VEGETABLES

25 g (1 oz) unsalted butter

175 g (6 oz) peeled potatoes

175 g (6 oz) peeled celeriac

115 g (4 oz) peeled carrots

1 onion, peeled

300 ml (10 fl oz) double cream

150 ml (5 fl oz) milk

115 g (4 oz) Cheddar, freshly grated

---

1 Preheat the oven to 220°C/425°F/Gas 7.

2 Ask the butcher to bone the saddle. You will then have the two eyes of meat, looking as they did before, just without the bones. Ask the butcher for the saddle bones as well as the fillets. Trim the flaps under the saddle to a length where they just overlap when folded under the saddle. Take out as much excess fat as you can from inside the saddle and even flatten the flaps with a meat hammer or large knife.

3 Open up the saddle and lay it upside down on the table. Mix the garlic and parsley together, and smear this on the inside. Season and lay the fillets on top. Pull the flaps up and together and then turn the saddle over. Tie with string in three places to keep the shape then place in a roasting tray on top of the saddle bones, to protect the meat from the heat.

4 Roast in the preheated oven for 10 minutes, then turn the temperature down to 180°C/350°F/Gas 4, and cook for about an hour. It should still be pink. Allow to stand for 10–15 minutes after cooking.

5 Meanwhile, grease an ovenproof dish and season it. Cut the potatoes thinly on a mandolin, and lay half of them on the bottom of the dish. Slice the celeriac and carrots, and shred the onion. Place these in layers on top of the potato and season well. Finish with a layer of potatoes and some seasoning.

6 Mix the double cream and milk together and carefully pour over the vegetables. Sprinkle with the grated cheese.

7 Bake in the preheated oven (at the lower temperature above), for about 40 minutes until everything is cooked and golden brown on top, and the cream has cooked and thickened.

8 Serve the lamb in slices, with spoonfuls of the vegetables.

☛ The French would call this vegetable dish a *dauphinoise*, which consists of layers of potatoes only, plus loads of garlic. I have done something more British, using our wonderful root vegetables, and there's not a whiff of garlic in sight (apart from that flavouring the lamb).

☛ The fact that it's a short saddle makes it easier to carve. Traditionally lamb saddle is carved lengthways in thin strips from top to tail, although cutting into slices across the grain wouldn't make much difference. Here, though, we have boned the saddle, so we have those two lovely eyes of meat.

Lamb Cutlets with Minted New Potatoes (see opposite)

Lamb Cutlets with Minted New Potatoes

Another celebration of spring and Easter lamb, but this is a marriage made in heaven, allying tender new lamb cutlets with the delicious new potatoes appearing now, fresh from the ground, and flavouring them with fresh mint. What more can I say, this is the simplest of dishes. On the long Easter weekend, preparing and cooking something like this means that you can spend more time on those walks, or talking to your guests. It *might* be warm enough to bring out the barbecue...

SERVES 4

12 lamb cutlets, trimmed	450g (1 lb) new potatoes	1 tbsp chopped fresh mint
1 tbsp groundnut oil	55g (2 oz) unsalted butter	salt and freshly ground black pepper

1 Clean the bones on the cutlets to the meat, and trim off excess fat. Tap the cutlets out with a meat mallet (use some clingfilm), so that all are of an even thickness.

2 Heat a ridged griddle pan, or bring the barbecue up to a good heat.

3 Meanwhile wash the potatoes, but keep the skin on. Put into cold water, add some salt, and bring up to the boil. Cook for 15–20 minutes, or until tender. Drain and allow to cool slightly.

4 If griddling or frying the cutlets, heat the oil in the pan; if barbecuing, coat the cutlets in oil. Lay the cutlets carefully in the pan or on the hot bars of the barbecue, and leave for a few minutes to mark them. Turn through 90 degrees, and mark again. Turn them completely over and repeat the double marking process. Cook them medium-rare – which will take about 5 minutes maximum – then season.

5 Melt the butter in a frying pan. Slice the potatoes into the pan, add the mint and some salt and pepper. Swill around to butter and season the potatoes.

6 Spoon the potatoes into the middle of each plate. Lay the cutlets on top and serve, dribbled with the excess butter and mint from the potatoes.

Irish Stew

Lamb again, but the combination of lamb, onions and potatoes is common throughout Europe. The most famous version is that from Ireland, where potatoes were such a staple, and sheep thrived on the lush grazing. Hogget or mutton was probably used at first and some say that kid was common as well.

The version here is unusual because of the cabbage, but that's how we used to do it at The Savoy Hotel, plating the lamb chops with a separate braised cabbage 'ball', the whole potatoes and the sauce, flavoured and thickened by the potato and cabbage (and sometimes enriched with cream). The celery leaves were the final touch.

SERVES 4

900 g (2 lb) large potatoes	salt and freshly ground black pepper	1 *bouquet garni* (bay leaf, parsley, thyme etc)
3 large onions	600 ml (1 pint) white stock (made from unroasted bones or vegetables)	1 tbsp chopped celery leaves
½ white cabbage		
8 large middle neck lamb chops		

1 Peel the potatoes and cut and trim into twelve even-sized pieces. Put to one side in water and keep the trimmings.

2 Peel and thinly slice the onions, and place in the bottom of a large, deep, heatproof stewing pan. Shred the cabbage and place on top of the onion. Put the chops on top. Slice the potato trimmings and scatter over the chops. Season with salt and pepper.

3 Cover the vegetables and meat with the stock and add the *bouquet garni*. Bring up to the boil, cover with a lid and cook slowly for 1–1½ hours on top of the stove.

4 Put in the trimmed potatoes, and gently simmer for another 20–30 minutes until the potatoes and the chops are cooked. Take out the chops and whole potatoes, put into a serving dish and keep warm.

5 Remove the *bouquet garni* and purée the liquor in a food processor. Check for seasoning and consistency.

6 Pour the sauce over the meat, sprinkle with the chopped celery leaves, and serve.

Pork Chop Schnitzel

A *Schnitzel* is much the same as the French and Italian escalope: meat that has been beaten flat, so that it cooks more quickly, and has often been tenderised in the process. Here I am using pork – we have wonderful pork in the UK – and applying a more continental approach to it, coating it with Parmesan breadcrumbs, and serving it with a pungent caper and anchovy sauce-relish. I am keeping the bone on for presentation, but you needn't. It does look quite spectacular, though.

SERVES 8

4 x 225 g (8 oz) pork chops on the bone, rind off

55 g (2 oz) plain flour

salt and freshly ground black pepper

2 eggs

175 g (6 oz) fresh white breadcrumbs

55 g (2 oz) Parmesan, freshly grated

1 tbsp chopped fresh parsley

1 tbsp olive oil

115 g (4 oz) unsalted butter

2 tbsp capers

juice of 1 lemon

4 canned anchovy fillets, finely chopped

1   Trim and clean the bone to about 4 cm (1½ in), using a strong knife. Put the chop between two sheets of plastic or clingfilm, and tap out to make the meat thinner, about 5 mm (¼ in) thick. Trim off to make a nice shape.

2   Season the flour with salt and pepper, and put on to a tray. Beat the eggs and put into another tray or shallow bowl. Mix the breadcrumbs, Parmesan and parsley and put on to yet another small tray.

3   Carefully coat the meat with flour, shaking off any excess. Put into the egg, shake off excess, and then put into the breadcrumb mix. Put on the table and tap with a palette knife to make sure the breadcrumbs are well stuck on.

4   Heat the oil and 25 g (1 oz) of the butter together in a frying pan and fry the chops on one side to a golden brown colour, about 3–4 minutes. Turn over and cook for another 3–4 minutes. A new pan or cleaned pan may be needed for each *Schnitzel,* but you'd need some more oil and butter then.

5   When all the *Schnitzels* are cooked, in a clean pan melt the remaining butter. As it colours, take off the heat and add the capers, lemon juice and anchovies. Pour over the *Schnitzels* and serve.

Smoked Haddock with Peas and Duck Egg

I love smoked haddock, I love peas, and I have a great fondness for duck eggs, which will be around now. They are fabulous together. And if you ever find a good supply of duck eggs, they make wonderful cakes. If you can only get hen's eggs – which should, of course, be organic and free-range – you might need more, as duck eggs are bigger.

SERVES 4

4 x 140 g (5 oz) smoked haddock fillets

65 g (2½ oz) unsalted butter

4 tbsp milk

4 duck eggs, beaten

2 tbsp double cream

salt and freshly ground black pepper

350 g (12 oz) frozen peas

1 Trim the haddock of all bones and skin.

2 Heat 25 g (1 oz) of the butter in a medium frying pan. Fry the haddock, bone-side down, for a few minutes, then turn over. Pour the milk into the pan and cook the fish gently for 4–5 minutes.

3 Heat another 25 g (1 oz) of the butter in another pan. Add the beaten eggs and cook, stirring, to scramble only until soft. Add the double cream and some salt and pepper.

4 Cook the peas in boiling salted water for about 6–7 minutes, then drain and mix with the scrambled eggs.

5 Put the scrambled eggs in the middle of each hot plate. Lift the haddock out of the milk on a fish slice, draining well, and place a piece on top of each portion of eggs. Rub the fish with a little butter, twist on some black pepper, and serve.

Stuffed Spring Greens

After the privations of winter, when there would have been nothing green to eat for months, spring and its burgeoning greenery would be welcomed with enormous pleasure. Most spring greens are cabbages, of the loose-headed spring cabbage variety, plucked a month or so before the head has a chance to form (although there are genuine non-hearting varieties). (Other leaves also sold as spring greens include Brussels sprouts tops, cauliflower tops and turnip or rape tops, the latter the lately fashionable Italian *cime di rapa*.) Here I have stuffed whole heads of spring greens, rather like we might cabbage, and I think this could be a dish that would get kids eating their vegetables.

SERVES 4

---

4 heads spring greens

1 chicken breast, skin off, minced

25 g (1 oz) fresh white breadcrumbs

½ onion, peeled, grated and squeezed (see p. 63)

a splash of Worcestershire sauce

2 rashers smoked bacon, cooked and finely chopped

salt and freshly ground black pepper

85 g (3 oz) unsalted butter

300 ml (10 fl oz) chicken stock

1 tbsp chopped fresh chives

---

1 Preheat the oven to 180°C/350°F/Gas 4.

2 Carefully trim the greens, keeping them whole, then plunge into boiling salted water for 1 minute. Take out and refresh in cold water.

3 Mix together the chicken breast, breadcrumbs, squeezed onion, Worcestershire sauce and chopped bacon, and season well.

4 Drain off the greens, and gently squeeze out any excess water. Holding the root end, open up from the other end of the greens, and spoon into each a quarter of the mixture. Fold the loose ends over to keep the stuffing in and shape nicely.

5 Using 25 g (1 oz) of the butter, grease a suitable ovenproof dish and some greaseproof paper. Lay the greens in the dish, pour the stock over, and cover the greens with the buttered paper. Braise in the preheated oven for about 20 minutes.

6 Take out of the oven. Keep them warm. Put the stock in a small pan and boil to reduce by about half. Beat in the remaining butter, add the chives and some seasoning. Pour over the greens and serve.

Mussels with Cream and Bacon

Mussels have always been popular: one of those foods that could be gathered from the coastlines, and full of taste and protein. This is one of my favourite ways of cooking them, with the full, salty flavour of the bacon and the smooth richness of cream. Mussels always remind me of the seaside, where they are best eaten. And they *must* be fresh.

SERVES 4

1.8 kg (4 lb) fresh mussels, cleaned	150 ml (5 fl oz) dry white wine	1 tbsp chopped fresh chives
55 g (2 oz) unsalted butter	4 tbsp double cream	salt and freshly ground black pepper
2 tbsp finely chopped onion	8 rashers back bacon	

1 Check the mussels for freshness: discard any that do not close when tapped. Scrub the shells well, and get rid of any wispy beards.

2 Put the shells into a pot in two or more batches, depending on the size of the pot. Put the lid on and turn on the heat. Shake occasionally until all the shells have opened. Discard any that remain closed. Strain through a colander into a bowl, then continue with the next batches of mussels. Keep the mussels warm.

3 Take all the juice from the mussels and strain through a muslin cloth.

4 Melt the butter in a clean pan, add the onions and sweat for a few minutes. Add the wine and boil to reduce by half. Add the strained mussel juice and the double cream and bring up to the boil.

5 Meanwhile grill the bacon until well done, then cut into chunky pieces.

6 Put the mussels back into the sauce, add the chives, then heat together and season. Spoon into bowls, pour the sauce over, sprinkle with bacon and serve.

☞ Some people might choose to take some of the mussels out of their shells, but I think sitting around a table, picking mussels up and sucking out their sweet flesh is half the fun. The mussels look more substantial in the bowl, they take longer to eat, and it's all nice and relaxing. And don't forget a glass of chilled Sauvignon Blanc.

Chicken Escalope with Asparagus and Butter

There has always been some confusion about the word 'escalope'. This is the word used in French and Italian cooking to denote a thin slice of meat (usually veal), and what we called it in Britain was 'collop' (often meaning collops of bacon). The word has nothing to do with scallops, the shellfish. Here, I tap chicken breasts flat, so that they cook more quickly, and serve them with one of spring's best products, English asparagus. Once again, it's a simple dish, the value lying in the quality of the produce.

SERVES 4

---

4 chicken breasts, boneless and skinless

25 g (1 oz) paprika

salt and freshly ground black pepper

1 tbsp olive oil

12 small asparagus spears

55 g (2 oz) unsalted butter

juice of ½ lemon

1 tbsp chopped fresh parsley

---

1 Take the breasts of chicken and tap flat between two sheets of plastic or clingfilm. Dust with paprika and some salt and pepper.

2 Heat the oil in a suitable frying pan, and add 25 g (1 oz) of the butter. When it has melted, add the chicken breasts, and colour and cook quickly, about 3 minutes. Turn over and cook for another 3–5 minutes. You may need to do this in batches. Keep warm on a platter.

3 Meanwhile cook the asparagus in boiling salted water for about 4 minutes, depending on the thickness of the spears. Drain well, and place three spears on each chicken breast.

4 Melt the remaining butter in a small pan, and heat to golden brown. Remove from the heat and add the lemon juice and parsley. Pour over the chicken to serve.

☞ To prepare asparagus: using a potato peeler or the back of a strong knife, scrape the lower two-thirds of the spears. Always peel from the tip end to the base and try to get uniformity in look. Much of the flavour and goodness is in the skin so you only want to remove the tough outer layer. Lay the spears side by side with the tips all levelled up and cut the lower parts of the spears off so that each spear is the same length. If cooking upright, tie into bundles.

Rice Pudding

A cereal 'pottage', a semi-liquid cooked dish, was everyday fare for rich and poor alike from the Middle Ages all over the country. In the north they would use oats (and 'porridge' is the dish still most similar to the medieval pottage); in the south, rye, barley and wheat. When rice was (expensively) introduced from Italy, it was mixed with milk and sweet spices and baked or boiled. Sometimes eggs were added for a richer result, and in Yorkshire, suet was often included as well. Our present-day rice puddings are not too different from these early originals. Whether they liked the skin then or not, I don't know...

SERVES 8

55 g (2 oz) Carolina short-grain rice	150 ml (5 fl oz) double cream	25 g (1 oz) unsalted butter
450 ml (15 fl oz) milk	55 g (2 oz) unrefined caster sugar	freshly grated nutmeg
	1 vanilla pod, split	strawberry jam

1 Put the rice, milk and cream into a thick-bottomed pan and bring to the boil, stirring all the time.

2 Add the sugar, the seeds from the vanilla pod and the pod itself. Simmer until cooked, stirring regularly, about 45–50 minutes. Remove the vanilla pod (and wash and use again).

3 Add the butter and nutmeg to taste, then pour into a dish and colour the top under a preheated grill until golden brown.

4 Serve with some good strawberry jam, perhaps putting a small spoonful in the middle of each portion.

☛ For a slightly fancier version, you could add a couple of eggs. When the rice is cooked, butter a pie dish. Beat 2 egg yolks into the rice. Whisk 2 egg whites and then fold them into the rice. Spoon into the pie dish and bake in the preheated oven at 160°C/325°F/ Gas 3 for 15-20 minutes. Sprinkle with icing sugar and serve.

Hot Cross Buns

British buns are made from a sweet yeast dough enriched with butter and eggs, dried fruit and spices. The basic mixture for these hot cross buns, Chelsea buns and many other traditional sweet breads is similar; the difference lies in what happens thereafter!

When I was a lad I worked during the school holidays, with Frank and Theo in the Glendale bakery, which sold its product to market stalls. Our busiest time was Maundy Thursday, preparing thousands of hot cross buns for Good Friday. We worked all night, moulding them by hand. Frank's late auntie was said to haunt the place, which gave me the willies!

The cross on top, traditionally associated with Easter, can be made simply by cutting into the dough and piping in a dough mixture, or by placing on a cross of separately made pastry, or lines of candied peel.

MAKES 16

1 recipe *Basic Bun Dough* (see p. 40)	**FILLING**	**TOPPING**
	55 g (2 oz) currants	55 g (2 oz) plain flour
	55 g (2 oz) sultanas	water
	¼ tsp ground allspice	115 g (4 oz) unrefined caster sugar
	¼ tsp freshly grated nutmeg	

1 Make the basic bun dough as described in steps 1–3 of the *Chelsea Bun* recipe on p. 40.

2 Knock the dough back and add the dried fruit, allspice and nutmeg. Form into sixteen even-sized balls, and flatten them slightly. Using a sharp knife, carefully cut a cross on top of each bun.

3 Mix together the flour and 1–2 tbsp water for the pastry crosses. Put into a piping bag, and pipe into the crosses on top of the buns. Place the buns on a greased baking tray, cover and allow to prove until doubled in size, about 30 minutes.

4 Preheat the oven to 220°C/425°F/Gas 7.

5 Bake the buns in the preheated oven for 15–20 minutes.

6 Meanwhile, boil the sugar and 150 ml (5 fl oz) water together to make a syrup.

7 Take the buns out of the oven and, while still hot, brush with the syrup to glaze them, giving the buns their characteristic sticky sheen.

Shrove Tuesday

Also known as Pancake Day, Fat Tuesday and Mardi Gras, Shrove Tuesday always falls on the day before Ash Wednesday, which is the first day of Lent in the Christian faith. Dates vary from year to year, as do the dates of Easter, but Shrove Tuesday usually falls in February, sometimes in early March.

The last three days before the beginning of Lent are known as Shrovetide. (The word 'shrove' comes from 'shrive', to confess, which is what all good Christians did before Lent.) Shrove Sunday, or Quinquagesima Sunday, is the 50th day before Easter. Collop Monday, or Shrove Monday, is named after the traditional dish of the day, collops of bacon served with eggs (no surprise there, we still eat it enthusiastically, but not just on Mondays). Shrove Tuesday was the day on which all fats, cream and other dairy products, including eggs, had to be used up, and was often the last day for a month on which one could eat meat and fish. Lent is a time of abstinence, of giving things up, so Shrove Tuesday was the last chance to indulge yourself, and making pancakes was a good way of using up the dairy perishables.

Pancake races are still held all over the UK on this day. They are said to date back centuries. A housewife heard the church bells ringing for the Shrove Tuesday service while in the process of making her pancakes; she ran out of the house, still carrying her frying pan and pancake, and carried on flipping until she reached the church. Now, in pancake races, competitors have to toss their pancakes at least three times during the race. Even the church bells, which used to summon everyone to confession, were known as pancake bells!

Shrove Tuesday, because it is a significant date in the Christian calendar, is celebrated all over the Christian world. The carnival to end all carnivals, Mardi Gras, is held every year in Rio de Janeiro, and the one held in New Orleans used to be similarly splendid. I believe the Russians have a *blini* week, called *maslenitsa*, which is much the same as Shrove Tuesday, a using-up of ingredients forbidden during the fasting time. Although the Russian *blinis* are very much smaller than our pancakes...

Basic Pancakes

There are a few pancake ideas already scattered through the book, and you could use one of them for your Shrove Tuesday pancakes, but this is a good basic. My mother used to do a pancake stew, with layers of meat in between. On Shrove Tuesday in Simpson's in the Strand we used to have to go early in the morning, and clear away the preparation tables and light the wood-burning stoves so that nothing would interfere with our production-line pancake service.

MAKES 8

140 g (5 oz) plain flour	25 g (1 oz) unsalted butter, melted
a pinch of salt	300 ml (10 fl oz) milk
1 large egg, beaten	vegetable oil, for cooking

1 Sift the flour and salt into a bowl. Make a well in the centre. Add the beaten egg, melted butter and half the milk to the well in the flour, then gradually bring together to make a batter, using a whisk. Slowly beat in the remainder of the milk, then allow to rest.

2 Heat a 20 cm (8 in) non-stick frying pan, and add a little oil. When it is hot, pour in just enough batter to cover the base of the pan (holding the pan facing slightly downwards, and pouring in the batter from a ladle from the top). Move the pan around to allow the batter to form a circle and completely cover the base of the pan. Your first may not turn out well, but you'll soon get the hang of it.

3 Let this colour for a minute or so, then turn the pancake over – toss if you dare! – and cook on for a few seconds.

4 Store the pancake in the folds of a tea towel to keep warm while you make more pancakes. Store them on top of each other until you have finished the batter.

☛ The traditional topping/filling is lemon juice and sugar. Sprinkle these on top of the pancake, then fold or roll up and eat. However, you can fill the pancakes with anything you like: see some of the suggestions here and throughout the book.

Scotch Pancakes

Pancakes – thin circles of cooked batter – exist all over Europe (think of the French *crêpes*), and the batter is very similar to that for Yorkshire pudding. In Scotland, though, what they call 'pancake' is actually a drop scone, made from a thicker batter, raised by baking powder, and cooked on a griddle to a fat circle rather like a crumpet (although this is yeast-raised). Eat freshly made: they are not so good cold and old. Serve them with cream and jam, or maple syrup or golden syrup and butter.

MAKES 12

225 g (8 oz) plain flour	25 g (1 oz) unrefined caster sugar	150 ml (5 fl oz) milk
1 tsp baking powder	1 egg, beaten	25 g (1 oz) unsalted butter, melted
¼ tsp salt	1 tbsp golden syrup	vegetable oil, for cooking

1 To make the pancakes, sift the flour, baking powder, salt and sugar together into a bowl. Make a well in the centre. Add the beaten egg and golden syrup, stir through, then pour in enough of the milk to make a stiff batter. Now add the melted butter along with enough of the rest of the milk to create a dropping consistency. Don't be afraid to add a little more milk if you think it needs it. This is the basic sweet Scotch pancake batter.

2 Heat a griddle or frying pan and brush with a little oil.

3 Using a tablespoon, 'drop' an amount on to the griddle and leave to set and colour. Turn over and cook the second side. Each pancake takes about 5 minutes to cook. Store the pancakes inside a tea towel while making the rest.

☞ A greased metal ring helps to keep the right shape and an even size.

☞ Although the pancakes are sweet, they go rather well with bacon, but make sure it is a sweet-cure bacon. Great for an American-style breakfast.

☞ In summer, these pancakes with marinated strawberries and raspberries, topped with clotted cream, make for a real treat.

Gingerbread Pancakes with Ginger Syrup

This uses the basic sweet Scotch pancake recipe, but with some surprisingly interesting additions: gingerbread and preserved ginger. If you're a ginger fan, then this is the one for you. (I'm actually addicted to those crystallised ginger chocolates they used to give out after dinner.)

SERVES 6

1 recipe *Sweet Scotch Pancakes* (see p. 249), batter only, do not cook!

225 g (8 oz) gingerbread, finely diced

vegetable oil, for cooking

6 tbsp golden syrup

3 pieces preserved ginger, finely diced

1 Make the batter for the Scotch pancakes, as described in stage 1 on p. 249.

2 Add the gingerbread dice to the pancake batter.

3 Cook the pancakes as described in stage 3 on p. 249. Make thin so as to cook through without burning.

4 Heat the golden syrup in a small pan, then add the ginger dice. Heat minimally through until warm.

5 Spoon the syrup and ginger sauce over the pancakes, and serve with whipped cream.

Apple and Rhubarb Pancakes

This is just one suggested filling for our basic pancakes. When I was doing the *Christmas Cook's Challenge,* for Rory Bremner I made a pancake filling of caramelised bananas and cream, and sautéed some diced plums to serve as a sauce. They were delicious.

SERVES 4

1 recipe *Basic Pancakes* (see p. 248)	**FILLING**	2 tbsp runny honey (or to taste)
	2 Bramley apples	2 tbsp Calvados
	225 g (8 oz) rhubarb	icing sugar
	55 g (2 oz) unsalted butter	

1   Preheat the oven to 180°C/350°F/Gas 4.

2   While making your pancakes, you could also be making this fruity filling. Keep the pancakes warm once made.

3   Peel and core the apples, then chop into large pieces. Trim the rhubarb, then cut into 2.5 cm (1 in) pieces.

4   Melt the butter in a medium pan. Add the apples and honey, and cook slowly for about 3–5 minutes.

5   When the apples just start to soften, add the rhubarb and simmer slowly for 5 minutes. Add the Calvados and cook on until the rhubarb still has a bite, about another 3–4 minutes.

6   Strain the mix through a sieve into a small pan. Put the juice back on to the heat and boil to reduce until sticky. Mix with the apple and rhubarb.

7   Put the pancakes on the table. Put an eighth of the mixture in the centre of each pancake, then fold half over to look like a semi-circle. Put on a baking tray, sprinkle with icing sugar, and warm through for 2 minutes in the preheated oven. Serve with ice-cream.

Index

THANKS   I must acknowledge the wisdom of so many books from so many years ago, but what I found fantastic this time were the three days or more I spent with Gerard O'Sullivan, my good friend, work-mate and chef. Between us we cooked the recipes for the photos in the book and over a period of time have cooked many, many more together. What a team, and what a great time we had.

I must also thank Susan Fleming, Lorraine Jerram and the team at Headline for organising, encouraging and pulling together all my thoughts. I am especially grateful to the wonderful Louise Hewitt for being able to read my writing, type my recipes, then read and re-read them all and push me to finish on time.

But I would like to give special thanks to my delicious grandchildren, Lily-Mae and Joseph. I have spent hours watching them eat, and it was they who inspired and convinced me that the recipes in this book need to stay in the repertoire of all British cooks and not be forgotten.